GUIDE TO
BRITAIN'S
WORKING PAST

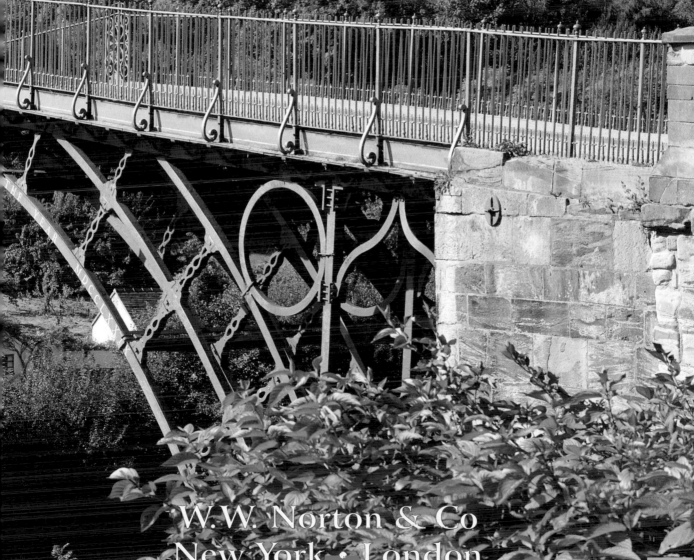

GUIDE TO
BRITAIN'S
WORKING PAST

Anthony Burton

W.W. Norton & Co
New York • London

First American edition 2003

Originally published in Great Britain under the title
THE DAILY TELEGRAPH GUIDE TO BRITAIN'S WORKING PAST

Manufacturing by Printer Trento srl
Book design by Robert Updegraff

Library of Congress Cataloging-in-Publication Data

Burton, Anthony, 1934–
Guide to Britain's working past / Anthony Burton.
—1st American ed.
p.   cm.
ISBN 0-393-32552-0 (pbk.)
1. Technology—Great Britain—History. 2. Industrial sites—Great Britain—Guidebooks.
3. Industrial archaeology—Great Britain—Guidebooks. 4. Industries—Great Britain—
History. 5. Industrialization—Great Britain—History.
6. Industrial revolution—Great Britain—History. I. Title.
T26.G3B87 2003
609.41—dc21
2003048783

W. W. Norton & Company, Inc., 500 Fifth Avenue
New York, N.Y. 10110
www.wwnorton.com

W. W. Norton & Company Ltd., Castle House
75/76 Wells Street, London W1T 3QT

1 2 3 4 5 6 7 8 9 0

Previous pages **The world's first iron bridge, crossing the Severn at Ironbridge.**

Opposite **The replica of Richard Trevithick's pioneering locomotive of 1813 in steam at the Ironbridge Gorge Museum.**

CONTENTS

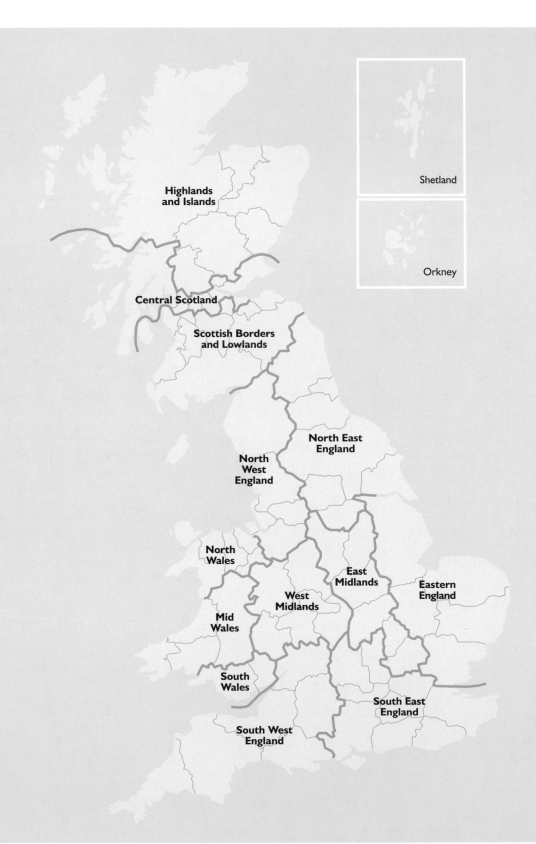

Highlands
and Islands

Central Scotland

Scottish Borders
and Lowlands

North East
England

North
West
England

North
Wales

East
Midlands

Eastern
England

West
Midlands

Mid
Wales

South
Wales

South East
England

South West
England

Shetland

Orkney

FOREWORD

The aim of this book is really very simple: to share my own enthusiasm for the places that are described in the hope that the reader will visit at least some of them and find as much pleasure and excitement in the experience as I have done. There have been huge changes since I first started hunting out old industrial sites some thirty years ago. Industrial museums were a rarity and inclined to worthy dullness, but there were a lot of places that were just there, features in the landscape but gently crumbling into obscurity and ruin. To take an interest in such places was considered eccentric if not downright suspicious. Today, places that were all but forgotten are being dubbed world heritage sites, buildings have been repaired, machines restored and set back in motion. If I had been writing this guide in those days, the directions for finding some of the sites would have sounded like a set of unusually complex instructions for a treasure hunt. Now the problem has changed. It is no longer a question of what to put in, but what to leave out. Somehow a card index that started with a couple of thousand or so entries had to be whittled down. The decisions that were taken give the book its present form.

The first decision was to limit the time scale. There is a good case to be made for saying that industrial life began in Britain back in the Stone Age, when men dug the first mines to reach choice bands of flint, but I have decided to leave prehistory to the archaeologists. At the other end of the time scale, the ever-accelerating rate of change means that places which were part of the working scene in my lifetime have already achieved museum status. Among the most impressive buildings of the twentieth century are the giant power stations, but who would have thought even a few years ago that one would end up as the Tate Modern? It is interesting, though, to note that visitors seem as impressed by the building as they are by the art. But I have taken a historical cut-off point at the end of the nineteenth century, or at any rate with the technology of the nineteenth century. So out go a whole range of topics from aviation to electronics. It still leaves an awful lot.

If you glance through the book you will see that there are a number of sites listed under the heading 'See Also'. This might suggest that they are also rans, second bests, but this is not the case at all. A major problem was what to do about the literally hundreds of watermills and windmills open to the public. To give each of them a full listing would have been both repetitious and would have resulted in a heavily unbalanced book. Consequently, there are sections on these mills in general, explaining the differences and similarities, so that the individual entries can be quite short and still give an excellent idea of what, for example, you might expect to see in one of the many working tower mills. Another piece of pruning will, I know, annoy a great many enthusiasts: I have not tried to list all the preserved railways in Britain. I could use the argument that a great many consist of twentieth-century locomotives hauling twentieth-century stock up and down short lengths of track, but that is not really the reason for their omission. There are, once again, simply too many, and there is no shortage of publications where they are all listed. So I have tried to concentrate on railway sites that have special historical or technological significance, which offer something much more than just a jolly puff down the line. The other limiting factor is accessibility. In general, I have steered away from places that are only open for a few days a year, unless there is an exceptionally strong case for their inclusion. One other area which has been excluded is the world of maritime history, simply because this is going to be dealt with in a separate volume. However, although old ships have been left out, sites which relate more particularly to manufacturing them have found a place. In the end, however, I have taken purely personal decisions. If I found a site interesting and exciting it went in, if not, however worthy it might seem, it was out.

Finally, the information is, I hope, accurate, or, more precisely, was accurate at the time the work was completed. Things do change: old sites close, new sites open, entrance charges rise – they seldom, alas, fall – and opening times vary. If you do find errors, please write to me at the publishers.

ANTHONY BURTON

INTRODUCTION

At the heart of this book is one of the great turning points in history: the Industrial Revolution. It was not a single event, but rather a coming together of a whole series of inventions and techniques, piling one on top of the other, building up to create a new type of society. Work moved out of the home and the small-scale unit into the mills and factories. One worker could tend a machine that did the work that had once been done by hundreds. New power sources appeared, new transport systems were developed and an irreversible movement began that took masses of people out of the countryside and into the towns. And it all began in Britain, round about the middle of the eighteenth century. When the poet Robert Southey went with his friend, the great engineer Thomas Telford, to see the building of the Caledonian Canal, he compared it to the Pyramids of Egypt, to the detriment of the latter. It may seem slightly farcical to compare what is now seen as quite a modest waterway to one of the greatest wonders of the ancient world, but one can understand what Southey meant. He was seeing the whole world change in front of his eyes, huge engineering works that were the marvel of the age. And we can still see those works today, and if they do not seem quite as grand as they did two centuries ago, a little exercise of historical imagination can make all the difference – for this, like the rest of the canal system, was built not with mechanical diggers but by men with spades and pickaxes. And that makes it really remarkable. The story of the Industrial Revolution is not just about giant machines: it is a human story as well.

The Industrial Revolution has no real starting date, no one year when you could say, 'Well that is the end of the old agricultural world, we're into the industrial age now.' Many of the changes were little more than developments of what had gone before, and the new industrial world

Animal power has been used for centuries for driving machinery. A horse walking in a circle turned the edge roller in this cider press at St Fagans.

makes little sense unless one has some idea of what the earlier age was like. There are certain key areas to look at, and the first is power. If anything distinguishes an industrial activity, it is the use of some sort of power greater than the human can manage on his or her own. Animals had been used since ancient times but are of only marginal importance in terms of what we can still see today. The real interest lies with the use of wind and water, and this still fascinates us. I have never met anyone who didn't at least pause to look at the spinning sails of a windmill or to enjoy the splash of water over a turning wheel. It is even more exciting to go inside to see the machinery, whether it is the familiar grindstones of the grain mill or the thumping of giant hammers in a forge. And this is surely one of the greatest appeals of the sort of sites I shall be looking at over the next few pages. These are machines that are not only enthralling to watch, but ones where anyone can easily understand what is going on.

These words you are reading were tapped out on a computer keyboard, put onto a disk and sent off for printing. It is all very familiar, but how many of us have any idea of what is really going on in the machine? Looking is no help. There are no moving parts inside the computer that we can see: the disc that is slipped in empty looks exactly the same when it comes out again, mysteriously full of words. The machines of an earlier age are not like that. The wheels turn, the gears mesh, this pushes at that and makes it do this. Sometimes it is very simple, sometimes a little more complicated, but it is all on show. Even something which looks really amazing, like one of my all time favourite machines, the spinning mule, is not really all that difficult. The mule may spin a hundred threads on a hundred spindles, but the mechanism would be just the same if you took ninety-nine of them away. If you look at a device which has been with us for centuries, the

One of Britain's few surviving charcoal-fuelled blast furnaces. The Dyfi furnace in Wales still has the water wheel originally used to power the bellows that blew air into the fire.

simple spinning wheel, you will see that it is essentially doing the same job as the complex machine of later years – taking fibres, stretching them out and twisting them together. This seems to me to be part of the joy of old machinery. Often it is most beautifully made and the interplay of moving parts is a pleasure to watch, sometimes a joy to listen to as well, whether it is the gentle murmur of wooden gears in a windmill or the hiss and puff of steam. But the great thing is that even the least technologically literate person can understand it with a bit of effort, and the best of the old machines have a very definite wow! factor. Recently I took my very young grandson to the Kelham Island Museum in Sheffield. Among the prize exhibits is a giant steam engine. It looked impressive just standing there, but then the steam was turned on and it came to life. Dan was enthralled, overawed and silenced, and believe me that is saying something for Dan. Three generations of Burtons stood there in delighted admiration, watching the technology of an earlier age, a vast machine of immense power, yet moving with a steady grace and fluid beauty. This is just one of the pleasures that are on offer to those who go off in search of the industrial past. A pleasure that is enhanced by knowing just a little about the background, the context of a site.

Beginnings

What were the first elements that were developed in the pre-revolution world of work? The first real fundamental, the basis for survival, was the turning of grain into flour or meal. The Domesday Book lists over 5000 grain mills, and the majority of those would have been powered by water. The mill had a central place in medieval life. The Lord of the Manor could, and did, demand soke rights, insisting that all the grain went to his mill, claiming a portion of it all. The miller also took his share, and most people believed a bit more as well. The line of dishonest millers in fiction goes right back to Chaucer. But there was nothing to be done: the poor needed bread to live, bread needed flour and the mill was the only place it could be had. So many old mills have survived simply because they remained important for so long, were built well and built to last.

The other essential of life was clothing. Britain was famous for its wool and its woollen cloth. It was on the back of the woollen trade that Britain's medieval prosperity was built. The yarn was spun, knitted and woven in homes, activities that have left only a few traces behind. But you can still see the prosperity, not in

Nailmaking in small individual workshops was an important part of the Black Country economy. This nailshop from Bromsgrove has been re-erected at the Avoncroft Museum.

industrial remains but in famous beauty spots – in the great churches of East Anglia, such as Lavenham, paid for from the profits of wool, and in the rich mansions of the clothiers of the Cotswolds. Indeed, the Cotswolds has a lot more to offer if you know where to look. Although most of the work of cloth making was carried out in workers' homes or small workshops, there was one activity that was mechanised. The cloth that left the loom was comparatively loosely woven and greasy. It had to be cleaned, the first stage generally involving scouring it with an easily obtained component: urine. This was collected on a regular basis from cottages and houses in the cloth making districts – not the most romantic of activities. Locals in those days didn't go out to 'spend a penny', they went out to earn one. The other great cleaning agent was also available in the area: fullers earth, also helpful in ridding the cloth of the stench of urine – which is why its main use these days is as cat litter. The job of thickening and shrinking the cloth involved pounding it in water. At first this was done by trampling it in a tub (hence surnames such as Walker), but it was soon realised that this chore could be mechanised. No one is quite sure when the first fulling mill was built, but there was certainly one in the twelfth century in the Cotswolds. Fulling stocks consist

of a pair of huge, very heavy wooden hammers. They were powered by a water wheel, which turned a subsidiary shaft with projections. As the wheel turned, the projections connected with the tails of the hammers lifted them, then as the wheel moved on, the hammers fell back onto the cloth in its trough of water. The hammers worked alternately and the ends were curved, so that the cloth was constantly dragged round and moved about. At the end of its long beating it was shrunk and thickened, ready for a final cleaning. Lastly it was stretched on frames to dry. These were tenter frames, which is why anyone who is feeling a bit stretched out and taut is on metaphorical tenterhooks.

For many centuries, when anyone spoke about a textile mill they meant a fulling mill; they were of huge importance. Stroud in Gloucestershire was one of the centres of the industry, and the streams and rivers in all the surrounding valleys were strung with mills, perhaps as many as 150 of them. There is a story here which is typical of so much of the whole industrial saga. In the centuries when transport ranged on a scale from poor to appalling, the main object was to have everything as close together as possible. Sheep roamed the Cotswolds and streams tumbled down the narrow valleys to power the wheels. As long as the water wheel was the main source of power, then the industry based on the rivers flourished. But with the arrival of steam, having a coalfield on the doorstep was suddenly more important than having a good, fast running, reliable stream – and with the advent of electricity, anything could go anywhere. Stroud's mills are still there, overlooked by the handsome houses of the clothiers who never strayed too far from their works; sadly, few are now involved in textiles. You can see what the area once was by driving out of Stroud on the Cirencester road or on the road to Nailsworth, or better still by walking the old canal towpath from Stroud to Chalford. A start has been made in trying to tell the world about this once vital industry – an industry which not only sent cloth all over Britain, but gave the dictionary a new word in the seventeenth century. A 'stroud' was defined as 'a length of cloth manufactured for trading with North American Indians'.

This book is not intended as a text book on industrial history, nor indeed on anything else, but I have dwelt on this one topic because it gives such a good demonstration of an industry that thrived, was of immense importance, dwindled to the point of being all but forgotten, yet has left a wealth of material behind. If anyone wants a Cotswold tour with a difference, away from the honey pots of 'quaint' villages where all the real shops have long gone and only antiques shops thrive, then why not have a look at the past that paid for all the pretty places and their grand houses.

Fulling mills were the first textile mills, and were used in the finishing process of woollen cloth. The fulling stocks can be seen at St Fagans.

The other major activity of the early years was getting minerals from the ground and working the ores to produce metals. Cornish tin was traded with the Phoenicians, or so they say; certainly the Romans came and mined for lead, copper, iron and even gold. Most people tend to think of coal first if they think of mining at all, but that was very much a late comer. The early references are all to 'sea coal', which was washed out of shallow seams by the action of waves, especially around the mouth of the Tyne. From there, some made its way to London – the name Seacoal Lane survives by the spot where it was landed from the coasters. Of all the metals,

iron was the most important, and the iron industry developed, rather like the woollen industry, in areas which we no longer think of as having any industrial connections whatsoever. Pre-eminent among these was the Weald of south east England, and the reason, once again, is that this is where the important raw materials were to be found. To get iron from its ore, it has to be smelted – heated to a high temperature in a furnace to release the metal from the oxide. Even if coal had been available, it would have been of little use: it simply introduces too many impurities. The fuel for the furnaces was charcoal, but the furnaces required a lot of it and charcoal making requires a lot of wood. So the furnaces were set up in among the forests. Then when the iron was produced, it still had to be worked under hammers. The forges were very similar to the fulling mills, using water-powered tilt hammers. Streams were dammed to create ponds to feed the water wheels, and many survive scattered throughout the area, their names surviving with them, for example, Hammer Pond, Furnace Pond, New Pond. Often this is all that remains of a once mighty industry. The coming of the Industrial Revolution did more than simply change how people worked, it changed where they worked as well. Whole industries died in one spot to be reborn in another. In the case of the iron industry, it was the discovery by Abraham Darby that if coal is turned into coke, it can be used in furnaces without ruining the iron. He had his first great breakthrough in Coalbrookdale in Shropshire, a place that has been recognised as one of the key centres of change. Suddenly, having forests near the iron ore was irrelevant: coal was what was needed, coal in huge quantities. A whole new generation of industrial centres grew up, and none was more important in this context than the valleys of South Wales. Production soared, new men learned new skills, new towns grew up and old towns settled down to obscurity. This was just one of the great discoveries of the late eighteenth century, and once it had been made, things could never be the same again.

The Industrial Revolution

So much happened so quickly in so many different areas of life that it is difficult to say where the impetus for change really began. A new power source appeared that was to prove of immense importance: the steam engine. Yet when the first 'modern' factories were built, they still depended on the old, reliable water wheel. But the steam engine didn't happen along by accident. It had its origins in another industry, coal mining, and that perhaps should be given the first say. Without coal, all sorts of things would never have happened – the iron industry could not have developed, the growth of towns would have been hampered for lack of fuel and, of course, the steam engine itself would also have lacked its own fuel.

Mines are wet places and the deeper you go, the wetter they tend to become. The steam engine was developed in the first instance to do no more than pump water out of mines, but that in itself was a huge achievement. It brought in the new age of deep mining. Although we can still visit mining museums, none of them can reproduce the conditions that existed down the pits in the early days – and visitors would not welcome the experience if they were offered it. I visited many working collieries while researching a book on miners and remember remarking to one of the men that I was still blowing coal dust out of my nose days after the last visit. 'Aye, lad,' he said, 'but it's what's not coming out that'll kill you.' We hear the horror stories of young children down the pit, but perhaps none suffered greater hardship than the women who worked in Scottish mines in the eighteenth century. They were the bearers, whose job it was to carry the coal on their backs from the coal face to the shaft, and, in the worst cases, to haul it up the near-vertical ladders to the surface. One man, Robert Bald, took the trouble to find out for himself, publishing the results in 1812. He measured one woman's load and found it was an astonishing 77kg (170lb). She carried this for 137m (150 yards) to the shaft, climbed ladders 36m (117ft) to the surface and then had a last 18m (20 yards) to go to the store. And she did this up to twenty-four times a shift, moving 2 tons of coal a day on her back. It is worth remembering stories like this when we go to a colliery museum, for however much it tries to give a notion of the reality of pit life, it can never reproduce the real horror of the actual working life of 200 years ago.

The steam engine that made deep mining possible also helped to alleviate some of the worst of the

These two engine houses occupy a spectacular location on the Cornish coast. They stand above the site of the Botallack copper mine, whose workings spread far out under the sea.

conditions. In time it was adapted to do more than just pump, it could be used to turn a wheel, and that could be used to wind workers and material up and down the shaft. But if a steam engine could turn a wheel at the pit head, then it could turn a wheel anywhere. The steam engine could take over the role of the old water wheel. It could work the machinery of a factory, and by the time the engine had been developed to take on the task, the factory age had already arrived.

The textile industry took the lead. The old system had continued on its way for centuries with minor changes and improvements. One of these improvements, which does not seem to be particularly revolutionary, was made in 1733 by John Kay of Bury in Lancashire. He invented his famous flying shuttle. In weaving, the warp threads are set in place on the loom and alternate threads are raised and lowered to allow the weft thread to be passed through, carried by the shuttle. Originally this was just passed through by hand, but when broadcloth was being woven, one man could not reach right across, so two pairs of hands were needed to throw the shuttle from one side to the other. John

A splendidly preserved example of a village built for textile workers. These were constructed by Samuel Greg of Quarry Bank Mill, Styal.

Kay's ingenious little device replaced the hands of the weavers by artificial hands or pickers, which could be operated by means of a handle suspended in front of the weaver. This had two immediate results. Firstly, in weaving broadcloth one man could now do the whole job on his own, and secondly, in all weaving the work was speeded up. Now the world of cloth making had two options. Make some of the weavers redundant, or supply them with more yarn to make more cloth. The latter was a good option, provided more yarn could be produced and the world wanted more cloth. The second requirement got a huge impetus thanks to the British move to empire building, which brought them to India and the colourful world of cotton textiles.

Now the search was on for new and faster spinning machines. The spinning wheel used one spinner to

spin yarn into one thread from one spindle. It was obvious that the answer was to be found in a system which allowed just one worker to manage to handle several spindles at the same time. The first success was the spinning jenny, which could still be used in the home or in a small workshop and was hand operated. However, the real advance came with Arkwright's water frame. This was something quite new, for it was designed to be worked by a water wheel. Spinning was moved from the home to the factory. It represented a social revolution as much as a technological one, because it changed everything. No one could decide for themselves when to start work and when to stop. When the wheel began to turn and the machinery whirred into life, everyone had to be there to tend it, and there they stayed until the wheel stopped or a new shift arrived. And because much of the work was unskilled, it was considered just the thing for small children. Because we look on the employment of the very young with such abhorrence, we find it difficult to see the situation as the worthies of eighteenth-century Britain saw it. Giving work to the parish poor was considered a very noble aim – even if the cynical might think that the greatest benefit came to the parishioners who saw the poor rates reduced. So we find a Vicar of Congleton in Cheshire offering his parish poor as apprentices in 1817: 'If you are in want of any of the above, we could readily furnish you with Ten or more at from nine to twelve years of age of both sexes.'

Quarry Bank Mill at Styal has one of the few surviving apprentice houses, and a very delightful building it is too, carrying that air of effortless grace which is the mark of so many Georgian buildings. Life for the inhabitants was not quite so effortless. We rarely hear first-hand accounts of life in such places, but if an apprentice had the effrontery to run away, then he would be hauled up before the magistrates to

Masson Mill at Matlock Bath is the best preserved of all the Arkwright cotton mills. Its elegant symmetry has been disturbed by later additions.

give an account of himself. Thirteen-year-old Thomas Priestley who ran away from Styal had this to say:

> *Our working hours were from six o'clock morning Summer and Winter till 7 in the evening. There were no nights worked. We had only 10 minutes allowed us for our breakfasts which were always brought to the Mill to us and we worked that up at night again – 2 days in the week we had an hour allowed us for dinner, while the machines were oiled, for doing this I was paid ½d a time, on other days we were allowed half an hour for dinner. When the Boys worked over time, they were paid 1d an hour.*

Just before he ran away he had a finger torn off in a machine. Styal, it should be said, was regarded as a model mill with unusually good conditions for the children.

Quarry Bank Mill is, like the apprentice house, a handsome building, a sort of oversized Georgian manor, and this is true of many of the early textile mills. One of the reasons for visiting them is that they are now extremely attractive places to see and the machinery inside them is a delight to watch. But it is

worth thinking as you watch a spinning mule, conducting its stately dance, backwards and forwards across the floor, of boys like little Thomas Priestley literally crawling in among the moving parts, mending broken threads and sweeping up waste.

In later years more machinery was added to the textile mills, weaving was added to spinning and the steam engine gradually came to take over the role of the water wheel. It was the birth of the factory age and the mill town which more than anything else epitomised the social upheaval of the Industrial Revolution. Another side to the rapid development of factories was the need for ever more machinery, and that in turn gave rise to an ever-increasing demand for iron. Once Abraham Darby had demonstrated that iron could be smelted with coke, the way was open for expansion. He produced cast iron, and others showed the way forward in developing wrought iron and steel. Once the iron was available, it was inevitable that new uses would be found for it. There is a logical circularity about some of the developments. The new machines made of iron were set in specially built mills, but the combination of moving machines, hot oil, highly combustible, greasy material and sparks made mill fires all too common. Iron came to the rescue. Fireproof mills were designed, using metal beams and columns as a frame, with floors carried on brick arches. There is a particularly fine early example in North Mill, Belper. From here you can trace a line of descent in the structural use of iron and steel frame buildings right through to the modern office block. One of the fascinations of this whole subject is seeing how one small change can lead to the most remarkable endings. John Kay tried to speed up the handloom, Abraham Darby wanted to make cooking pots, and today we have finished up with Canary Wharf.

Other industries thrived and changed during the same period. For example, men such as Josiah Wedgwood set about transforming pottery manufacture from a craft to an industry. One result of all this activity was a need to move materials around the country cheaply and efficiently. Road improvement got under way with the new Turnpike Trusts who were empowered by Parliament to build toll roads. Many modern roads follow the old routes, and the tollhouse with its bay jutting out to give a good view is a familiar feature. Men such as Thomas Telford and John Loudon McAdam gave the country roads with good, firm surfaces. We can only get an idea of what such roads were like in a museum setting, as at Blists Hill, Ironbridge, where a section of Telford road has been reconstructed. But we can still see other mementoes of those days, because one of the requirements laid down by Parliament was that the roads should include such novelties as milestones, and these survive all over the place, in a fascinating variety of shapes and forms. Some are plain stone, some elaborately carved and lettered; others have metal plates let into stone, while some have post and lettering cast in a single piece. It is always worth looking out for them on the roadside. The most impressive survivors of this time are the bridges, particularly those which made use of the new materials. The bridge that gave the town of Ironbridge its name is the best-known example, though it was far from revolutionary in the way it actually used the iron sections. However, the most important transport routes of the age were the new canals.

One of the five-lock staircases on the Leicester Arm of the Grand Union Canal at Foxton. The locks all interconnect and have side ponds for water conservation.

Water transport was not new in the eighteenth century. Rivers had been used in transport for thousands of years. Navigation had been improved by the use of locks and weirs, but a limit had been reached. If water transport was to spread throughout the country, then it would have to be by wholly artificial canals. The British public's enthusiasm for investing in canals was first roused when the young Duke of Bridgewater built a canal to link his mines at Worsley to Manchester. The great attraction was the aqueduct across the River Irwell at Barton. Here was the astonishing sight of barges on the river while boats passed high above them on a splendid watery bridge. People were amazed. Some had declared it an impossible fantasy – totally ignoring the fact that such aqueducts had already been built in France a hundred years earlier. Now, in a period of little more than half a century, the whole of Britain was, it seemed, united by watery threads. Locks were grouped together in longer and longer flights, cuttings and tunnels dived through the ground and embankments soared above the fields. Spectacular aqueducts were built in stone and iron, and intriguing devices such as inclined planes were constructed to lift boats from one level to another. It was the greatest explosion of engineering energy that Britain had seen since the Romans marched away. The canals linked the industries of the Industrial Revolution together. Because we use them for pleasure boating, it is easy to underestimate their importance. They seem ridiculously slow, and the boats that used them, mostly the famous narrow boats, are absurdly small. But think of them as they were seen by an industrialist setting up in business two centuries or so ago. His best available power unit for moving goods was the horse. The best he could expect from a cart on one of the new improved roads was that a horse would be able to pull 2 tons in a wagon – and good roads were still not that common. If he was forced to turn to a packhorse, he would need a string of sixteen animals to do the same work. Yet one horse could pull a narrow boat on the canal over long distances with a load of up to 30 tons. The canals may seem modest today, but they were the wonder of the age, which is one reason why travelling the canals for pleasure today is still as good a way as any of getting a glimpse into the world of the Industrial Revolution.

The Victorian Heyday

In many ways the nineteenth century represented a continuation of the trends begun in the eighteenth century, a period of development rather than innovation. Yet in one aspect, the differences were more crucial than the similarities. The steam engine had been improved throughout the former period, but it was in the latter years that it not only drove machinery, but also moved itself. It revolutionised transport.

It all began with the steamship. There were a number of experiments where the engine drove paddle wheels. The earliest experiments took place in France in 1775; by 1788 a paddle steamer was puffing its way down a Scottish loch, with Robert Burns himself on board to take notes. Come 1812 a commercial steamer, the *Comet*, was at work on the Clyde – the engine of that pioneering vessel can be seen in London's Science Museum. Yet the real success story of the steamship deals not with the tourist trade along picturesque Scottish waterways, but with the ocean-going steamer and the genius of Isambard Kingdom Brunel. From his first paddle steamer, designed for the Atlantic trade, the *Great Western*, he went on to build the first truly modern liner, the SS *Great Britain*, with iron hull and screw propeller. This splendid old ship is now undergoing restoration at the yard where she was built in Bristol. Although ships as such are not dealt with here, their construction does get a mention, alongside some of the associated trades such as rope making.

The development of the steamship was comparatively slow and was overtaken by the other great development of the steam engine – the railway locomotive. In 1801 the engineer Richard Trevithick built a little road locomotive, which successfully steamed up Camborne Hill in his native Cornwall. A replica has been built to celebrate the bicentenary and proved just as successful in storming up the steep hill. It is now a regular and popular visitor to many sites and events. There was no great enthusiasm for letting steam engines loose on the public highway, but in

1804 Trevithick was able to demonstrate that one of his engines could also run on iron rails and drag a considerable load behind it. The railway age was, or should have been, born. But there was a snag. The only railtracks available at that time were built out of cast iron – brittle, fragile things, designed for use by horse-drawn trucks, which cracked under the weight of the engine. Another twenty years were to pass before rail technology and steam technology came together. In 1825 the Stockton & Darlington Railway was opened, using steam locomotives for all freight traffic, even though passengers had to make do with a stage coach fitted with flanged wheels and still pulled by horses. In just a few years the first inter-city line was completed, connecting Liverpool and Manchester, with a regular service entirely run by steam. It signalled a huge period of expansion, during which the rail network spread out across Britain and from there to the rest of the world. Probably no aspect of the industrial past has aroused more enthusiasm and passion than the steam railway. Preserved lines flourish, although that is only a part of the story. The railway age has left us some great civil engineering features, not as museum pieces, but still in use, still carrying rail traffic. The great railway termini remain among the most daring buildings of the nineteenth century, extending building technology into whole new regions. Think of St Pancras Station in London, and most people think of the Gothic hotel stuck on the front. The greater marvel lies behind, the immense glazed arch of the train shed, 73m (240ft) across, and supported on 580 tons of iron work. Designed by William Henry Barlow in the 1860s, it remained the world's widest constructed span for a quarter of a century.

The other defining issue of the Victorian age was the provision of public utilities. Although there may not be anything obviously romantic about sewage disposal or even fresh water supply, they probably did more for the health of the nation than could have been achieved by an army of doctors. Steam was once again a key factor, powering the pumps that took fresh water in and

The first passenger railway: Trevithick's Catch-me-who-can gave rides in London in 1808 near the site of the present Euston Station.

The steam engine was of immense importance in the improvement of public health. The grand engines at Crossness played a vital role in sewage treatment in nineteenth-century London.

effluent out. The city fathers who paid the bills not only wanted to do good, they wanted to be seen to do good. So one finds great pumping stations fitted out with all the elaborate trappings that one might expect in the grandest of town halls or even in a new cathedral. Elaborate decoration was the order of the day, even if no one apart from the few staff responsible for the works was ever likely to see it. There are those who like their steam unadorned, happy with the steady rhythm of the engines themselves, their gleaming metal work and austere beauty. Others delight in the settings, wonders of Gothic taste. It is hard to pick a winner in this contest of extravaganzas, but there are some splendid contenders. My awards for the most elaborate buildings go to Ryhope, all gables and pinnacles, and for the interior to Papplewick, a gloriously over the top mélange, where not a surface is left undecorated and stained glass windows cast their multi-coloured light over the great beam engines. A third prize could be added for the Abbey works in Leicester, which show that even a sewage station could be a thing of beauty.

This was an age where Britain ruled the industrial world with supreme self confidence. The technology developed in these islands was spread out far and wide, and although it falls outside the scope of this book, the evidence remains. It still comes as a visual shock to find that perhaps the most elaborate of all Victorian railway stations, and one which bears her name, is not to be found in London, but in Bombay. These were the years when things were built bigger than ever before and no one felt the need to apologise for boasting about them. The refined simplicity of a Georgian cotton mill gave way to an often riotous elaboration. The former Templeton Carpet Factory in Glasgow, now used as offices, is an Arabian Nights fantasy of coloured tiles, minarets and elaborate windows, which gives no hint of why it was built and what went on inside. A personal favourite, tucked away down a Bristol side street, is Edward Everard's Printing Works. The decoration is just as grand, but this time the theme of exotica is at least allied to devices related to the work of the building. Such places serve as useful reminders that hunting out the remains of old industries need not mean looking through the grime of ages to some glum reminder of a doom-filled past: it can be colourful, fun and hugely rewarding.

This has been something of a dash through industrial history, but hopefully it has given a context to the entries that follow shortly. Most of the main topics will be covered in more detail at the appropriate places in the rest of the book.

Locomotives on parade: this is just a small part of the collection on display at the National Railway Museum in York.

About this book

The County Chapters

In an ideal world there would be a separate chapter for every county, but this is not practical here. Firstly, the sites are not evenly distributed: you can hardly expect to find the same number of industrial sites in Dorset as you would in Lancashire. Even more problems have been created by the nation's bureaucracy, where some counties vanish altogether, new counties are created and mysterious entities known as unitary authorities have now appeared to complicate the scene. I personally find it confusing, and I suspect many readers will feel the same. To try and make sense of the complexities, the material has been grouped into regions: seven for England and three each for Scotland and Wales. In some cases, within these broad categories the counties have been grouped together – all the new Yorkshires have been amalgamated as just one Yorkshire, for example, and some of the southern counties of England have been given en bloc. It seems to me to be the best way of achieving the aims of the book.

Readers who want to know what an area has to offer will be able to find the information with the minimum of trouble.

Listings Within Chapters

The entries are generally arranged alphabetically, but the occasional entry which requires a full page or more may slip out of the order. This should not be a problem. All the sites are listed in the index and all are located on the maps. Those sites listed in the Features sections are shown as main sites on the relevant county map.

The 'See Also' Sections

As explained in the Foreword, these are not to be thought of as second-rate sites, rather as sites that do not necessarily need a long description. The list also includes sites which may not be open to the public and can only be viewed from the outside, but are interesting and important and well worth seeing.

Ownership

Unlike ancient monuments, only a minority of industrial sites is under the care of national bodies. The description will show those that belong to the following: English Heritage (EH), The National Trust (NT), CADW, Historic Scotland (HS) and The National Trust for Scotland (NTS). As usual, members of these organisations will generally get in free of charge.

Most of the other sites and museums are either privately owned or run by specialist organisations, such as The Trevithick Trust who have done splendid work in Cornwall. A small minority of sites is simply there to be seen by anyone who cares to go and look for them, and these are indicated as 'Open access'. If you want more information on the sites owned or run by these organisations, you can look them up on the internet:

English Heritage: www.english-heritage.org.uk
National Trust: www.nationaltrust.org.uk
Trevithick Trust: www.trevithicktrust.com
CADW: www.cadw.wales.gov.uk
Historic Scotland: www.historic-scotland.net
National Trust for Scotland: www.nts.org.uk

Prices

Because prices change all the time, anything written now could well be out of date before publication. I have given a rough indication of the price band in which admission charges fall at present. They may tip over into a different band – for example, a charge of £2.40 might rise to £2.60 – but the £ sign should serve as a good guide. These are the approximate price bands indicated by the symbols.

£	£2.50 or under
££	£2.50 to £5
£££	£5 to £7.50
££££	Over £7.50

You should perhaps note that some in the top price bracket are big museums, where you can easily spend a whole day and where special family admission rates often apply, so that they can offer really very good value for money.

Opening Hours

Again, these change all the time, so the best we can do is to give the information available at the time of writing. In general, opening times only vary by a small amount from year to year; the site that is open daily is unlikely to revert to once a week and vice versa. The vast majority of sites add Bank Holidays to their regular opening times, and in the case of windmills and watermills, on National Mills Weekends. If in doubt, check with the local tourist board.

Directions

The directions should enable you to find the place you are looking for using an ordinary road atlas, and, in many cases, once you get within range, there are signposts to help in finding the exact location. There are one or two lonely sites that are open access and not signposted at all. In these cases, I have added a map reference giving the number of the appropriate Landranger Ordnance Survey Map, followed by the reference itself expressed in the standard way – if in any doubt what that is, then all O.S. maps have an explanation in the marginal notes. As an example, the Haytor tramway is given as 191/769776, which is the point shown on map 191 where the tramway can be located from the minor road from Haytor Vale to Manaton.

Please Note

Every effort has been made to make sure that the information is up to date and accurate, but one can never be absolutely certain. I well remember a book I wrote some years ago in which one particular building was singled out for praise. I had a call from a local paper on publication day: the demolition crew had moved in that morning! I trust, and hope, the same will not happen again. As I stated in the Foreword, if readers find any errors in the information supplied, please do let me know by writing care of the publishers.

SOUTH WEST ENGLAND

CORNWALL

Think of the industrial landscape of Cornwall and inevitably, and rightly, the first thought is of the engine houses rising above the remains of old tin and copper mines. But that is not quite the whole story. The mines gave rise to engineering companies, which were to become major manufacturers of steam engines and mine equipment, firms such as Harvey of Hayle and Holman of Camborne. And other workings have also left their mark, from the immense crater of Delabole slate quarry to the 'Cornish Alps', the gleaming white spoil mountains that tower above the china clay pits of St Austell.

The 10.7m (35ft) water wheel and balance bob originally used to pump clay slurry at Wheal Martyn china clay works.

CAMBORNE
King Edward Mine, Troon

Trevithick Trust; Easter week, June to September Sunday to Friday; Tel: 01209 614881

This is a most unusual site: a real mine but not quite a real mine. In 1897 the Camborne School of Mines was desperate to have somewhere, under the control of the college, where the students could acquire practical skills. They took over the former South Condurrow mine, which had closed following a col-

The engine house and other buildings at the former King Edward copper mine, which became a mining school – now a museum.

lapse in tin prices. It was worked just as a commercial mine would have been worked, with all the machinery for ore dressing, as well as genuine underground working. Now it has been re-opened yet again, this time as a unique museum.

CARTHEW
Wheal Martyn China Clay Heritage Centre

Trevithick Trust; ££; May to September daily, April and October closed Saturday, winter Sunday to Wednesday; Off the B3274, St Austell-Bodmin road; Tel: 01726 850362; Website: www.wheal-martyn.com

The gleaming white mountains of quartz sand dominate the area round St Austell. They are the waste from an important industry, the extraction of china clay, and what this site is all about is the separation of the sand from the clay. That probably sounds a bit dull but it is actually just the opposite. Above all, it is a wonderful example of the ingenuity with which water power can be used. The works date back to the nineteenth century.

The clay was obtained by removing the surface soil to reach the kaolin, a form of decomposed granite, and gradu-

ally an ever-deeper pit was formed from which the clay was washed out as a slurry. In theory, all that was now needed was to get rid of the water and separate out the unwanted sand in settling tanks. The first problem to be solved was to get the slurry from the pit, and here the work was done by water power. The trouble is that the splendid 10.6m (35ft) diameter water wheel is roughly 1.6km

(1 mile) from the pit and the pump it has to work. The wheel works a crank that transmits power through a series of flat rods snaking away across the site and through a short tunnel, all the way back to the pump at the pit. This is not the only water wheel needed to keep the slurry on the move from settling tank to settling tank. Finally, when the sand has been separated out and removed, the clay is spread out in the vast kiln where underfloor flues from the furnace dry it out. Now the clay is cut into blocks and is ready to be taken away to the coast for shipment.

One of the appeals of this site is that it is so attractive; even the settling tanks with their milky liquid have an eerie beauty. You can get a glimpse of the industry of today. A woodland walk ends at the edge of the site, and you emerge high above a deep clay pit, where the trucks at the bottom look like toys. And all this massive industrial effort started because a gentleman called William Cookworthy discovered in the eighteenth century that this was just the material to make that most delicate of all pottery: porcelain.

COTEHELE
Mill

NT; ££, the charge for the mill also allows admission to the grounds of Cotehele House; April to July afternoons, September to November daily except Friday, July and August daily; Tel: 01579 351346

The riverside estate on the banks of the Tamar was a busy spot, dominated by the

There has been a mill at Cotehele since medieval times, but the present stone building and mill house were built in the nineteenth century.

magnificent house, begun in the fifteenth century. The community that grew up around it was served by its own mill, built in the late eighteenth century, and powered by an overshot wheel. At one point there was a second wheel used to work a saw mill. The gentle climate of the Tamar valley proved a good place to grow strawberries, and here the wood was cut for punnets. There is still a saw pit and forge at the site. Lime was an important feature of agricultural life in the area, and there is a fine set of kilns down by the river.

Quay and Museum

NT; £; April to October daily

The quay has a small stone warehouse housing an outpost of The National Maritime Museum, but the finest exhibit can be seen out on the water: the ketch rigged sailing barge *Shamrock*, built in 1899. In her working days she had the unromantic but valuable job of carrying animal manure down to Plymouth. The sites are all within walking distance and set in pleasant countryside.

DELABOLE

Free; Open access

The land to the east of the little town has been eaten away to create an immense hole. The earliest written records show quarrying for slate was already well under way here in the fourteenth century, and it has been going on more or less ever since. In 1882 at the peak of its productivity the quarry was already 120m (400ft) deep and was employing 500 workers. Today it is 150m (500ft) deep, and it is possible to walk all the way round on a fenced path that runs for 2.4km (1½ miles) round the perimeter. You can peer down to the startling blue lake at the bottom and see the complex of levels and inclines. It is an extraordinary sight. Nearby is an imposing example of the marriage of very old and very new technology, with the whirring rotors of a big wind farm, with a visitor centre.

PENDEEN

Geevor Tin Mine

Trevithick Trust; ££; April to October daily except Saturday, winter closed weekends; Tel: 01736 788662

I have a slight feeling of sadness about this site, because when I first visited here it was a working mine – and that was not so very long ago. Now the men I last saw splashing through the yellow water to reach seams deep underground and drilling away at the rock face act as guides for visitors. There is a chance to see the underground world, but only in a comparatively shallow adit. Above ground, the old surface plant where the ore was treated is on show, and the museum gives an excellent picture of the mine through film and models.

Levant Steam Engine

NT with Trevithick Trust; ££; January to April plus October and May Tuesday and Friday, June Sunday and Wednesday to Friday, July and August every day, September Sunday to Friday; Access down a road and track, signposted off the road in Pendeen; Tel: 01736 786156

This is a wonderfully romantic site, with a little engine house perched on the edge of the cliffs among the surface remains of the old Levant copper and tin mine. The sea sweeps into a deep chasm, and you can still peer over the edge to see the steps cut into the cliff face. It was down these that the miners made their way to reach the adit. The workings ran out right under the sea bed, and in later years the miners were carried down on the man engine, a form of steam-powered lift, rather like a vertical wooden beam with small open, wooden platforms onto which the men stepped. In October 1919 the engine broke and thirty-one miners were killed and another eleven seriously injured. Part of the engine is preserved as a reminder of the tragedy. A rather happier experience is to be had at the engine house, where the little beam engine built by Harvey of Hayle in 1840 is not only preserved but regularly steamed. Unlike most Cornish engines, the whole of the beam is inside the house. This was a winding engine, and visitors have a chance to look down the alarmingly deep shaft.

The view down the shaft at Levant mine provides a rare opportunity to see the depths from which Cornish engines pumped up water. The Levant engine is tiny by Cornish standards.

Although it has all the appearance of a beautiful natural cave and lake, the Carnglaze cavern was created by slate miners.

POOL

Cornish Mines and Engines

NT with Trevithick Trust; ££, admission charge covers both sites; April to November Monday to Saturday (open Sunday in August); Trevithick Road, TR15 3NP; Tel: 01209 315 027

You cannot miss the old engine house in the centre of Pool, right on the main road. There are so many engine houses in Cornwall, but this one is immediately obvious as being very different, for one end of the beam can be seen sticking out through the wall and is quite likely to be nodding up and down. The outside beam ends in a sweep arm, fastened to the drum used for winding in the now capped shaft of East Pool Mine. Inside is the fine beam engine, built by Holman Brothers of nearby Camborne in 1887. There is a Cornish boiler, but no steam is supplied power comes rather sneakily from an electric motor that actually turns the drum and causes the working parts of the engine to move, just the opposite of how the engine originally worked.

The second engine is across the main road and reached rather incongruously through the supermarket car park. But what a marvel it is. This is a giant of an engine, built by Harvey in 1892, though it started life elsewhere and was moved in the 1920s. A stumpy beam pokes out through the bob wall, and inside is the huge cylinder, 2.3m (90in.) in diameter. This

worked on the Taylor shaft, and in its latter days the mine had reached 290 fathoms (530m or 1740ft to non-miners) below the level of the drainage adit. It is overseen by the bust of Richard Trevithick, the man who brought high pressure steam to Cornish mines.

PORTREATH

Tolgus Tin

Trevithick Trust; ££; November to March Sunday to Wednesday, April to November daily except Saturday; The site is on the Portreath-Redruth road at the Cornish Gold site; Tel: 01209 215185

Although this is not a mining site, it is still part of the mining story. Tin ore survived in small quantities in mine waste heaps, and stream works were set up to recover it. Tolgus was established in 1865. What is entailed is a system of separating out the heavy ore from the lighter rock by washing and crushing, until the end product was sufficiently concentrated to send to the smelters. In among the various pulverisers and washing tables are the stamps. This was the first stage in the process, crushing the ore under a row of iron-headed columns powered by a water wheel. It was said that in their working days they could be heard over a mile away, steadily pounding up and down. The other imposing machine is the round frame, last survivor of a set of six, used to concentrate the tin particles.

ST NEOT

Carnglaze Slate Caverns

££; Monday to Saturday during school holidays; Tel: 01579 320725

I first visited this magical spot many years ago with my young children, who by then had already been towed round many industrial sites, and yet they still loved it. No one can be certain how long the area has been worked for slate – a historian of the region writing in 1856 described them as 'ancient' even then. Unlike many mines, these excavations have produced immense caverns, the largest rising over 15m (50ft), and the underground tour takes visitors down to a lake of intense blue. There was one curious episode in the history of the caverns. In World War II they were used to store the Navy's most prized possession – the rum rations.

SALTASH

Royal Albert Bridge

Free; Open access

This is a fitting monument to one of Britain's greatest engineers, Isambard Kingdom Brunel, and his last major work. This is the bridge that took the famous broad gauge railway across the Tamar into Cornwall, and it is a remarkable structure. In essence it is a suspension bridge but made rigid enough for trains by two immense, hollow wrought iron struts. On the end is the date 1859, the year it opened and the year Brunel died. Stand and admire.

Brunel's last great work: the Royal Albert Bridge across the Tamar.

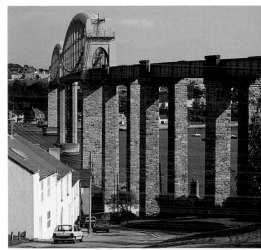

TIN, COPPER AND STEAM

Tin and copper have been a part of Cornish life from a time long before the first records were written. In the earliest days the ore was gained by streaming. Alluvial deposits fanning out from a vein close to the surface were worked and particles of ore could even be collected from the sea shore – as it still is in the very last streaming works at Blue Hills in Trevellas Coombe. Because the ore is heavy, it could be separated out from the small stones and gravel by washing in a stream, much as the men of the Klondike panned for gold. The ore could then be crushed and smelted (heated in a furnace to release the metal).

The top of the cylinder of the East Pool engine, a typical Cornish beam engine, built by Holman Brothers of Camborne.

In time, the easily worked deposits ran out, and deeper and deeper veins or lodes had to be worked. Thus streaming gave way to deep mining. All mines face a common problem: at some point you will reach water, and unless you can get rid of the water, work must come to a halt. The easiest method is to dig a tunnel from low ground, which can act as a drain or adit. This was a particularly useful method when a mine was near the shoreline, as the adit could be opened up from the cliff face. You can see one below the cliffs at Levant. But the further down you go, the greater the problem becomes, and pumps had to be used to bring the water up to adit level. Soon extra power was needed to do the work, and water wheels were used to power the pumps. However, the relentless move still continued into ever deeper mines. Mining was no longer about individuals scraping what they could from the ground: it needed capital to pay for big, expensive machines. Fortunately, there has always been an element of independence about the Cornish mining industry. In most mining communities, workers were paid wages, but the Cornish miner lived by different rules. They negotiated a contract with the owners, and how much they earned depended not just on how hard they worked, but also on how astute they were at assessing both the labour that was going to be needed and how valuable the ore would prove to be. Although everyone took their share of the prosperous mine, everyone also shared the risk of failure.

By the late seventeenth century the limit of what could be done by existing technology had just about been reached. A Dartmouth blacksmith, Thomas Newcomen, made tools for the local mines and saw what was happening. He set himself to finding a solution, and in doing so he set in motion one of the crucial periods of development of the Industrial Revolution. He built a new type of pump powered by steam. The idea was simple. The engine consisted of a giant pivoting beam, from one end of which the pump rods were suspended. Gravity dragged that end of the beam down. What he needed was a force to lift them up again. At the other end of the beam he set a cylinder and piston. Steam was passed into the cylinder, then condensed with cold water. The result was a partial vacuum below the piston. Now air pressure acted on the top of the piston, forcing it down and raising the pump rods at the other end. The first engine was installed at a coal mine at Dudley in 1712, and a working replica now has an honoured place at the Black Country Museum. Appropriately, an original engine can be seen in the engineer's home town of Dartmouth. The Cornish were early enthusiasts for the new engines, and soon the great beasts were nodding their heads over shafts throughout the county. They made deep mining possible, but at a price: they were extravagant users of coal. Repeatedly cooling and heating the cylinder was wasteful of fuel, and Cornwall had no coal of its own to waste. It all had to be brought in from outside. This was why the ore was seldom smelted in the county. It was cheaper to send the ore to a coalfield area, such as South Wales, than it was to bring the coal to Cornwall.

Then in the late eighteenth century a young Scotsman working on a model Newcomen engine at

Glasgow University realised that he could make a vast improvement in the Newcomen engine. His name was James Watt. Instead of condensing the steam in the cylinder, he used a separate condenser. He did more: he closed off the top of his cylinder so that steam could be admitted above as well as below it. This meant he could use steam pressure instead of air pressure to do the work. He had made a steam engine.

This should have been wonderful news for the Cornish, yet there was a certain scepticism among the locals that an outsider could do better than one of their own. However, the hugely increased efficiency of engines made by Watt with his partner Matthew Boulton could not be ignored. Soon there was not a Newcomen engine left in Cornwall, and the county had developed its most famous landmark – the engine house. You can see them all over the place, but there are just a few places where they seem especially dramatic – the cliffside houses at Botallack or St Agnes, or the remains high among the moors of Caradon Hill. The reason they have survived is that these were always more than just covers to keep the weather at bay, they were a structural part of the machine itself. The giant beams, wood in the first engines, metal in the later versions, were balanced on one of the end walls, the bob wall. Half was inside the house, rising up above the cylinder, the other half was outside, attached to the pump rods leading down the shaft. The Watt engine, however, could do more than just pump. If the pump rods were replaced by a sweep arm and a crank, then it could drive machinery. So the winding engine, or whim engine was added to the pumping engine, and sometimes even a third engine was added to work the stamps for crushing the ore. Look at an engine house today, and you can still see the massive bob wall, both shorter and thicker than the others. The boiler house has usually gone, but the tall chimney that ensured a good draught to the fire

Although the first successful steam pumping engine was built by Thomas Newcomen of Dartmouth, it was installed at Dudley. This working replica can be seen at the Black Country Museum.

survives, either separately or as an integral part of the engine house.

Soon the Cornish manufacturers began building engines of their own, including famous firms such as Holman of Camborne and Harvey of Hayle. There are a few fragments left of the great Harvey works in Hayle itself, but happily some of their mighty engines do survive. Even so, if you want to see the biggest of them all, then you need to head across the sea to Haarlem Mere in Holland to see the Cruquis pumping engine, with its 3.6m (12ft) diameter cylinder – so big that when it left Cornwall it was towed across the Channel instead of being stored in the hold.

Boulton and Watt dominated the steam engine world of the eighteenth century, thanks to an all-embracing patent that effectively prevented anyone else doing anything at all. When it came to an end in 1800, eager young Cornishmen leaped at the chance to try their own ideas, and at their head was Richard Trevithick. He invented a whole new generation of high pressure engines, with steam produced by his own Cornish boiler. Then he went a stage further. He realised that his new, smaller, versatile engines could not only move a lot of different machines, they could also move themselves as well. In 1801 his first road locomotive charged up Camborne hill; you can see a statue of the great man clutching a model of his engine at the foot of the slope in Camborne. He went on to set his engine on iron tracks and the steam railway was born.

Trevithick was born at Illogan near Camborne, but the family soon moved to a nearby cottage at Penponds. Although it is occupied, one room has been preserved. This is the old parlour, which with its panelled walls show that the Trevithicks were people with status in the mining world. It is owned by the National Trust and is open on Wednesday afternoons in summer.

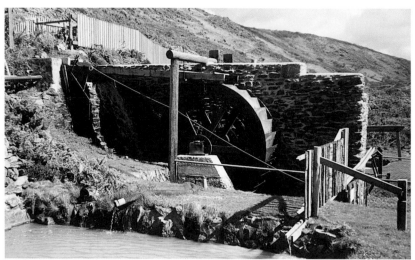

The overshot water wheel is not a museum exhibit, but is still in regular use powering ore crushers at Blue Hills.

is pounded under water-powered stamps, then taken to a shaking table (which is just what its name suggests). Here the ore from the stamps is washed and separated from the debris. After that it is smelted in a tiny furnace and cast into giftware: from beach to brooch on just one site. And all this is in a splendid, wild setting surrounded by the ruins of old mines.

WENDRON

Poldark Mine and Heritage Complex

£££; Easter to October daily;
Tel: 01326 573173;
Website: www.poldark-mine.co.uk

Based on a mine complex at the heart of what was once the richest tin mining district of Cornwall, this has become a mixture of industrial museum and theme park. Among the prime exhibits is the Greensplat beam engine built around 1830 and the last to continue at work in Cornwall, pensioned off in 1959. Today visitors can go underground, see a reconstructed mining village and a wide range of mining artefacts.

TREVELLAS COOMBE, ST AGNES

Blue Hills Tin Streams

££; April to October daily; Leave St Agnes on the B3285 Perranporth road and turn left by Wheal Kitty to the deep valley running down to the sea (map ref. 204/725515); Tel: 01872 553341; Website: www.bluehills@freenet.co.uk

This is an extraordinary survivor and it is not a museum but a real workplace. It just happens to use methods dating back a century and more. Local tin ore is used. Some of it is literally picked up off the beach, and you can tell when a bucket is full of ore if you try and lift it. No ordinary seaside pebbles were ever that heavy. The ore

See Also

An inescapable feature of the Cornish industrial landscape is the ruined engine house – there are so many that it would be impossible to list them all. They can be found grouped all round the great mining districts of Camborne and Redruth, some of the most spectacular are to be seen on the coast. A walk out to St Agnes Head provides views of several fine survivors; however, perhaps the most exciting is to be found down the coast from the Levant mine at Botallack (map ref. 203/362333) with one house on the cliffs, and a lower one perched on a seemingly impossibly small ledge above the waves. Inland one important site is Wheal Busy at Chacewater (map ref. 204/741449), where a Newcomen engine was installed in 1725, followed by a succession of other steam engines. For a different landscape, visit Caradon Hill (map ref. 201/2770) where the old mineral railway can be walked on its way past the mines

Bude Canal

Free; Open access
One of the few canals with a lock providing direct access to the sea. The towpath can be followed inland to the site of an inclined plane. There is also a small museum on the wharf.

Melinsey Watermill, Veryan

£; April to October daily;
Tel: 01872 501371
A mill with overshot wheel, agricultural museum and craft centre.

Wayside Folk Museum, Zennor

£; April to October daily;
01736 796945
The museum, based on a watermill, has exhibits covering many aspects of local life, including mining.

A ruined engine stands high on the moors at Caradon Hill.

DEVON

'Glorious Devon' is famed as the county of rich red soil, wild moorland and a superb coastline, not at all the sort of place where you expect to find very much in the way of industry. This is true, though areas such as Dartmoor are famous for their quarries and some of the copper mining activity has spilled over the Tamar from Cornwall. But if there is not very much here, then at least what there is has an extraordinary variety. Therefore all the main sites listed are of quite outstanding interest.

DARTMOUTH
Newcomen Engine

£; Open daily; Royal Avenue Gardens; Tel: 01803 834224; Website: www.enquire@dartmouth-tourism.org.uk

This is the oldest surviving steam engine in the world, erected here as a monument to the Dartmouth man who invented it, blacksmith Thomas Newcomen. Strictly speaking, it is an atmospheric engine, since the work of pushing the piston down in the cylinder is done by air pressure, but it is easy to see it as the forerunner of all the beam engines of the south-west. It started its working life around 1720 at a colliery near Coventry, then moved to Hawkesbury Junction where the Coventry and Oxford Canals meet – and where its old engine house still stands. The engine is demonstrated, but not with steam, and does a little gentle pumping. It is one of the most important monuments of the Industrial Revolution.

Paignton & Dartmouth Steam Railway

£££ return fare; Easter to October

Just across the estuary at Kingswear is a quite different steam experience. This is a beautiful little line, offering a delightful mixture of riverside scenery and marvellous views out to sea. Those who want the best view of all can travel in the special Pullman observation car – very grand.

HAYTOR DOWN
Haytor Granite Tramway

Free; Open access; The line of the tramway can be found near Haytor Vale, by walking a short way up the minor road to Manaton. The tramway heads off to the north of Haytor rocks (map ref. 191/769776)

This extraordinary line was built in 1820 to carry stone from the Dartmoor quarries to the Stover Canal at Teignbridge. It was a tramway, an early railway on which trucks were hauled by horses. Normally tramways were built with cast

The immense overshot water wheel at Morwellham Quay was originally used to provide the power for a manganese mill.

iron rails. Unfortunately, iron was expensive in Devon, but stone was plentiful, hard wearing and cheap. So the line was constructed with granite rails made up of shaped blocks each up to 2.4m (8ft) long. You can follow the line out across the moor, find sidings, branch lines to the old quarries and even points, where swivelling metal plates once allowed trucks to move from one line to another. And all this in the setting of some of Dartmoor's finest scenery.

MORWELLHAM QUAY

££££; Open daily but limitations in winter; Tel: 01822 832766; Website: www.morwellham-quay.co.uk

This was once the great copper shipping port of the Tamar, but with the collapse of the industry the quays fell silent and decay set in. Now after a great deal of restoration effort one can see the scale of the enterprise. It was above all a communications centre, where tramways connected to the Tavistock Canal, emerging from a long tunnel high on the hillside, and trucks ran down an incline to cross the quay on wooden trestles. The dock scene has been recreated, which now includes a berth for the restored Tamar ketch,

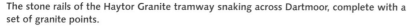

The stone rails of the Haytor Granite tramway snaking across Dartmoor, complete with a set of granite points.

STICKLEPATH
Finch Foundry

NT; ££; April to November open daily, except Tuesday; Tel: 01837 840046

An odd name for a start, because this isn't a foundry at all but a forge where William Finch began making agricultural tools in 1814. You know you are in for a treat even before you step inside, as a series of three water wheels turn under the splashing outpourings of an overhead launder, or water trough. The first wheel powers a fan where the metal is heated, a simple improvement over the familiar blacksmith's hearth and bellows. The hot metal is cut by mechanical shears and slid under one of the two giant tilt hammers. Held in a massive frame, kept in place by a bewildering array of wedges and struts, the hammer pounds away a dozen or more times for each turn of the second water wheel. It all looks crude and higgledy-piggledy, but it has stood the test of time. It is a perfect example of the 'if it's not broken, don't mend it' school of thought, and a splendid sight to see as the floor shudders with each blow of the hammer. The final stage is grinding, where the third wheel comes into play. The grinder lies on a board, holding the blade in front of him, literally with his nose to the grindstone, and having tried it I can vouch for it being a rather disconcerting experience.

One of the great charms of Finch's is the fact that everything is so easy to understand: what you are seeing is a smithy, where the power of water has taken the place of human effort – a blacksmith's shop for a giant.

The great hammers used to shape the metal at Finch Foundry, powered through a complex of belts and pulleys.

Garlandstone. A water wheel remains that once ground manganese ore, and many of the port's buildings, from cooperage to assay office, have been recreated. Coming up to date, there is a chance to visit the hydro-electric station of 1933. There is also an opportunity to go underground, riding a train into the old George and Charlotte Copper Mine, last worked in the 1860s. The 'model' village, complete with pub, is not a museum piece but still lived in. The whole site has been much extended over the years to bring in extra buildings, from a Methodist chapel to a Victorian farm complete with animals.

This has been an extraordinary attempt to bring a remarkable industrial port back to life. Like many large open air museums, this has been extended to costumed guides, and whether you find this helpful or mildly embarrassing is a matter of personal taste. There is so much here that is really interesting that I am happy to overlook suggestions that I might also want to dress up in a genuine replica of a Victorian costume.

UFFCULME
Coldharbour Mill

£££; April to October daily, November to March closed weekends;
Tel: 01884 840960;
Website: www.coldharbourmill.org.uk

This is a woollen mill and an altogether splendid place. Because the woollen mills of Yorkshire are so well known, it is easy to overlook the West of England trade. But here is a lonely survivor, tucked away in the countryside at the edge of a peaceful Devon village. They started making woollen cloth here in the 1790s and manufacturing continued up to 1981. What you get today is essentially a Victorian factory, much as it was when work ended, with most of the old machinery still in place and in working order so that everything can be demonstrated. What I really like is the no frills approach, no attempt to tart the old lady up: she is what she is, a working lass.

The first thing you see is that this began as a water-powered mill. There is an impressive leat from the River Culm, leading down to a big breast shot wheel. That did the job right up to 1910, when the steam engine was brought in. This is a really fine sight, a big engine, still steamed, and driving the rope race that carried the power to all the different floors of the mill. Inside there is the full range of machinery, from the combing shed where the fibres were prepared for spinning to the looms that turned out worsted cloth. It looks like a working mill, and when the different machines spring into life, it is a working mill.

See Also

Branscombe Mill

NT; £; April to November Sundays, July and August plus Wednesday;
Tel: 01392 881691
Preserved watermill, but the village also has an old working bakery and a thatched forge still used for making ornamental ironwork.

Hele Mill

£; April to June, September to October daily except Saturday, July to August daily; Wartermouth Road; Tel: 01271 863185
Working watermill, which also has a porcelain roller mill and 1928 diesel engine.

The remains of the former gunpowder mills on Dartmoor.

Otterton Mill

£; Open daily; Tel: 01395 568521
A working watermill with two breastshot wheels, providing flour for its own bakery.

Powder Mills

Free; Open access; Near Two Bridges, off B3212 Moretonhampstead Road (map ref. 191/628769)
The remains of a once important gunpowder manufacturing centre in a moorland setting.

Wheal Betsy

NT; Free; Open access; Off A386, north of Mary Tavy
Engine house and remains of a former lead mine on the edge of Dartmoor.

DORSET AND SOMERSET including Bath

This is an area of contrasts, from the Somerset Levels to the heights of Exmoor. The former bears the marks of a centuries-old struggle to keep the low lying land clear of water, while the latter has a now largely forgotten history of mining. Often the industries seem almost to have slipped away from the landscape altogether, but walk the Mendips, for example, and you are likely to find reminders of old lead mines all over the place. I have a lump of what looks like shiny black jet, picked up on a stroll, which is, in fact, slag from old lead workings. It makes a useful paper weight.

BATH

Museum of Bath at Work, Julian Road

££; April to November daily, November to March weekends only; Tel: 01225 318348; Website: www.bath-at-work.org.uk

This houses a splendidly bizarre collection, a masterpiece of organised muddle. At its heart is the reconstructed works of J.B. Bowler who set up business in Bath as 'engineer, plumber's and general brass founder, gas-fitter, lock smith and bell hanger'. As that seemed to be not quite enough to keep him busy, he added soda water machinery and manufactured aerated

water. Nothing was ever thrown away, no machinery ever discarded. And here it all is in glorious confusion to our eyes, but no doubt arranged in a perfectly logical sequence that made sense to Mr Bowler and his descendants. New exhibits have been added, including a display on Bath stone, a cabinet-maker's workshop and the Horstmann Car Company

J.B. Bowler's office, preserved much as it might have been when he started his business in Bath in 1872.

CHARTERHOUSE, MENDIP

Blackmoor Educational Nature Reserve

Free; Open access; Charterhouse is a hamlet to the north of the B3371. There is parking at the visitor centre or at the end of the lane alongside (map ref. 182/502557)

Lead has been mined in the Mendips since Roman times, and there is a just about discernible Roman fortlet by the mining site. This is a place to wander and make discoveries. What appear to be little limestone cliffs are rakes, where the old miners dug down from the surface to extract the ore. Hollows in the land are the remains of buddles where the ore was washed and separated. Shafts can be located and piles of slag abound. The most interesting remains are the old condensing flues. The ore was heated and the vapours passed up and down the flues, where the lead condensed. One of the attractions of this site is that it would be a real pleasure to walk round, just to enjoy the scenery, even if there were no historical remains at all.

Claverton Pumping Station

£; May to October Sundays and Bank Holidays; Approached down Ferry Lane, a cul-de-sac off the A36, west of Bath; Tel: 01225 483001; Website: www.katrust.org

This one really is unique. When the Kennet and Avon Canal was built in the 1790s it had to be supplied with water. The canal was set on the hillside some 12m (40ft) above an obvious source of water: the River Avon. There was already a watermill at Claverton, fed by a leat running from above a massive weir. The mill was bought and the pumping station built on the site. Power comes from an immense water wheel, 5.2m (17ft) long and 7.3m (24ft) wide. Gears mesh, cranks turn and a pair of beam pumps nod up and down. It seems rather charmingly quaint, but it was hugely efficient, able to shift 100,000 gallons up from the river to the canal every hour – and all without paying for fuel. It is regularly demonstrated.

PORTLAND

Free; Open access

There is a small and very good local history museum in Easton, but the main interest is in the widespread remains of the quarries, which have provided stone for famous buildings from St Paul's Cathedral to Broadcasting House. Portland was an island until 1839, so stone had to be shipped out. The task was eased in 1826 when the island got its first railway, The Merchants' Railway. It had an incline, down which the loaded trucks were lowered to the harbour at Castletown. It is still a prominent landmark feature, and traces of the old tramway system can be found, with the rows of stone blocks that held the rails

The square chimney stands above the annealing furnace at Saltford Brass Mill, a rare survivor from a once important industry.

as confirmation. It can easily be followed as a cliff path leading down the west side towards the Bill. The quarries are everywhere with their vast blocks of stone, and there are spectacular reminders of just how much has been hacked away in the ledges on the eastern side by the Bill, where the cliffs have simply been removed. There is a splendid opportunity to take a seaside walk with a difference by following the cliff paths on either side of the island.

Saltford Brass Mill

Free; Second Saturday in month or by arrangement; Tel: 0117 9862216

The name 'mill' gives the clue of where to look for this – down by the river, crossed by an imposing weir. This is a brass mill, one of many that once lined the Avon valley all the way up from Bristol. The industry developed here because zinc ore was available from the Mendips and there was copper in plenty in the West Country. In essentials, the brass mill is not unlike any foundry, with an annealing oven in place of the blast furnace, but with the same use of water to power the machines for working the alloy. Nothing was wasted here – the slag was shaped into blocks and used for building construction. Someone was impressed by local transport improvements, for they carved the message 'Begun Diggin The Rail Road Juncn 1836' on one of the walls. Although

The ledges at Portland Bill were created by quarrying, sometimes leaving isolated stacks behind. The latest of the three Portland lighthouses can be seen in the distance.

public access is limited, group visits can always be arranged, and the site is included here as a survivor of a once vital industry of the region.

Westonzoyland Pumping Station

£ static, ££ in steam; Sunday afternoons and summer Thursdays, check locally for steaming days; Tel: 01823 275795; Website:www.btinternet.com/~wzlet/index.htm

I have to admit to a certain amount of prejudice here. When you approach the site, the most obvious landmark is the tall stack rising above the boiler house, rebuilt a few years ago – and I was the one who clambered up the scaffolding to lay the last brick. But then I was already an enthusiast for this site. It is located at the heart of that strange area of wetlands, the Somerset Levels. Steam pumps were added to the complex system of banks and dykes in the nineteenth century, and this is a grand survivor. The engine, by Easton, Amos and Son, is a vertical two-cylinder engine that drove a centrifugal pump. It is still regularly steamed, and a number of smaller steam engines are on display. The great virtue of this site is that you can instantly see what it is there to do – hold the water at bay, and in its heyday it was able to keep over 800 hectares of land drained.

See Also

There are many watermills in the area, of which the following are the most interesting:

Alderholt Mill
£; Easter to October weekends; Tel: 01425 653130; Website: www.smoothhound.co.uk
The mill sits across a tributary of the Avon that forms the boundary between Hampshire and Dorset. It has been recently restored and produces wholemeal flour.

Piles Mill, Allerford
NT; Free; Open access; Tel: 01643 862452
Sixteenth-century cruck frame on the Holnicote Estate.

Mangerton Mill, Bridport
Free; Easter to October Tuesday to Sunday; Tel: 01308 485224
Three-storey mill with museum and craft workshops.

Burcott Mill
NT; Free entry, £ Guided tour; Open daily; Tel: 01749 673118; Website: smoothhound.co.uk
Working mill, producing flour.

Dunster Mill
NT; £; April to November daily; Tel: 01643 821759
Mill with two overshot wheels, producing flour.

White Mill, Shapwick
NT; £; April to November weekends; Tel: 01258 857184
Not working but has original wooden machinery.

Sturminster Newton Mill
£; Easter to September all day Saturday to Monday and Thursday; Tel: 01258 473760
An old mill but powered by a 1904 turbine.

Two other different mills can be added to the list:

Stembridge Windmill, High Ham
NT; £; April to October Sunday, Monday and Wednesday afternoons; Tel: 01458 250818
Britain's only surviving thatched windmill.

Wookey Hole Papermill
£££, Price includes caves and other amusements; All year; Tel: 01749 672243; Website: www.wookey.co.uk
Paper is made using water-powered machinery.

Brendon Hill
Free; Open access
From the little hamlet on the B3224, a straight track can be seen heading off down the hill for 1.2km to Comberow. This was an incline on the West Somerset Railway. It was opened in 1858 and was used to take ore from the Brendon Hill iron mines to Watchet for shipment round the coast to South Wales. It is still a remarkable landscape feature.

West Somerset Railway, Minehead
££££ return fare; June to October daily, April, May and October Tuesday to Thursday, weekends
This is the complete branch line, all 32km (20 miles) of it, from a junction at Taunton. It has all the atmosphere of the GWR of old, with splendid scenery thrown in.

Stembridge windmill, built in 1822, with its distinctive boat-shaped cap carrying the sails. It worked until 1910.

WILTSHIRE

This was once the heart of a thriving woollen industry that had its golden age before the Industrial Revolution had gathered its full momentum. It is still not too difficult to see towns such as Trowbridge as former textile centres, and the mill buildings in the town are easily identifiable. It comes as rather more of a surprise to find the popular tourist town of Bradford-on-Avon was an equally important centre of the woollen trade. Almost all the grand houses were clothiers' houses, while the beautiful houses on the hillside, known as the Torys – no political connotation – were homes of the merchants who employed the domestic workers of the surrounding area. The mills came later, and there is a fine mill, dating from the very end of the manufacturing period, down on the river by the bridge. Abbey Mill was built on the site of an earlier mill in 1874. And the very first site on the list that follows is one of my personal favourites.

CROFTON
Pumping Station

££; April to October, steaming weekends once a month; Tel: 01672 870300; Website: www.katrust.org

This is home to two beam engines, built to supply water to the Kennet & Avon Canal. One was built by Harveys of Hayle in 1845, but the other is even more venerable, a Boulton and Watt engine of 1812, which can claim the honour of being the oldest steam engine in the world still in its original building and still able to do the job it was built to do. It is extraordinary to think that when this engine started its working life, Napoleon was just starting on the long trudge back from Moscow. And, unlike the majority of preserved engines, these really do still perform, so not only can you watch them at their steady labours, but you can also see the result as water gushes out to fill the channel leading to the summit level of the canal.

DEVIZES
Kennet & Avon Canal Trust Museum

£; All day, closed January; Couch Lane, SN10 1EB; Tel: 01380 721279; Website: www.katrust.org

The small museum, housed in an old building on the town wharf, which in its time has been a granary and bonded store, tells the story of the Kennet & Avon Canal from construction to the present. But the site has more to offer. Follow the towpath out to the west and you will find a lock, then another and another until a whole string appears, charging off down the hillside, with side ponds sculpted alongside to keep them topped with water. This is the Caen Hill flight of locks, not Britain's longest, but certainly one of the most impressive.

Pewsey Heritage Centre

Free; April to October weekdays and Saturday mornings

The centre is based on the old Whatley foundry, built around 1870. The company produced engineering castings of all kinds, but especially for water wheels, pumps and mill gears. At the heart of the present collection stand the surviving machine tools. Local history is well covered and there is an outstanding collection of traction engine models.

See Also
Dundas Aqueduct, Limpley Stoke
Free; Open access (map ref. 172/785625)
A handsome, classically styled aqueduct on the Kennet & Avon Canal, by the entrance to the Somerset Coal Canal.

Avon Mill, Malmesbury
Free; Exterior view only
A particularly handsome, water-powered woollen mill, now converted into apartments.

A splendid motley array of exhibits on display at the former Whatley foundry in Pewsey. Parts of the original line shafting can still be seen.

The pride of the Great Western Railway, locomotive No.6000, *King George V* was built in 1927 and withdrawn from service in 1962 after completing nearly 2 million miles. The engine now stands in the former workshops of the GWR at Swindon, and as a special treat visitors can climb on to the footplate.

SWINDON
Steam

£££; Open daily; Follow brown signs for Outlet Centre and Museum; Kemble Drive, SN2 2AT; Tel: 01793 466646; Website: www.steam-museum.org.uk

This, for me, is a model of what a good, modern museum should be. Housed in the former workshops of the Great Western Railway, it is so much more than just a collection of locomotives and carriages. It tells the story of the works themselves, how the machines were built, right here in these buildings, and the story is brought to life by videos and recordings of the people who worked here. So you follow a natural progression and get the finished product right at the end. It is well worth waiting for, as it includes such giants of the steam age as the locomotive *King George V*. This is a museum you don't even have to be a railway buff to enjoy. Outside the museum walls is New Swindon, the village built by Brunel and the GWR to house the new workforce. It is a good place for wandering round to see how well provided for they were compared with other industrial workers in the nineteenth century.

GLOUCESTERSHIRE including Bristol

If Wiltshire has a history as an important area for manufacturing woollen cloth, then the same can be said of Gloucestershire, only more so. Textiles are not yet dead, as mills look for niche markets. In Stroud, for example, they make the green baize on which virtually all snooker champions demonstrate their skill – as do lesser players; and Stroud fabric gets whacked around the courts of Wimbledon, stretched as the cover of tennis balls. But many of the mills have been adapted to other uses. One of the finest of them all, Ebley Mill, now houses the Council Offices. It is not open to visitors as an attraction, but it has been preserved and forms a splendid centrepiece to the town, having something of the air of a French chateau. Bristol has been the hub of many activities, as a busy port and as a centre for lots of industries from brass making in the past to the aero industry of the present.

BRISTOL

Industrial Museum, Prince's Wharf

Free; April to October Saturday to Wednesday, November to March weekends only; City Docks BS1 4RN; Tel: 0117 925 1470; Website: www.bristol-city.gov.uk/museums

The location helps to make this museum rather special, situated right at the heart of what was until not very long ago a busy working harbour – and the museum spreads out beyond the walls of the building. This is very much a Bristol museum, telling the story of the city and in particular its outstanding engineering tradition. So in transport you have the story of road vehicles from the horse-drawn age through to the first experiments with steam on the road and on to the imposing Bristol car. Then there is the Great Western Railway and exhibits relating to the aeronautics industry – though if you want to see Bristol's very first plane, you have to go up the hill to the City Museum. For the shipping story, the real interest lies outside in the docks. Old cranes line the wharf and include the Fairbairn steam crane, which has been restored to working order. A small train puffs to and fro on the dock railway. Visitors can even take a trip round the harbour on the steam tug *Mayflower* and see the firefighting vessel *Pyronaut* put through its paces, sending jets of water skywards.

No one should really leave the city without taking at least a look at the works of Isambard Kingdom Brunel. The original GWR station is now home to a new museum telling the story of the Empire and Commonwealth; his pioneering iron steamer, the SS *Great Britain* is undergoing restoration in the dry dock where she was built, and it is open to the public. It is certainly well worth making the trip up to Clifton village to see his famous suspension bridge crossing the Avon gorge.

The Bristol Industrial Museum is situated in the heart of the city docks. A steam railway runs in front of the main building in the shadow of the cranes, and the museum's preserved craft are by the wharf.

COLEFORD

Hopewell Colliery Museum

££; Easter to October daily; On the B4226, between Coleford and Cinderford; Cannop Hill, Speech House Road; Tel: 01594 810706

The Forest of Dean has a long tradition of 'free mining', which allows anyone born in the area who has worked for a year and a day in a mine to work a claim of their own. The result is a lot of small coal mines, mostly drift mines, just a few of which survive. Hopewell Colliery is one of them. Visitors get a full underground tour, following the steeply inclined seams and leaving to return to the open air along an old level, dug in from the hillside early in the nineteenth century. The walk back is along the line of an old tramway. This is an ideal starting point for anyone keen to follow the history of the miners – and if you want to know what an ancient miner looked like, you can see his image in the stained glass of the Rising Sun pub, nestling under the shadow of spoil heaps transformed into viewpoints in the heart of the forest.

GLOUCESTER

National Waterways Museum

££; Daily; Llanthony Warehouse, The Docks, GL1 2EH; Tel: 01452 318054; Website: www.nwm.org.uk

With the opening of the ship canal from Sharpness in 1827, Gloucester became an inland port. It thrived in the nineteenth century, when a new dock was built, surrounded by tall warehouses. It is one of these that houses the Waterways Museum. There are really two quite distinct parts to this museum: inside are the displays telling the story of Britain's canals, how they were built and how they were run in the days when they were the country's most important transport routes. The rest of the story is told outside in the big exhibits, the narrow boats and barges out on the water, a collection which includes a steam dredger, still in working order, and a concrete barge not a barge to carry concrete, but one built with a concrete hull. There is a chance to take a boat trip on the canal itself, and visitors can roam around the docks. The Mariners' Church is a reminder that this was, in effect, a seaport.

A restored narrowboat is one of the many floating exhibits at the National Waterways Museum at Gloucester Docks.

NAILSWORTH

Dunkirk Mill

£; Two weekends a month in summer (details from Stroud tourist board); On the road between Nailsworth and Stroud, but access is by footpath from the car park behind Egypt Mill, Nailsworth; Tel: 01453 765768; Website: www.stroud-textile.org.uk

This is the heart of the old woollen mill area. Even before you reach Dunkirk, you get a glimpse of Egypt Mill with its romantic mill pond, now a hotel but once a woollen mill. Dunkirk is altogether grander. There has been a mill here since at least the end of the seventeenth century, but this is the 'New Mill', a mere two centuries old. It has been mainly converted into housing but part has been kept as a reminder of the past. The mill had no fewer than four water wheels, and one is now used to power machinery, including a rare gig mill, part of the finishing process. It is a small exhibit, but it makes a good introduction to a really fascinating region.

UPPER SOUDLEY

Dean Heritage Centre

££; Daily; Camp Mill, GL14 2UB; Tel: 01594 822170; Website: www.fweb.org.uk

The main building is a watermill. Built in 1876, it has certainly enjoyed a varied history – grain mill, leatherboard mill and sawmill. The aim of the centre is to tell the story of the working world of the Forest of Dean and bring it to life.

So this is, for example, one of the few places where you can see charcoal being made in the traditional way. Displays also include a section devoted to the coal mines of the Forest, many of which were worked by Free Miners, often on a very small scale. The tiny drift mines can still be found in the surrounding area. The arrival of steam power is also covered, from the first pumping engines for the bigger mines to the steam railways. There is still a preserved line, the Dean Forest Railway, running between Lydney and Parkhead. It seems an unlikely place to be thinking about industry, but there was a forge and a foundry here as well, right back in the seventeenth century. Poke around in the nearby woods and you can find the traces. Even if you don't recognise any of the signs, it is still lovely countryside, so the effort won't have been wasted.

See Also

Chalford
Free; Open access
Not only can many fine old woollen mills be seen in the valley at Chalford, but also one of the unusual circular lock cottages of the Thames & Severn Canal. A towpath walk down the canal is as good a way as any of getting views of the mills and the often imposing mill houses.

Sapperton Tunnel, Coates
Free; Open access
Highly decorated portal of Thames & Severn Canal tunnel, with boat trips inside the tunnel on some summer weekends. The pub is a former navvy lodging house.

Tewkesbury
Abbey Mill stands on the Mill Avon, the former course of the river. It is very impressive from the exterior, with two out of the original four water wheels surviving, though all the internal machinery has gone. In St Mary's Lane is a row of framework knitters' cottages, with typical long windows on the first floor. They can be viewed from the outside, but one is let out to holidaymakers by the Landmark Trust.

SOUTH EAST ENGLAND

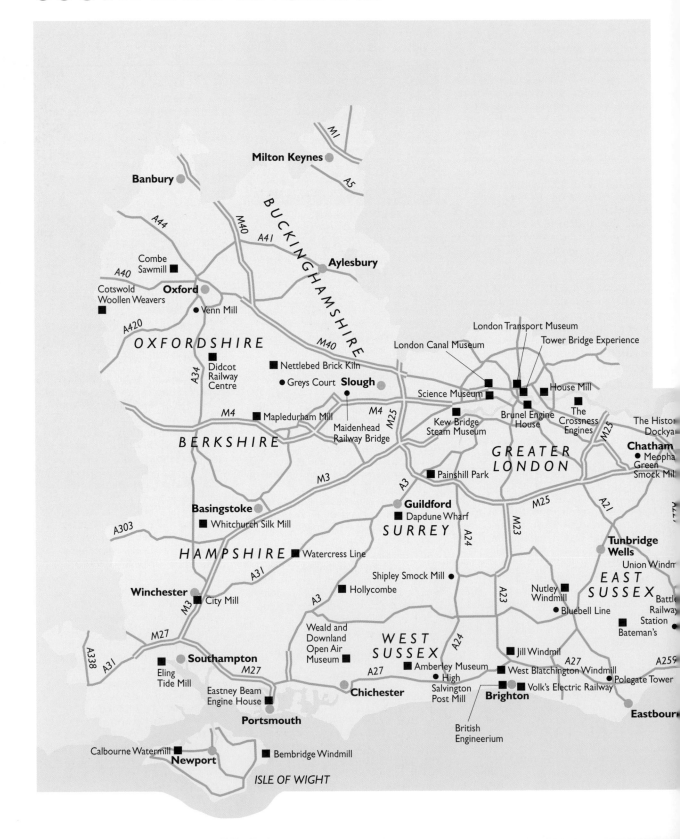

Milton Keynes

Banbury

M1

A5

BUCKINGHAMSHIRE

A44

M40

A41

Combe
Sawmill

Aylesbury

A40

Cotswold
Woollen Weavers

Oxford

A420

Venn Mill

OXFORDSHIRE

M40

A34

Didcot
Railway
Centre

Nettlebed Brick Kiln

Greys Court

Slough

A4

M4

Mapl   Mill

Maidenhead
Railway Bridge

M4

M25

A3

London Transport Museum

London Canal Museum

Tower Bridge Experience

Science Museum

House Mill

Kew Bridge
Steam Museum

Brunel Engine
House

The
Crossness
Engines

The Histor
Dockya

Chatham

Meopha
Green
Smock Mil

BERKSHIRE

M3

Painshill Park

GREATER
LONDON

M25

A21

M25

A303

Basingstoke

Whitchurch Silk Mill

Guildford

Dapdune Wharf

SURREY

A24

M23

Tunbridge
Wells

Union Windm

HAMPSHIRE

Watercress Line

A31

Shipley Smock Mill

A23

Nutley
Windmill

EAST
SUSSEX

Winchester

City Mill

A3

Hollycombe

Bluebell Line

Battle
Railway
Station

M3

Weald and
Downland
Open Air
Museum

WEST
SUSSEX

A24

Bateman's

Jill Windmill

A259

M27

A338

A31

Southampton

M27

Eling
Tide Mill

Eastney Beam
Engine House

Portsmouth

A27

Chichester

Amberley Museum

High
Salvington
Post Mill

West Blatchington Windmill

A27

Brighton

Volk's Electric Railway

Polegate Tower

Eastbour

British
Engineerium

Calbourne Watermill

Newport

Bembridge Windmill

ISLE OF WIGHT

HAMPSHIRE and the Isle of Wight

That this is not a very industrial area is perhaps exemplified by the first entry. The railway got its name because its main freight came in the form of watercress grown locally for the London market, which seems to say it all. Yet there are sites of the greatest importance. At Funtley on the River Meon near Titchfield, Henry Cort had a foundry where in 1775 he invented the process of converting cast iron into wrought iron by 'puddling'. Sadly, there is nothing left to see. Another landmark in industrial history was passed in 1802 when Sir Marc Brunel and Henry Maudslay installed machinery for making standardised blocks for ships at the Portsmouth dockyard. The building still exists and a few pieces of the thirty-two machines, but it is not, as yet at any rate, open to the public. It seems a shame that when the great ships themselves are preserved, there seems to be less interest in how they were made in the days of sail.

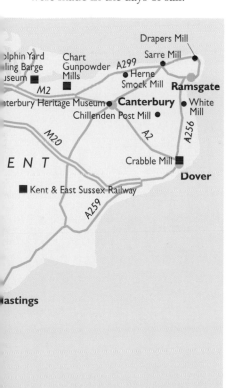

ALRESFORD
Watercress Line

£££; February to November;
Tel: 01962 733810;
Website: www.watercress.co.uk

This preserved steam railway is only 16km (10 miles) long, but noted for the steep gradients that earned this section the nickname 'The Alps'. It provides a genuine test for the powerful locomotives, including classic Southern Railway giants from the Merchant Navy, Battle of Britain and West Country classes. The run to Alton is through attractive countryside. The station originally had a junction with the short-lived light railway to Basingstoke. However, the line, and the station, achieved a certain fame when Alton was transformed into Buggleskelly and the line became the mythical Southern Railway of Northern Ireland in the Will Hay classic, *Oh, Mr. Porter!*

BEMBRIDGE
Windmill

NT; £; April to June, September to October daily except Saturday, July and August daily; Tel: 01983 873945

Perched on a little hill at the far eastern tip of the Isle of Wight, the old mill looks out to sea, the last surviving windmill on the island. Built somewhere around 1700, this is a handsome building, a well known landmark for sailors and a lure to artists, including the great Turner who painted it. A tower mill, it comes with a set of wooden machinery.

LIPHOOK
Hollycombe

£££; April to October Sundays, August daily; Iron Hill, Midhurst Road, GU30 7LP; Tel: 01428 724900; Website: www.hollycombe.co.uk

Steam at work and steam at play on offer in abundance. The fun part is the fairground, with steam yachts and gallopers, steam chair-o-planes and swings and even a steam-powered big wheel. Prize of the collection is Mr Field's Steam Circus, built in the 1870s and probably the oldest

All the fun of the steam fair! The big wheel, c.1914, driven by a portable Clayton & Shuttleworth engine is one of the popular attractions at Hollycombe.

surviving steam ride in the world. The miniature railway also comes into the fun category, though steam enthusiasts will find the serious railway side just as enjoyable There is a narrow gauge quarry railway and a standard gauge line. The steam farm not only has traction engines at work, but also has a stationary engine and line shafting to work a whole range of farm machinery. Add to this a steam sawmill, a variety of road engines and even a paddle steamer engine, and you have just about as varied a collection as you could wish to find.

WATER POWER

The water wheel was almost certainly first brought to Britain by the Romans, and it was a type of wheel first suggested in the first century BC by Vitruvius. This is the one with which we are all familiar, where the wheel rotates vertically round a horizontal axle. There was another tradition that reached these islands with the Vikings: the Norse wheel. In this version the axle is vertical and the blades of the wheel are set directly into the stream or river, where they turn horizontally. There may well have been a number of these in the country at one time, but now they are only found in the northern islands of Shetland and Orkney. Elsewhere, the Vitruvian wheel is the norm. Many watermills survive, but nothing like the number there once were. The Domesday Book records an astonishing 5,624 at work in England south of the Trent. Southern England still has enough mills left to give an idea of their rich diversity.

The earliest vertical water wheels were mainly of the type known as undershot, where the bottom of the wheel is immersed in a stream of water that pushes the wheel round. At its simplest the wheel is turned directly by the river or stream itself, but this presents a few difficulties. There is no means of controlling the flow or of quickly stopping the wheel. The alternative is to control the flow, either by creating a mill pond or by building a weir across the river and diverting water into a specially cut channel or leat. This can be controlled by sluices, and after passing the wheel, the water is returned to the river along the tail race. An alternative is the overshot wheel. The wheel itself is different in that instead of the paddles it has 'buckets' set round the rim. The water comes from a source at a higher level than the mill, carried in a trough, known as a launder. It falls onto the wheel, filling the buckets, making one side of the wheel heavier than the other so that it begins to turn. There is also an intermediary version, the breast shot wheel, with buckets like the overshot but with water arriving at the level of the axle. It was only in the eighteenth century that engineers led by John Smeaton carried out a scientific investigation into the efficiency of different types of wheel. The overshot was the clear winner, but as with so many things, the best is not always the most practical. It is often far easier to provide water for an undershot wheel and simply accept that it is going to be less efficient – and the miller had the consolation that there was no extra charge for using water inefficiently.

There was one problem that faced all millers, however: what to do in a drought when the water supply dried up. One answer was to use a source of water that never dried up, the tides. In a tide mill, such as that at Eling in Hampshire, the rising tide is allowed to flow into the mill pond. At high tide the

The watermill at Bateman's seen across the mill pond. It was built by a local iron master in the seventeenth century and restored in the 1970s to full working order.

sluices are closed, trapping the water, which can then be released to flow past the wheel. It solves the water shortage problem but carries its own built-in disadvantage. The times the mill can work are decided by the tide table, not the clock, making for a curious working schedule.

In the Norse mill the grindstones can be set directly onto the turning shaft, but in all the other mills, the grindstones have to be turned horizontally by a vertical wheel. The mills need gears. The introduction of gears is one of the great advances in technology. You can not only change the direction of motion, you can adjust the speed as well. If, for example, you have a large slow moving gear wheel and you mesh it with a small one, then the small one will turn several times for each turn of the big gear. It will go faster and will drive machinery faster. In most watermills the gearing looks fascinatingly complex but is really very simple. First comes the pit wheel, attached to the wheel axle and turning vertically with the wheel. This engages with the wallower, a second wheel set at right angles to it. Now we have a shaft turning vertically, as is needed. At the opposite end of the shaft is the great spur wheel, which is still turning quite slowly but that engages with the smaller stone nut, actually controlling the speed of the grindstones themselves. It sounds a bit complicated when it is all written out, but in practice it is very straightforward. It is an arrangement you will find repeated in watermills throughout Britain.

It was soon realised that once you could control a turning shaft, you could use it to power all sorts of things, not just the machinery of a grain mill. One of the earliest applications was to work hammers. A tappet wheel could be turned by the shaft. This is just a wheel with projections on the rim. At its simplest, the wheel turns, the projection hits the end of the pivoted hammer and pushes it down, lifting the head at the other end. Then as the projection clears, the hammer is released and the head crashes down. This was a system that was widely used for the iron industry of the Weald, where the metal was forged under the tilt hammers. But southern England also has examples of the versatility of water power. At Faversham, grinding mills were not concerned with grain for the table but ground the ingredients for gunpowder. Ingenious men even found new uses for the modern age. When Rudyard Kipling moved into a Jacobean house, Bateman's at Burwash in East Sussex, he also became the owner of an old grain mill in the grounds. He had no desire to grind his own flour but he did want modern amenities in his house. So the old watermill was adapted to turn a generator and Kipling could enjoy the benefits of electric power. It has been restored now and is back to its old role as a grain mill, which is rather a pity.

The final stage in the development of water power appeared with the turbine, in which the wheel has cups round the rim and the whole mechanism is enclosed within an outer casing. Water is injected through a nozzle and the wheel whizzes round at high speed. At first this had few applications, but it came into its own at the end of the nineteenth century, when turbines were used in hydro-electric schemes. Very few old turbines have survived, but they can still be found.

A selection of watermills in south east England

Bateman's, Burwash, Sussex
NT; ££, the admission price includes the house and gardens; April to November daily; Tel: 01435 882302
The mill with an overshot wheel was built in 1634, and is worked on most Saturday afternoons to grind flour. The water turbine used by Kipling to generate electricity can still be seen.

Calbourne Watermill, Isle of Wight
£; Easter to October daily; On the B3401 road towards Freshwater; Tel: 01983 531227
The building is seventeenth-century, though the machinery is quite modern by comparison, just over a hundred years old. The wheel is overshot, and instead of driving grindstones, it works more modern rollers.

Crabble Mill, Dover, Kent
£; Easter to September daily, October to Christmas and February to March Sundays only; Tel: 01304 823292; Website: www.invmed.demon.co.uk/mill
A big, six-storey weather-boarded watermill built in 1812, with five pairs of stones, three of which are still used to produce wholemeal flour. There are craft and art galleries on site.

Eling Tide Mill, Totton, Hampshire
£; Wednesday to Sunday; Tel: 01703 869575
The first tide mill here was recorded in the Domesday Book, though the present mill is a Johnny-come-lately of the eighteenth century. There are two iron water wheels and milling is done daily, but to see the machinery at work requires scrutiny of the tide tables

Mapledurham Mill, Oxfordshire
£; Easter to September weekends; Tel: 0118 947 8284; Website: www.mapledurham.co.uk
A delightful situation by the Thames adds to the charm of this little mill. The undershot wheel works wooden machinery that grumbles softly through the working day. It is still at work producing wholemeal flour.

City Mill, Bridge Street, Winchester, Hampshire
NT; £; April to October Wednesday to Sunday, March weekends; Tel: 01962 870057
Built as a tannery in 1744 and later converted to a grain mill, this is a delightful building of mellow red brick and tile, straddling the River Itchen in the heart of the city. The machinery has been recently restored.

The handsome Georgian façade of Whitchurch Silk Mill on the River Test, still at work more than two centuries after it was built.

PORTSMOUTH

Eastney Beam Engine House

£; Last weekend of each month; Henderson Road, Eastney, PO4 9JF; Tel: 02392 827261

Perhaps there are few less enticing offers than a suggestion of a visit to the local sewage pumping station, however worthy such a place might be. The Victorians didn't see it like that. They considered it to be a major advance in public health and were proud of their efforts. They had every right to show off the machines that did the work, a magnificent pair of beam engines built by James Watt & Co. in 1887. These are unlike the familiar beam engines, in that they are compounds, in which steam passes first to a high pressure cylinder and then exhausts into a second cylinder to add an extra effort. All very impressive.

Although it falls outside the scope of this book, few visitors will want to miss out on Portsmouth's historic ships, which have their own industrial story to tell. They range from the all-wooden construction of the Tudor *Mary Rose* (paradoxically the structure is much clearer in her present condition than it would be with a complete ship), through the famous *Victory* to the Industrial Revolution's answer to the battleship, the armour-plated *Warrior*. As mentioned in the introduction, not all the historic dockyard is open to visitors.

WHITCHURCH

Silk Mill

££; Tuesday to Sunday; 28 Winchester Street, RG28 7AL; Tel: 01256 893882; Website: www.whitchurchsilkmill.org.uk

This must be one of the most attractive textile mills you could ever hope to find. It is unmistakably Georgian, effortlessly elegant, its rich red brick set off by the clear waters of the River Test. The most modern part of the exterior is the clock, installed to celebrate the Battle of Waterloo, and taking over the duties of time-keeper from the spiky little bell tower. Silk was woven here, using water-powered machinery right up until the 1950s, at which point a little modest modernisation took over. I visited in 1985, when just one weaver was left at work, and it seemed a century and a half of tradition had ended. But now it has been reborn: machinery, some of it more than a century old, has been restored, and work goes on with the reproduction of speciality silks – a cause for celebration if ever there was one.

EAST AND WEST SUSSEX

The counties of downland and seaside have rather more to offer than one might expect, and provide an opportunity to see the development of power sources over the centuries, from windmill and watermill to mighty steam engines and Britain's very first electric railway.

AMBERLEY

Amberley Museum

££; March to November closed Monday, Tuesday except for school holidays; Close to Amberley Station; Tel: 01798 831370

The setting is spectacular: old chalk pits in the middle of the South Downs, which gleam and glisten in the sun. A good deal of the interest lies with this old working site, where railways disappear into cliff faces and huge banks of lime kilns stand below the chalk face. The workshops now house a variety of crafts, from cobbling to pottery, and there are some unusual exhibits, including a working village telephone exchange.

BRIGHTON

Volk's Electric Railway

£; Easter to mid-September daily; Tel: 01273 673201

This is Britain's first electric railway and one of the first electrically powered transport systems in the world. A miniature electric line was demonstrated in Berlin in 1879. Magnus Volk was an enthusiast for the idea and he built his 2.4km (1½ mile) track along the sea front in 1883. It has been extended and modified over the years, but still offers a novel way of enjoying the delights of the seaside.

CLAYTON

Jill Windmill

Free; May to September Sunday afternoons, winter second Sundays

Three for the price of one here. High on the Downs above the village are two windmills, Jack and Jill. The latter is a little post mill, built in 1821, which first turned its sails in Brighton. It has been restored and is opened on summer Sundays. Neighbouring Jack is a tower mill of 1866, but not open. It is rare to have two mills together for comparison. The third site is at the foot of the hill, where the London & Brighton Railway was pushed through the ridge of the Downs in a 2km (1¼ mile) long tunnel.

A cluster of old buildings that have been dismantled and re-erected as part of the Weald and Downland Open Air Museum

It was a great engineering achievement by John Rastrick, and the company's architect, David Mocatta, made sure that the world knew about it. The north portal by the main road had the full Gothic treatment, with turrets, arrow slits and battlements. The tiny cottage on top was home to the tunnel keeper.

HOVE

British Engineerium

££; Open daily; Off Nevill Road; Tel: 01273 554070; Website: www.britishengineerium.com

The Goldstone pumping station was built in 1866 to supply water to the town, and that meant ordering mighty steam engines to do the job. The engines were given a suitably dignified setting. On first walking in, you enter a

The gleaming brass of the Barnstaple horse-drawn fire engine, one of the many steam engines at the British Engineerium.

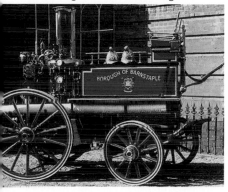

hall of immense grandeur, beautifully restored. All the main features of the works have been kept, from the underground railway that brought coal to the four Lancashire boilers, to the two huge beam engines, of 1866 and 1876, both compounds, which brought water up from a 49m (160ft) well. Sometimes statistics do help to give a notion of size. The piston of the low pressure cylinder of the 1876 engine, which moves so smoothly, together with its connecting rod weighs $2^{1}/_{2}$ tons. And when it moved it could lift 150,000 gallons of water an hour up to the reservoir. This is just a part of the story, for the old works have become the centre for a magnificent steam collection, with everything from fire engines to models. For the best of the museum, try and visit on one of the steam days, held regularly throughout the year, and see the engines come to life.

West Blatchington Windmill

£; May to September Sunday afternoons; Holmes Avenue, just south of the A2038; Tel: 01273 776017

A short distance from the Engineerium is this older source of power, an unusual hexagonal smock mill, standing on top of a brick and flint tower. There is also a good milling museum attached.

NUTLEY

Windmill

Free; March to September last Sunday afternoon in month; From the village, take the A22 going north and turn right towards Crowborough (map ref. 188/451291); Tel: 01435 873367

Although the mill is seldom open and not even easy to find, it is included because it is such a good example of an open trestle post mill. The seemingly fragile buck balanced on its trestle frame could be the model for a medieval illustration. In fact it was built some time in the seventeenth century. Flour is still milled occasionally.

SINGLETON

Weald and Downland Open Air Museum

£££; March to November daily; winter Wednesday, Saturday, Sunday; Chichester, PO18 0EU; Tel: 01243 811363; Website: www.wealddown.co.uk

This is a huge site, the kind of place where you can easily spend a whole day. It is a sort of retirement home for old buildings, buildings which were destined for demolition but rescued and brought here piece by piece and put together again. The aim is not to present a theme park atmosphere, but to provide an opportunity to study the buildings themselves, and in particular see just how they were put together. These are not the grand architectural statements, but the ordinary buildings our ancestors would have known, places of good, solid worth. In among them is a working watermill, a small wind pump, a tollhouse, a blacksmith's forge and a whole range of houses and farm buildings.

See Also

Railway Station, Battle

The station is still in use and is as good an example of Victorian Gothic as any, even extending to a vast baronial fireplace in the waiting room. The name is not inappropriate, since the town itself is named after the Battle of Hastings.

Bluebell Line, Sheffield Park

£££ return fare; May to September daily, school holidays; Uckfield, TN22 3QL; Tel: 01825 722370
One of Britain's oldest preserved steam railways. The immaculate period reconstructions run through everything from stations to rolling stock.

There are a number of windmills in the area, and the following are worth a detour:

High Salvington

£; April to September 1st and 3rd Sunday afternoons; Tel: 01903 260218
A post mill of *c*.1700, producing flour.

Polegate

£; Easter to October Sunday afternoons, August plus Wednesday afternoons; Tel: 01323 734496; Website: www.steali.co.uk
A tower mill with oat crushers as well as millstones; museum of milling.

Shipley

£; Easter to October 1st and 3rd Sundays; Tel: 01043 730439; Website: www.shipleywindmill.org.uk
Big and very handsome smock mill, once owned by Hilaire Belloc. Even when closed, it is worth going to see the outside.

KENT

The importance of Kent to the brewing industry can be seen in the many hop gardens that still flourish, and in the characteristic shape of the oast houses in which they are dried. This fits well with the image of the Garden of England. But Kent was once the centre of one of the country's most important industries.

CHATHAM

The Historic Dockyard

££££; April to November daily, November, February and March Wednesdays and weekends; Tel: 01634 823800; Website: www.chdt.org.uk

There has been a naval shipyard here since the middle of the sixteenth century, when the Admiralty decided the fleet needed a home nearer to London and came to 'Jillyingham Water' and the tiny hamlet of Chatham. The first dry dock was built in 1581, and soon ships were being built as well as repaired. Perhaps the most famous survivor of all Chatham's ships is not here but at Portsmouth: HMS *Victory*. So this is a place with a great story to tell. The emphasis now is on the ships themselves, including the twentieth-century destroyer HMS *Cavalier*, but the most interesting exhibits for this visitor were the ones that showed how ships were built and fitted out, and nothing is more impressive than the Ropery. The oldest part of the complex was built in 1729, and extension and improvement went on into the nineteenth century with the introduction of machinery and steam power. In effect, this is not unlike a textile mill, taking fibres, aligning them and twisting them together – except that the scale is far more massive. At the heart of it all is the forming machine, built by the famous engineer Henry Maudslay, which travels down the length of the ropewalk, forming the strands which can be up to 243m (800ft) long. Amazingly, it is still in use and you have the chance to see a process that has not changed for 150 years. There is a lot more to see on the shipbuilding side, but it is the rope making that you never forget.

There is one other very special attraction at Chatham, the paddle steamer *Kingswear Castle*, a picture of Victorian elegance – even if she was actually built in the 1920s! Her coal-fired boiler sends steam to the compound engine, which turns over quietly and smoothly with little more than a hiss of steam above the splash of the paddle wheels.

CRANBROOK

Union Windmill, Benenden Road

Free; April to October Saturday, mid-July to end of August plus Sunday afternoons; Tel: 01580 712984; Website: www.cranbrook.kent.sch.uk

This is one of the grandest of all Britain's windmills. A seven-storey smock mill, and the country's tallest, it lords it over the centre of the town, rising high over the rooftops. It looks splendid and it still works.

The majestic Union Mill lords it over Cranbrook. The seven-storey smock mill was built in 1814 and restored to full working order in 1960.

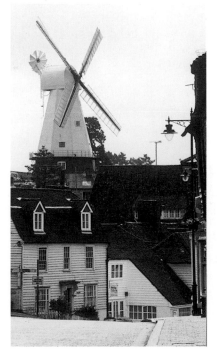

IRON AND THE WEALD

Ironmaking in the Weald, the lowland area between the North and South Downs, was already established when the Romans arrived. Iron was available in the Wadhurst clay, and the heavily forested area was ideal for producing charcoal in large quantities. Early extraction was carried out in bloomeries – open hearths where the ore was heated with charcoal, the temperature raised by bellows. It produced a spongy mass, which was reheated and the impurities hammered out as slag.

The first big change came in the early Tudor period, with the introduction of the blast furnace. It still depended on heating charcoal and ore, but was now enclosed in a furnace with a powerful blast blown through. The temperature in the furnace was so high that the metal became molten and could be tapped off and run into moulds. This could either be cast directly in shaped moulds or hammered out in forges. What the industry now required was a power source that would work the bellows for the blast of the foundries and power the hammers of the forge. The obvious answer was the water wheel. So streams were dammed to create ponds, in the same way that they had been dammed to provide mill ponds for grain mills. Furnaces and forges were established throughout the Weald, spreading across the boundary between Kent and East Sussex.

Vast quantities of charcoal were used in the furnaces of the Weald. Coppiced wood was carefully built into stacks that were covered over to smoulder slowly. This very old practice is still demonstrated at the Weald and Downland Museum.

began using coke instead of charcoal for his furnaces. It was the death knell of the Wealdland industry. There seems at first to be nothing left of a once great industry, but take out one of the Ordnance Survey maps covering the region – 187, 188 and 198 and you will see it dotted with small, triangular-shaped ponds. Often they have names, such as Hammer Pond or Furnace Pond, to show just why they were formed, though many remain nameless. But they all conform to the same basic pattern. The short side of the triangle is the dam holding back the water, which would then be released through sluices to the water wheel. They can appear singly or in a series, strung one after another down a stream. There are particularly good examples in the woods to the east of Crabtree, where two names appear, New Pond and Furnace Pond. It is an interesting area to explore, and you can find a substantial bridge across a stream and ruined sluices (map ref. 198/228247). There are traces of buildings, but only excavation would reveal the exact nature of the site. The other important part of the enterprise was charcoal making. This involves making a pyramid-like structure out of evenly cut logs, which when lit are covered over so that they smoulder under carefully controlled conditions. This is an

The industry began to decline in the seventeenth century. It was still strong enough in the early eighteenth century for people to begin to worry that the timber of the Weald was being used up, and soon there would not be enough left to build the ships for the navy. Then, up in Shropshire, Abraham Darby activity that leaves little evidence, as the charcoal burners worked in the heart of the woodland, for the very good reason that it is much easier to bring away the light charcoal than it is to carry substantial logs. The ancient craft is still demonstrated at the Weald and Downland Museum.

FAVERSHAM

Chart Gunpowder Mills

Free; Easter to October weekends; Off Stonebridge Way; Tel: 01795 534542; Website: www.faversham.org

Faversham is a beautiful market town, full of elegant old buildings, which makes it all the more remarkable that it was once the centre of a great explosives industry. Gunpowder consists of a mixture of charcoal, saltpetre and sulphur ground together. Here the little mill has been preserved with an overshot wheel to power the grindstones. The building is flimsy, so that if things did go wrong, it would disintegrate without causing too much damage. Even so, there is a mass grave in the town cemetery where 73 of the 108 victims of a great explosion in 1916 are buried. The mill is only a part of the story. There are far more extensive works in the woods between Faversham and Oare, and a walk through the trees can pro-

An old Thames sailing barge undergoing restoration at the Dolphin Yard Sailing Barge Museum workshops.

vide glimpses of the explosive past, from the blast walls to contain the violence to the waterways along which the gunpowder punts made their way. Water transport was safe compared to road traffic, so much of the powder went by water, and there are still sailing barges to be seen on the creek in the town centre. It is hoped to develop a full museum in the area shortly. For the time being the story of Faversham is told in the Fleur de Lis Heritage Centre, which also contains a village telephone exchange from the days before the electronic revolution.

SITTINGBOURNE

Dolphin Yard Sailing Barge Museum

£; Easter to end October Sundays; Crown Quay Lane, ME10 3SN; Tel: 01795 423215

The museum is approached along Milton Creek, where humps in the mud represent the last resting-places of old barges. In the nineteenth century there was an important brick and cement industry here, and the most efficient method of getting the finished product to booming London was by sailing barge. The barges were repaired here, at Dolphin Yard. The Thames barges are things of beauty, but they were also supremely practical, capable of being worked by a two-man crew and, at a pinch, single-handedly. Visitors can see the simple machinery needed to keep them afloat, and the loft where sails were made and repaired. When the museum was set up, someone had the brilliant idea that the best way to make it interesting was to set it to work, so barges still come here for restoration and essential work. It is impossible to say what will be here at any one time, but something will, and it will be splendid, as all Thames barges are.

TENTERDEN

Kent & East Sussex Railway

£££ return fare; May to September daily; Easter to May and October weekends; Tenterden Town Station, TN30 6HE; Tel: 01580 765155; Website: www.seeth.org.uk/kesr

This is a preserved railway of special significance. As the railway map filled

One of the last of the old electro-mechanical telephone exchanges at the Fleur de Lis Heritage Centre, Faversham.

in during the nineteenth century, several small towns were left outside the net, not grand enough to merit the splendour of a main line, nor even a branch line. So they got the poor relation, a light railway, built and run on the cheap. King of the light railway empire was Colonel Holman Fred Stephens, who ran his different railways from offices on the Kent & East Sussex at unromantic 23 Salford Terrace, Tonbridge. This is a line that typifies the Stephens ethic – nothing fancy and with the minimum of facilities. The little tank engine *Bodiam* is typical of the line, for it was already twenty-eight years old when it started here in 1901. This is more than just another steam railway though: the little museum tells the story of the eccentric Colonel Stephens and the strange array of railways that he ran on a rather frayed shoestring.

See Also

Canterbury Heritage Museum, Stour Street, Canterbury

£; June to October daily; November to May Monday to Saturday

The museum is housed in the medieval splendour of the Poor Priests Hospital, and has one outstanding exhibit from the world of technology. On 3 April 1830 the Canterbury & Whitstable Railway was opened, the first in the world to offer a regular passenger service behind a steam locomotive. That first locomotive was Robert Stephenson's *Invicta*, Number 12 on the works list and not quite as famous as Number 11, *Rocket*. The old engine has a place of honour in the museum.

More windmills to admire:

Chillenden

Free; May to September Sunday afternoons; Tel: 01304 812320
A rare example of an open trestle post mill.

Herne

£; Easter to September Sunday afternoons, July and August plus Thursdays; Tel: 01227 361326
A smock mill of 1789 with original machinery.

Drapers Mill, Margate

£; May to September Sunday afternoons, July and August plus late afternoons Thursdays; Tel: 01843 226227
Another smock mill but with additional gas engine.

Meopham Green

£; May to September Sunday afternoons; Tel: 01474 813518
A hexagonal smock mill with a small museum of milling.

White Mill, Sandwich

£; Easter to mid-September Sunday afternoons, January to end November Friday mornings, all year Sunday mornings; Tel: 01304 612076; Website: www.kent-museums.org.uk
A smock mill of 1760 with original machinery and folk museum.

Sarre mill

£; All year daily but closed Mondays in winter; Tel: 01843 847573
This is a working smock mill producing flour, together with a museum and traction engines.

SURREY and Greater London

Many old industries have been swept away in the changes that have engulfed the area in recent years. The shipyard where Brunel's *Great Eastern* was built has gone; the Spitalfields silk weavers' garrets are fashionable residences. Fortunately there are still survivors to see and enjoy.

COBHAM

Painshill Park

££; April to October Tuesday to Sunday, November to March as before but closed Friday; Tel: 01932 868113; Website: www.brainsys.com/cobham

This is not quite what you might think of as an industrial site, but it is a charming eighteenth-century estate full of follies and grottoes, and graced with a lot of water – which is where we come in. The water was supplied from the River Mole courtesy of pumps installed by Bramah in 1835. Power comes from an immense 11m (36ft) diameter water wheel. It filled the lake and produced an ornamental cascade. An even older device was used to send water to the big house – a horse engine. There is also a conventional watermill, just off Cobham High Street, but it only opens for a few days a year.

GUILDFORD

Dapdune Wharf

NT, £, Extra charge for boat trip; April to November Thursday, Saturday and Sunday; Wharf Road, GU1 4RR; Tel: 01483 561389

The opening up of the River Wey to Thames barges was begun by Sir Richard Weston, who put up most of the money and supervised operations, in 1651. It involved building ten locks, 14.5km (9 miles) of artificial cutting and a new wharf at Guildford. Dapdune wharf has one of the few surviving treadmill cranes and is home to the sailing barge *Reliance* and an exhibition on the life of this historic waterway. There are trips by electric launch from the wharf.

Dapdune Wharf on the River Wey Navigation. The mobile hand crane is an unusual and attractive feature.

LONDON'S RAILWAYS

The capital was the great lure that drew enthusiastic railway promoters, and each and every one of them made their London terminus into a showpiece, an architectural statement of superiority and grandeur. There was one exception: London's very first line. This was the Surrey Iron Railway, the very first public railway to be authorised by Act of Parliament. That, however, was in 1801, before the very first steam locomotive had ever run on rails. It was a tramway, running for just 9.6km (6 miles) from the Thames at Wandsworth to Croydon, and later extended. Virtually nothing has survived, though anyone fortunate enough to be able to pay a visit to Young's traditional brewery in Wandsworth will find some of the old stone sleeper blocks built into the yard wall.

The first of the great railways to arrive was Robert Stephenson's London & Birmingham, which began running trains out of Euston in 1838. Rather appropriately, the station was built very near the spot where Richard Trevithick ran his little engine *Catch me who can* in 1808 in a failed attempt to interest Londoners in his new invention. As befitted the first London station, it was given a monumental entrance, a Doric arch with adjoining lodges. In 1846 the station was improved with the construction of the Great Hall, an equally grand monument with a sweeping double staircase, from the top of which George Stephenson's statue looked down on the crowds. Sadly, arch and great hall have gone,

One of the most flamboyant works of the Gothic revival, Sir Gilbert Scott's station hotel at St Pancras. It stands in contrast to the unadorned engineering of the station itself, which was the work of William Henry Barlow.

demolished in the name of modernisation, which might have been acceptable if something truly splendid had been built in their place. All we have is the sort of bland, featureless architecture at which nobody would ever pause in admiration. Happily, other stations still display the proud self-confidence that characterised the best of Victorian architecture. When looking at stations, there are usually two very different elements to bear in mind: the façade and the train shed. The former is the bold face shown to the world, where architects aim for an effect; the latter is more likely to be the work of engineers, who had to solve the problem of how to build immense roofs to cover the multitude of tracks. Sometimes the two blend into a harmonious whole, as at King's Cross, but not always. There is nothing much in the face of Paddington, for example, to indicate the grandeur that lies inside. The following selection gives some idea of the qualities that can be found in the very best of London's stations.

King's Cross

Opened in 1852 and designed by Joseph and Lewis Cubitt, it looks the least Victorian of all the great stations. It was built for the Great Northern, a line not noted for extravagance; so instead of stone, generally favoured to give a sense of eminence, the designers settled on brick. And where some went for elaboration, they opted for simplicity. The train shed consisted of two curved roofs, carried on iron supports springing from the brick walls. This was then reflected in the two glazed arches of the frontage.

Paddington

The London end of Brunel's Great Western has been transformed in recent years with a new concourse. Fortunately, nothing of great importance has been lost. It is the train shed that demands attention, a glorious cathedral of steam, complete with aisles and crossings. Here one can see the hand of Brunel, but the details such as the odd little Tudor-style oriel window on Platform One is the work of the architect Matthew Digby Wyatt.

St Pancras

What most people think of as Victorian Gothic at its most flamboyant is not the station as such but the station hotel, the work of Sir Gilbert Scott. Although it was once fashionable to mock such extravagance, the circle has turned again and it is now generally admired. When the Midland Railway opened the station in 1868, the train shed, designed by William Henry Barlow, had the biggest station roof of them all, and it was an engineering triumph. An odd feature can be found under the station itself: the vaults specially designed to hold hogsheads of beer sent down from Burton-on-Trent.

Liverpool Street

Sir John Betjeman described this as 'the most picturesque and interesting' of the London termini, and I am not about to take issue. It is certainly one of the most complex. A near contemporary of St Pancras, the Great Eastern terminus went for a less ornate Gothic but an even more cathedral-like train shed, with aisles of cast iron pillars, and complex patterns of arches seeming to go off in every direction.

Isambard Kingdom Brunel described what he wanted for Paddington Station, the London end of the Great Western Railway: 'an enormous conservatory in a railway cutting'. And that is what he got.

There is one other aspect of the London railway story that should not be missed. The first underground opened between Bishop's Road and Farringdon in 1863. The Metropolitan was run with steam locomotives, having two gauges of track to accommodate the standard gauge and Brunel's Great Western broad gauge. The stations were little more than platforms in tunnels, but recent refurbishment has shown a certain dignified simplicity in the brick arches and ventilation shafts. Those who complain about travelling by tube might like to contemplate the effect of steam engines in place of electric. The best of the old Metropolitan stations is Baker Street.

London

ABBEY WOOD

The Crossness Engines

££; See below; Belvedere Road, Abbey Wood, SE2 9AQ; Tel: 020 8311 3711; Website: www.tanton.ndirect.co.uk/crossness

This is an industrial museum in the making, and at present can only be visited by appointment; but it is included here because it represents both the majesty of steam and a masterpiece of Victorian decorative ironwork. There are four immense beam engines here, built in 1864 as compounds and made even more efficient in 1899 when they were converted to triple expansion.

House Mill, Bromley-by-Bow

£; March to December first Sunday in month, May to October also open other Sunday afternoons; Three Mills Lane, Three Mills Island, Bromley-by-Bow, E3 3DU; Tel: 0208 980 4626; Website: www.leevalleypark.org.uk

The island in the River Lea was once home to an interesting industrial complex, which included a gin distillery and grain mills. Outwardly little has changed, but the former bottling plant is now a café, where a copper still has been preserved, and other buildings now house film and TV studios and a theatre. House Mill ground the grain for the gin distillery. It is a tide mill built in 1776 and an unusually grand affair, five storeys high, the upper storeys marked by dormer windows in the steeply pitched roof. There were originally twelve pairs of millstones and four wheels, but six pairs of stones have been removed. The adjoining Clock Mill also retains its wheels. Altogether, this is one of the grandest watermill complexes in Britain.

London Canal Museum

£; Closed Mondays; New Wharf Road, N1 9RT; Tel: 020 7713 0836; Website: www.canalmuseum.org.uk

Even without the museum, this would be an interesting spot. It started life in the 1860s as Carlo Gatti's Ice House. Gatti wanted to make ice cream, but how did you manage in the days before the refrigerator? The answer was to hack great lumps of ice in Norway, send them by ship to Limehouse Dock, London, and then on by canal to be stored in the vast wells at the bottom of the Ice House. Now the museum tells the story of London's canals.

The back cabin of a narrowboat at the London Canal Museum. This tiny space was the living and sleeping accommodation for an entire family.

Brunel Engine House

£; April to October weekend afternoons, November to March Sunday afternoons; Railway Approach Road, Rotherhithe, SE16 4LF; Tel: 020 8806 4325; Website: www.brunelenginehouse.org.uk

Not Isambard this time, but his eminent father, Marc Brunel, who was the man responsible for building the first tunnel under the Thames, between 1825 and 1842. A steam engine was installed to pump the works on this site, and here the museum has its home. One of the main exhibits is the horizontal V steam engine, the last of its kind, built by John Rennie. The original entrance to the tunnel was via a spiral ramp. Part of the original on the opposite bank can be seen at Wapping Underground Station, for the old tunnel now carries tube trains.

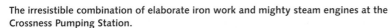

The irresistible combination of elaborate iron work and mighty steam engines at the Crossness Pumping Station.

Tower Bridge Experience

£££; Open daily; Tower Bridge, SE1 2UP; Tel: 020 7403 3761; Website: www.towerbridge.org.uk

Tower Bridge has come to epitomise London, much as the Eiffel Tower does Paris. It has a faintly comical air about it, a mock medieval exterior hiding what was, at the time, state of the art technology. The problem was to cross the Thames by a bridge that would still allow ships to use the river. The answer was a bascule bridge, with hydraulic machinery that would raise the two immense platforms carrying the roadway. Power was supplied by a pair of compound engines built by the leading company in hydraulic engineering, Armstrong Mitchell of Newcastle. A high-level walkway provides one of the best views in London.

London Transport Museum

£££; Open daily; The Piazza, Covent Garden, WC2E 7BB; Tel: 020 7379 6344; Website: www.ltmuseum.co.uk

The name tells you exactly what to expect – the story of London's transport from the days of horse-drawn

London buses of various vintages on parade amid the decorative columns and tracery of the old Covent Garden Market, now home to the London Transport Museum.

Just a part of the magnificent 90 in. (230cm) Grand Junction steam engine built for the Kew Pumping Station in 1846.

vehicles to the present, with exhibits ranging from the very first omnibus, introduced by George Shillibeer in 1829, which ran between Paddington and the city, to the steam locomotive that once worked on the Circle Line. The setting is itself of historic interest, being the old flower market that once made Covent Garden one of the busiest and liveliest places in London.

Kew Bridge Steam Museum

££; Open daily; Green Dragon Lane, Brentford, TW8 0EN; Tel: 020 8568 4757; Website: www.kbsm.org

No problem finding this place – just look out for the tower, rising high above the rooftops and stopping just short of the 61m (200ft) mark. This is not, as you might think, a chimney for the old water pumping station, but the Standpipe Tower. Like so many of the Victorian pumping stations, this one has a sense of style, as befits a building that was to house what was in its day the biggest steam engine in the world. This is the 100-inch engine built by Harvey of Hayle, that began work in 1857. If 100 inches doesn't sound very big, remember that this is just the diameter of the steam cylinder, and the giant was able to pump water at a rate of 717 gallons, not per hour, not per minute but at every single stroke. And this is only one of the engines on show. The oldest of the original Kew engines is a Boulton and Watt of 1820, and the other engines provide a splendid array of steam, from the 'upside down' Bull to the elegant Maudslay. As if there wasn't enough here already, other engines have been brought in, big and small, including a wonderful Hathorn Davey triple expansion, with three cylinders. In recent years a narrow gauge railway has been added as an extra attraction, which runs on special days throughout the year. Visiting Kew is about as close as the steam enthusiast will ever get to entering paradise.

Science Museum

Free; Open daily; Exhibition Road, South Kensington, SW7 2DD; Tel: 020 7942 4000; Website: www.nmsi.ac.uk

It is difficult to know what to say about this, other than that it is one of the most important collections of its kind in the world. If you are interested in any aspect of the history of technology, you are bound to finish up here sooner or later. In recent years it has become rather more all singing, all dancing and includes an IMAX cinema. But it is still a serious collection with a host of unmissable exhibits.

BERKSHIRE, BUCKINGHAMSHIRE AND OXFORDSHIRE

These are essentially rural counties, though there have been important industries in the region in the past. Oxfordshire, for example, had a number of thriving brick works that survived well into the twentieth century and were at the peak of activity in the period from 1860 to 1880. There were eighty-three brickyards in the county. Little now remains, apart from the bricks themselves, which are often found used in particularly distinctive ways. In Oxford itself, for example, the area known as Jericho contains terraces of houses where walls have been given a checkerboard effect by alternating grey bricks with the more familiar red. Even more impressive effects can be seen in Oxford's well-known buildings, as in the polychrome brickwork of William Butterfield's Keble College Chapel.

Brick was also to be the favoured material for generations of engineers who brought transport routes through the area. The neat

little brick bridges of the Oxford Canal and the Grand Union are easily overlooked, but each is a good example of the fine effect that can be achieved in simple structures, using appropriate local materials. Even grander things appeared with the coming of the railways. Brunel's bridge over the Thames near Maidenhead is a masterpiece, with its wide, low arches, each with a span of 39m (128ft).

COMBE, OXFORDSHIRE
Sawmill

££; March, May, August, October 3rd Sundays; On the River Evenlode, near Combe Station (map ref. 164/416150); Tel: 01608 643377

Although the site is only open for a few days a year, it is worth the effort to try and get to see it since there really is nothing else quite like it. The sawmill was built to serve the huge estate of Blenheim House at some time around 1850. It worked on the 'belt and braces' principle. At one end of the building is a water wheel, driving various woodworking machines through a belt and line shafting. At the opposite end of the building is a beam engine, able to work the same mechanisms. The water wheel was favoured, since water is free, and steam was used in times of drought. This could produce some interesting results, as water levels could drop to the point where there was not enough to feed the condenser. This produces spectacular clouds of steam, and the whole place soon resembles a sauna.

DIDCOT, OXFORDSHIRE
Didcot Railway Centre

££££ (depending on special events); All year weekends, April to October and school holidays daily; By Didcot Parkway Station, OX11 7NJ; Tel: 01255 817200; Website: www.didcotrailwaycentre.org.uk

Housed in the former GWR engine shed, this is home to a major collection of Great Western Railway locomotives and rolling stock. The old

The steam beam engine at Combe sawmill. The work of running the machinery is shared with a water wheel.

A GWR locomotive having its tender filled with coal at Didcot.

Radstock station and signal box have been re-erected on the site. Representatives of the famous locomotive classes are here – the Kings, the Castles, the Manors and the Halls, some of which are given outings under steam. There is one special feature: a recreated length of the famous Brunel broad gauge track.

FILKINS, OXFORDSHIRE
Cotswold Woollen Weavers

Free; All year Monday to Saturday, Sunday afternoon; Tel: 01367 860491; Website: http://ds.dial.pipex.com/wool.weavers

This is a real working mill where cloth is made and sold in the shop and it is the last bastion of an old tradition, for the wool that is used comes from the now rare breed of Cotswold sheep. Here you get to see the whole process virtually from fleece to cloth. The process begins when the cleaned wool is thrown into the scribbler, a venerable machine built in 1862, where the fibres are separated by vicious-looking wire-studded rollers. Then the wool passes through all the different stages of carding and spinning to be prepared for the looms. The main work is done on big Dobcross looms, and there is one giant 3.3m (130in.) loom used for weaving articles such as bedspreads. The mill is generally at work, and what you see depends on what happens to be going on. Machines here are run because they are needed, not as demonstrations for visitors, and for me that makes it all the more interesting.

NETTLEBED, OXFORDSHIRE
Brick kiln

Free; Open access; In the centre of the village

To be honest, there is not a great deal to be seen here, simply what looks

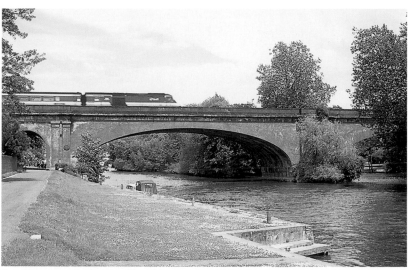

Brunel's railway bridge over the Thames at Maidenhead is famous as an example of engineering, and is also the scene for Turner's painting *Rain, Steam and Speed*.

very like a bottle oven strayed across from the Potteries. And that is essentially what it is, except that it served what was once a substantial local industry making bricks. The square chamber at the heart of the kiln could hold up to 12,000 bricks. Once they were in, the entrance was stopped and the furnace fired up. Perhaps not worth a long journey to see, it is certainly worth a detour, for it is a solitary survivor.

See Also
Venn Mill, Garford, Oxon
£; April to October 2nd Sunday in month; Tel: 01367 718888
Particularly traditional country watermill grinding local wheat.

Greys Court, Rotherfield Greys, Oxon
NT; ££ Gardens only; Daily, except Sunday and Monday, April to October; Henley-on-Thames, RG9 4PG; Tel: 01494 755564
A fine house but the interest for this book is the donkey wheel, used to raise water from a 61m (200ft) well. Unlike the treadmills found in gaols, for example, this was a wheel in which the donkey walked on the inside.

Maidenhead railway bridge, Berks
Free; Open Access
Brunel's bridge crosses the Thames on two broad, flattened arches. Critics of the day claimed it would never stand but here it is as elegant as ever.

West Midlands

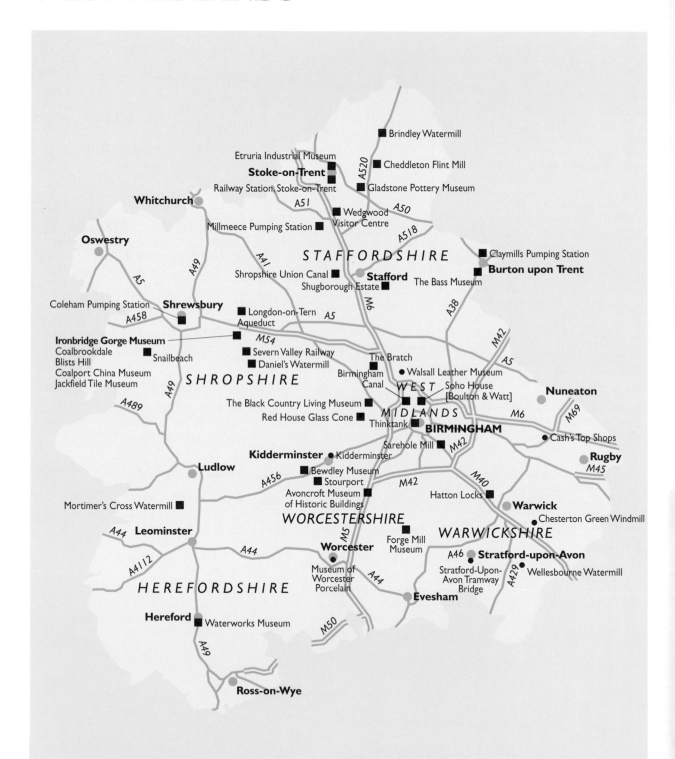

Brindley Watermill

Etruria Industrial Museum

Cheddleton Flint Mill

Stoke-on-Trent

Railway Station, Stoke-on-Trent

Gladstone Pottery Museum

A520

A51

A50

Whitchurch

Wedgwood Visitor Centre

Millmeece Pumping Station

A518

Oswestry

Claymills Pumping Station

STAFFORDSHIRE

A41

A49

Shropshire Union Canal

Stafford

Burton upon Trent

A5

Shugborough Estate

The Bass Museum

Coleham Pumping Station

Shrewsbury

M6

A38

A458

Longdon-on-Tern Aqueduct

A5

A42

Ironbridge Gorge Museum

M54

A5

Coalbrookdale
Blists Hill
Coalport China Museum
Jackfield Tile Museum

Snailbeach

Severn Valley Railway

The Bratch

Daniel's Watermill

Birmingham Canal

Walsall Leather Museum

A49

SHROPSHIRE

WEST

Soho House
[Boulton & Watt]

Nuneaton

A489

The Black Country Living Museum

MIDLANDS

M6

M69

Red House Glass Cone

Thinktank

BIRMINGHAM

Cash's Top Shops

Sarehole Mill

Kidderminster

Kidderminster

M42

Rugby

M45

Ludlow

A456

Bewdley Museum

Stourport

M42

Hatton Locks

M40

Warwick

Avoncroft Museum
of Historic Buildings

Chesterton Green Windmill

Mortimer's Cross Watermill

WORCESTERSHIRE

WARWICKSHIRE

A44

Leominster

A44

M5

Forge Mill
Museum

Worcester

A46

Stratford-upon-Avon

A4112

Museum of
Worcester
Porcelain

A44

Stratford-Upon-
Avon Tramway
Bridge

A429

Wellesbourne Watermill

HEREFORDSHIRE

Evesham

Hereford Waterworks Museum

M50

A49

Ross-on-Wye

HEREFORDSHIRE AND WORCESTERSHIRE

These are largely agricultural counties, but they have odd pockets of industry: needle making round Redditch, carpets in Kidderminster and there was once an extensive salt trade from Droitwich, served by the Droitwich Canal, currently being restored.

BEWDLEY

Museum

£; April to November daily; The Shambles, Load Street, DY12 2AE; Tel: 01299 403573

Hard to believe now, but Bewdley was once a major port on the River Severn, and its story is told in a museum housed in the old butchers' Shambles, which, considering what a noisome place this would once have been, makes a very attractive setting. The most important section has a preserved brass foundry and there is a little piece of machinery of great charm. A water wheel drives a pump that supplied water to the house of Joseph Tangye, a name widely admired as a builder of mighty steam engines.

The elegant masonry bridge over the river was designed by Thomas Telford.

The old shambles in Bewdley now provide an attractive setting for the town museum.

The original machinery is still in place in the eighteenth century watermill at Mortimer's Cross.

HEREFORD

Waterworks Museum, Broomy Hill

££; April to October Tuesdays, April to October steam days on last Sunday in the month, June to October plus second Sunday; Breinton Road, HR4 0JS; Tel: 01432 344062

A tall water tower rising above the banks of the Wye marks the site of the old waterworks. Unlike most pumping stations now open to the public, the original beam engines have gone. The first replacement was a vertical triple expansion engine of 1895, which could pump a million gallons of water in a twelve-hour shift. This monster of a machine was supplied by Worth, Mackenzie & Co of Stockton-on-Tees. A beam engine has now been added to the collection, a Simpson of 1851, and coming more up to date, a National Gas engine of 1912. There is even an overshot water wheel, bringing memories of older forms of power. The biggest change in recent years has not been the addition of a new engine, but rather the arrival of a whole new water pumping station, brought over from Leominster and re-erected here, now housing a 1932 Tangye diesel pumping engine from Pembroke Dock. This really is a museum that tells the whole story of water supply.

MORTIMER'S CROSS

Watermill

EH; £; April to October Thursday and Sunday afternoons; Tel: 01568 708820

An eighteenth-century watermill with all its machinery in working order.

REDDITCH

Forge Mill Museum

£; Easter to September Monday to Friday and Saturday afternoons, February to Easter and October to November Monday to Thursday and Sunday afternoons; Off the A441, Alvechurch Road; Needle Mill Lane, Riverside, B98 8HY; Tel: 01527 62509

I fell in love with this site when I first visited it back in the 1970s and it is even better now. The machinery, which was then marvellous but static, is now back in working order. The great attraction is the ingenuity with which a simple power source, the water wheel, has been harnessed for quite different tasks. The first stage of needle making takes coils of wire, straightens them and then points them. This was done at powered grindstones, each grinder holding bundles of up to a hundred wires at a time. It was lethal work. The dust got into the pointers' lungs, and it was a lucky man who lived to see his thirtieth birthday. There was also a danger from breaking

STOKE HEATH, BROMSGROVE

Avoncroft Museum of Historic Buildings

££; April to December daily; Tel: 01527 831363; Website: www.avoncroft.org.uk

When in an act of architectural vandalism all too typical of the 1960s permission was given to demolish the magnificent fifteenth-century Merchant's House in Bromsgrove, local enthusiasts managed to save all the timbers. The house was repaired and re-erected, the first occupant of this 6-hectare (15-acre) site. More have been added through the years of all kinds and varieties, from a cockpit to a corrugated iron mission church, from medieval hall to prefab. Even a collection of telephone kiosks has been moved here. There is a fine nineteenth-century post mill, still producing flour, and a perry mill where the stones used for crushing pears and apples are powered by a horse. All the buildings are interesting, and in among them are two that epitomise the work of the Black

Country. The first is a nailer's workshop. Small outbuildings like this were attached to cottages, and the work was very basic. The iron was heated in a hearth, then shaped by an 'oliver', a hammer worked by a foot treadle. Dies were used to give the correct size and shape. The chainshop from Cradley Heath is basically similar, but has moved up several scales of magnitude. Again, metal was heated and shaped, first bent into a U, then the ends were reheated, overlapped and welded together. Small chains were often made by women, the big chains, up to anchor chain size, by men. There are occasional demonstrations. Oddly enough, children seldom remember the grandest buildings, but always recall the humblest on site – the three-seater loo.

The chain-making shop at the Avoncroft Museum of Historic Buildings. The building originally stood at Cradley in the heart of the Black Country. Chains of all sizes were made here, the smallest under half an inch by women, the rest, up to the size of anchor chains, by the men.

The eighteenth-century needle mill at Redditch.

stones. They spun at around 2000 r.p.m., and in 1812 one broke and shot off, leaving a fragment buried in the wall. It carries the date 1816 and the initials, E.M., of the grinder it killed. The needles were stamped, holes were cut and the eyes created. The last bit is the best, the scouring mill. Here the needles were cleaned by being shaken together with scouring agents. The great wooden boxes rock to and fro, powered by water, using a mechanism given a lovely name from the noise it makes – the 'whee whaw'. The mill was in use for over 200 years, and it has a strange beauty at odds with its lethal history.

See Also

Kidderminster

This is an important carpet manufacturing centre. The best way to see the mills is to walk the towpath of the Staffs & Worcester Canal on its way through the town. But hurry: they are being demolished at an ever greater rate. It is worth looking at Park Lane, a most unusual development of carpet manufacturers' houses.

Museum of Worcester Porcelain, Severn Street, Worcester

££; Daily; Tel: 01905 23221
Royal Worcester Porcelain was founded in 1749, and parts of the present factory date back to 1792. The museum displays two centuries of ware and there are tours of the modern works.

WARWICKSHIRE AND WEST MIDLANDS

We have now arrived at a very heavily industrialised area, part of which earned itself the title of Black Country from the pall of smoke that rose above it. Based originally on small workshops turning out a variety of goods, from nails to fancy ware, Birmingham and the surrounding area began to develop rapidly during the Industrial Revolution. It became the hub of the English canal system in the eighteenth century, and was criss-crossed by railways in the nineteenth century. Collieries fed the new steam engines with coal; a strong tradition of engineering was carried on through from the days of Boulton and Watt into the age of the motor car and motor cycle. The very success of the area means that the old is constantly being pushed aside to make way for the new. On a recent visit to the Birmingham Canal I found that an area I thought I knew really well was so changed that I lost all sense of where I was, and it was only when I reached the top of the Farmer's Bridge locks that I got my bearings. Fortunately, the past is still preserved in some exceptional museums, and even the old craft tradition lives on in areas such as the Jewellery Quarter in Birmingham.

BIRMINGHAM

Sarehole Mill

Free; Open every afternoon except Monday; Cole Bank Road, Hall Green, B13 0BD; Tel: 0121 303 4698; Website: www.birmingham.gov/bmag

A watermill with a difference, for it has seen a variety of uses. There has been a corn mill here since the sixteenth century, but in the 1750s it was taken over by Matthew Boulton and used for metal rolling. By the 1760s it had been rebuilt and used both for corn again and for grinding edge tools. In the 1850s a steam engine was installed, as well as the two water wheels, one high breast shot and the other overshot. The old steam engine has gone but the chimney remains a prominent feature. Thanks to restoration, the machinery is all in good order, and there are occasional milling days.

Sarehole Mill still has two water wheels and, as the tall chimney indicates, once had a steam engine as well.

CANALS

The rationale for canal building was clearly spelled out in the eighteenth century, thanks to a series of simple experiments. How much could you move using one horse to do the work? Put your load on the back of a pack horse and you could shift perhaps no more than 136kg (300lbs). Put it in a cart on one of the new surfaced roads and you went up to an impressive 2 tons. But fill a boat and set it down on a river and the load shot up to 30 tons. The trouble was that by the middle of the eighteenth century the country had run out of navigable rivers that could be tamed for transport, leaving whole areas untouched, and those were often the areas where the new industries were burgeoning. The only answer was to build wholly artificial canals.

The idea of canal construction was not new. Over in France, an impressive canal network had already been building up for over a century, so Britain was quite late in the day in discovering the benefits of this new type of waterway. But once the first canal had been completed, canal building went ahead at an astonishing rate, reaching a peak in the early 1790s when in a period of just three years work began on no fewer than thirty-nine new canals. It all began when a young nobleman, Francis Egerton, third Duke of Bridgewater, decided that he had had his fill of life in the fashionable world and returned to his estates near Manchester. Here he had a good income from his coal mines at Worsley, and he knew that he would have even greater profits if he could get his coal

efficiently and cheaply to rapidly developing Manchester. So he promoted and paid for his very own canal. It began underground in the mine workings before setting off on its modest 11km (7-mile) journey, but in the course of that journey there was one major obstacle to be overcome, the River Irwell. It was crossed on a high aqueduct, the wonder of the age. Tourists came to stare at the improbable sight of boats on the canal crossing high above others on the river. Even more impressive for would-be investors was the effect of the opening in 1761 – the price of coal in Manchester was halved.

The engineer who had worked on the Bridgewater Canal, James Brindley, found his skills in demand for other canals up and down the country. The first canal had been built to take barges from the local rivers, particularly the Mersey flats, roughly 21m (70ft) long by 4.2m (14ft) beam. Now Brindley was involved in a far greater project, the Trent and Mersey, a canal that was to be 153km (93 miles) long. Inevitably there were to be many changes in level, but engineers knew the answer to that. Locks were already in use on river navigations. Basically, the lock is a very simple device. A chamber is closed at both ends by watertight gates, and water can be let in or out through sluices. To go downhill, the lock has to be filled, after which the top gates can be opened and the boat moves in. Then the water is let out, and when levels are equal the boat can leave. To go uphill, the sequence is simply reversed. But Brindley had a new problem to face: a ridge running right across the line of the canal that simply could not be conquered by locks. He had only one choice. He would have to go through Harecastle Hill in a tunnel. No one had ever built a canal tunnel to this scale, over

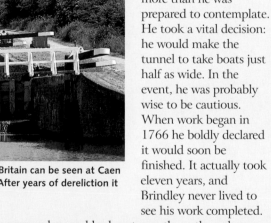

One of the most spectacular lock flights in Britain can be seen at Caen Hill, Devizes on the Kennet & Avon Canal. After years of dereliction it was re-opened in 1990.

2.4km (1½ miles) long. The idea of making it big enough to take 4.3m (14ft) wide boats was more than he was prepared to contemplate. He took a vital decision: he would make the tunnel to take boats just half as wide. In the event, he was probably wise to be cautious. When work began in 1766 he boldly declared it would soon be finished. It actually took eleven years, and Brindley never lived to see his work completed.

It was narrow, low and had no towpath, so the only way in which boats could be moved through was by 'legging'. The boatmen lay on their backs and walked their feet along the tunnel wall, while someone else, often one of the children, led the horse over the top.

The decision taken at Harecastle had huge repercussions. If the widest boat that could pass through the tunnel was going to be roughly 2m (7ft) beam, then there was no point in anything else on the canal being built to take larger vessels. So locks were built narrow as well, and a special type of boat was developed – the narrow boat. Today it seems incredible that the most important transport system of the whole Industrial Revolution depended on such puny craft. But just think back to those statistics quoted at the beginning: the narrow boat could in fact take a good load, ideally suited for just one horse. No one can blame Brindley if he failed to look ahead to the days of power and the steam railway that still lay half a century in the future. His narrow canals and narrow boats did everything that was asked of them, and towns such as Birmingham prospered on the basis of the new system. Indeed, Birmingham itself lay at the very heart of a great web of waterways spreading throughout the Midlands. A new generation of boating families grew up who abandoned life on the land and spent all their time on the boats. The back cabin was a miracle of organisation, with an entire family squeezed into a space usually no more than 3m (10ft) by 2.1m (7ft).

The first burst of canal building died away in the economic slump that accompanied the disastrous – as far as the British economy was concerned – war with America. When it resumed in the 1790s there was a new generation of canal engineers with new ideas. The Brindley age was dominated by what is known as contour cutting, following the natural lie of the land so that a canal would wander across the face of the countryside, squirming round hills in immense detours. The new generation would have none of that. Nowhere is this clearer than in Birmingham itself. Brindley built the first Birmingham Canal, a typically meandering affair, which proved inadequate for the growing commercial traffic. So Thomas Telford was called in to build a new main line. This cut through the line of the old waterway, almost arrow straight. Instead of rounding hills, it sliced through them in deep cuttings; it strode over valleys on high embankments. And new materials were brought in. The early engineers had relied exclusively on the materials of the local district through which the canal was to pass. In

stony areas they opened quarries and built stone bridges, in other areas they dug clay pits and made bricks. Now a new construction material was available – iron. This had a huge advantage. If the canal is made to a uniform width, then you can have a uniform bridge to cross it. All through the Birmingham network of canals you will find little identical bridges, all using the same castings, provided by the local Horseley Iron Works, and the idea spread to other canals. But engineers also like to show off, and you can see far more spectacular use of iron by taking a trip to Smethwick. Here are two splendid structures, the high arched iron bridge carrying Galton Street over a deep cutting, and the Engine Arm aqueduct, a resplendent affair of ornate Gothic decoration. The latter is considerably different from the very first iron aqueduct, also designed by Telford, which carried the now defunct Shrewsbury Canal across the river at Longdon-on-Tern. He went on to join William Jessop in creating the mightiest iron aqueduct of them all: Pontcysyllte, near Llangollen.

The canals struggled on through the railway age but traffic slowly died away, and the coming of the motorised truck, offering door-to-door service, finished almost all commercial carrying. Yet the network lives on, used now for pleasure boating. The modern narrow boat comes with all mod cons and a powerful motor instead of a plodding horse. But the canal system remains remarkably unchanged. There is still a huge amount of great historic interest to see. I have listed some of the more important sites in the vital area of the West Midlands, and all are well worth visiting. But the best way of all to see the canals is to see them by boat. It is by witnessing the system at work that everything really begins to make sense, and even in this modern age the pace of life remains what it was over two centuries ago. You still travel at the speed set by the horse-drawn working boats of the past.

A selection of canal sites in the West Midlands

All these sites are accessible and can be reached down the towpaths.

Birmingham Canal
The canal runs from the heart of the city to Wolverhampton. The most interesting section to explore is at Smethwick, and can easily be reached from Smethwick station. This stretch includes Galton Bridge, the Engine Arm aqueduct and the Galton Valley Canal Heritage Centre by Brasshouse Lane.

The Bratch, Staffs
A curious little flight of locks on the Staffs & Worcester Canal, set so close together that the locks almost touch. The scene is completed by a lock cottage and an elegant octagonal tollhouse.

Hatton Locks, Warwicks
This is an immense flight of locks on the Grand Union Canal. There are twenty-one locks, all packed close together, rising up alongside the A4177. They look impressive to a visitor, daunting to anyone in a boat who faces the challenge of working through the whole lot.

Longdon-on-Tern Aqueduct, Shropshire
The first cast iron aqueduct looks like a prototype, with a rather crude trough carried on spindly iron supports. It can be seen close by the bridge carrying the B5063 across the River Tern.

Stourport, Worcestershire
Brindley brought his Staffs & Worcester Canal here to make a junction with the Severn. There was scarcely a hamlet here at the time, but a whole Georgian town grew up around the canal basins and here it is today, a real canal town, centred on the basins and locks.

Giant steam engines dominate the ground floor exhibition at Birmingham's brand new museum, Thinktank – from a beam engine of 1778 to the locomotive *City of Birmingham*.

Thinktank, Millennium Point, Curzon Street

£££; Open daily except Friday; Digbeth, B4 7XG; Tel: 0121 303 1655; Website: www.thinktank.ac

This is Britain's latest major museum to be devoted to science and technology. It opened in the autumn of 2001 and it is very much the modern, interactive place that one would expect, housed in a very unmuseumy building of steel and glass. There are three main areas, dealing with the past, the present and the future. The history of technology section is dominated by steam engines, and appropriately the most important exhibit comes from the famous Birmingham company, Boulton & Watt. The 1778 beam engine is the oldest of its kind still in steam, and a grand sight it is too. But it is by no means the only really interesting engine here: other gems include a compound beam engine and the odd little geared engine, built by Murray in 1802. The transport section covers a wide range – bicycles, motor cars and up to the age of flight – though disappointingly for Birmingham, little on canals. But by way of compensation the railway section houses the massive Pacific locomotive *City of Birmingham*, and a Spitfire and a Hurricane are suspended overhead. The final section is a reflection of Birmingham's engineering past, when small workshops made a bewildering variety of things. This part is presented in quite a traditional way, appropriate for the past, but the present and future exhibition areas are where the designers have clearly had fun – there are great areas for children. And who could resist a drum-playing robot?

DUDLEY
The Black Country Living Museum

£££; March to October every day, November to February Wednesday to Sunday; Tipton Road, DY1 4SQ; Tel: 0121 557 9643; Website: www.bclm.co.uk

This is a major museum with a strong industrial element At its heart is the Dudley Canal and the famous Dudley tunnel. The canal tunnel ate its way deep into the hillside and linked together limestone quarries and mines. One of the real treats on offer is the boat trip to this astonishing structure, which alternates vast caverns with narrow bores for the boat to slip through with scarcely more than inches to spare. The canal basin's immense range of lime kilns forms a focal point for a recreated Black Country village, with workshops, church and pub, shops and houses.

The main industries are well represented, especially coal mining, with a chance to go underground in a drift mine. But there was one special event that gives Dudley great historical significance. Thomas Newcomen came here in 1712 and built his very first steam engine to pump water from the mines on Lord Dudley's estates. In 1986 work was completed on a full-scale working replica, together with a recreation of the original engine house.

It is regularly steamed, a chance to step back and see the very beginning of the steam revolution. It is a splendid achievement. This is a big site, but the problems of getting around to everything are much eased by the electric trams. Like other museums of this type, characters in costume wander around and help recreate the life of the past, but happily no one has ever lost sight of the fact that this is a museum, not just based in an industrial area, but based on one of huge importance.

WORDSLEY, STOURBRIDGE
Red House Glass Cone

Opening Easter 2002; High Street, DY8 4AZ; Tel: 01384 812750

The glass cone dominates the whole area, rising high above the Stourbridge Canal. Superficially, it looks like a pottery kiln, and it does also have a furnace at its heart. But in practice it is very different. Men worked inside the cone, taking molten glass from the central furnace for blowing, keeping it hot in annealing hearths at the side. Built in the late eighteenth century, there were once many such cones, but this is now a rare survivor. Recent renovation has opened it all up for visitors. The sparkling end products of the local glass industry can be seen in the nearby Broadfield House Glass Museum.

Chain-making by hand is demonstrated daily at the Black Country Living Museum's traditional chain shop.

See Also

Cash's Top Shops, Coventry
Exterior only
If one could actually get inside the complex, this would have been a major entry, but the best way to see it is only from Cash's Street or the Coventry Canal towpath. These were cottage workshops. What appears to be a perfectly normal row of terraced houses with neat gardens have a continuous workshop running above them. Workers could go to work without a journey – just pop upstairs. The company is known to generations of parents as manufacturers of name tabs for school uniforms.

Chesterton Green windmill
Exterior only
A curiosity: a former working mill built like a folly, raised on a circular arcade.

Stratford-upon-Avon Tramway Bridge
Free; Open access
The nine-arched river bridge carried the lines of the Stratford and Moreton Railway, built to carry horse-drawn trucks in 1826. It now carries pedestrians.

Walsall Leather Museum
Free; All year, closed Sunday morning and Mondays; Littleton Street West, WS2 8EQ; Tel: 01922 721153
Housed in nineteenth-century workshops, the museum tells the story of an important local industry, with demonstrations.

Wellesbourne watermill
££; Easter to September Thursday to Monday; Tel: 01789 470237
Grinds flour commercially, but also shows wood- and iron-working machinery.

BOULTON AND WATT

Matthew Boulton and James Watt formed one of the most famous partnerships in industrial history, totally controlling the manufacture of steam engines in Britain throughout the latter part of the eighteenth century. Boulton was the manufacturer and entrepreneur, Watt the inventor, and they complemented each other to perfection. Matthew Boulton built a new factory beside the recently completed Birmingham Canal, on what is now the Soho Loop of that waterway. It was here that some of the great events of the age occurred, including a first full-scale display in Britain of the new wonder of the age: gas lighting. What made the works world famous, however, was the development of the steam engine, from a rather primitive device that could only be used for pumping water to a flexible power source that could turn the wheels of industry. Watt was dedicated to his inventions but Boulton's

The end of the beam of one of the Papplewick engines. It shows the parallel motion, which James Watt considered to be one of his finest inventions.

interests ranged far wider. He was one of the driving forces behind the Lunar Society of Birmingham – so called because they met at the full moon – a society of scientists and manufacturers, which included such luminaries as Erasmus Darwin and Joseph Priestley. In many ways they represented all that was thrusting and radical in eighteenth-century Britain.

The former Soho works are now incorporated into Avery's, the well-known manufacturers of weighing machines of all kinds. There is a historical museum that can only be visited by appointment. Soho House, where the Lunar Society met, is, however, now open to the public.

Soho House
£; Closed on Mondays; Soho Avenue, Handsworth, B18 5LB; Tel: 0121 554 9122
It has been refurnished as it was in Boulton's time, and there are exhibits on his industrial activities.

THE IRONBRIDGE GORGE

The area has been given many titles over the years, but mostly on the theme of the birthplace of the Industrial Revolution. Such a complex movement could never have had just one place where everything began, but enough did begin here to make some sense of the claim; and enough still remains to make this a mecca for every enthusiast. There is so much, in fact, that it is scarcely possible to see everything in this quite small area in a weekend, let alone a single day. How did it all come about? It was largely a case of the right natural resources being available in the right place. Here there was coal, iron ore, clay and ironstone, all situated close to what was then a navigable part of the River Severn. From these beginnings, great industries evolved. Coal and iron ore were dug to feed the furnaces; clay was used to make pottery and tiles. But what gave the area its real significance was the arrival of Abraham Darby, an industrialist from Bristol who wanted to make iron pots by a new method of casting. He bought an old foundry in Coalbrookdale in 1708. Like all iron furnaces of that time, it used charcoal as a fuel because coal introduced too many impurities into the iron. Darby had a new idea: if he took the coal and converted it into coke first, then he had an alternative fuel. As it turned out, the local coal was ideal for the purpose, and his experiments were hugely successful. The iron works prospered, and from humble cooking pots he went on to produce cylinders for the first steam engines, including Richard Trevithick's pioneering steam locomotive of 1803, and in later years Coalbrookdale became famous for its ornate castings, notably a magnificent fountain for the Great Exhibition. But by far the most famous castings were made in 1777 for the world's first iron bridge that was to give the area its name. It still stands today, spanning the Severn in a great semicircular arch. The iron works were centres of innovation, not just by the Darbys but by the Reynolds as well, who helped pioneer other uses of iron, from boats to aqueducts.

A number of crafts are preserved at the museum, which have largely been lost to the modern world. This workshop from Broseley was used for making clay pipes.

The local clay was the other valuable resource. It was used for such comparatively mundane, if useful, activities as brickmaking. But what the area became really famous for was its ornamental work. The Coalport Pottery was started in the eighteenth century but reached its peak in the nineteenth when it began to turn out 'jewelled' ware, all shining gilt and enamel, and elaborate porcelain. Scarcely less grand were the decorative tiles produced at the Jackfield works. All these different aspects of the age are represented in the Ironbridge Gorge group of museums.

££££ (the admission covers all sites and remains valid until all have been visited); Daily; Ironbridge Gorge Museums, Telford, TF8 7AW; Tel: 01952 433522 / 432166 / 0800 590258; Website: www.ironbridge.org.uk

Coalbrookdale

The Museum of Iron is situated at the old Darby works, and at the heart of it is the furnace itself, where the first iron was smelted with coke and the parts of the iron bridge were cast. It has all been restored and probably looks a good deal smarter now than it did when Abraham Darby first took it over. The whole site is undergoing a major refurbishment, but the elements remain much the same. This is the place to come to marvel at the range of work, from the early humble cooking pots to cast iron statues. There are splendid cast iron Victorian stoves, and their modern successors, the Agas, are still made here. Other buildings are spread out down the dale, and down by the Severn is the splendidly absurd castellated warehouse, which tells something of the transport story and the role of the river in the development of the area.

Blists Hill

This big open air site has shifted its emphasis from the purely industrial to the recreation of a Victorian town, which is undeniably popular and pulls in the crowds. Happily, for this visitor at least, the industrial past has not been forgotten. Among the most exciting exhibits is a replica of the Trevithick engine, built here in 1803, the first locomotive in the world to run on iron rails. Driving it is, to say the least, an interesting experience, as it has no brakes, just regulator and reversing handle – and to add to the problems, there is no way of knowing which way the engine is going to go when the steam reaches the cylinder at the start of a run. An even earlier transport route winds round the site: the Shropshire Canal – not to be confused with the Shropshire Union. This had iron tub boats, and when they reached the top of the slope above the Severn they could be floated onto wheeled wooden cradles and hauled up and down the very imposing Hay inclined plane. Another reminder of water transport is the restored sailing barge, a Severn trow. It sits rather glumly in a shed, a fact that is particularly mournful since she is quite able to take to the water and sail away. Eighteenth-century road transport is recalled in the relocated Telford tollhouse.

Other major remains include a mine with steam winding engine, blast furnaces with a really splendid steam-blowing engine and a wrought iron works. When visited for the writing of this guide, plans were in hand for demonstrations of rolling iron, a spectacular sight, with the hot metal zipping backwards and forwards as it is squeezed down to the right size and shape. There is an iron foundry still used for casting, and a lot more, and always something going on somewhere on the site.

Coalport China Museum

This sits at the bottom of the Hay incline. The present works were begun in 1796 and are dominated by the bottle kilns. The museum shows how the ware was made and is full of examples. Whether you admire the simpler patterns of the early days or the full blown rather blowsy creations of the Victorians is a matter of taste

Jackfield Tile Museum

Quite a latecomer by Ironbridge standards, the works were only begun in 1874 but quickly established a reputation as the leading manufacturers of encaustic tiles, based on medieval patterns, just the thing for the Gothic revival. Decorative tiles were no less popular, and at its height the works were turning out 20 million a year. The museum is a delight.

Other Sites

The most important is the iron bridge itself, well worth a really close look for its unique construction. No one had ever attempted anything like it before, so the parts were cast like timbers for a conventional bridge, and slotted and fitted together with woodworking joints. Other sites can be seen around the area through trail maps. What happened here in earlier days is extraordinary, and the way in which it has been brought back to life in just a few years is scarcely less remarkable.

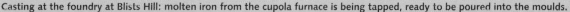

Casting at the foundry at Blists Hill: molten iron from the cupola furnace is being tapped, ready to be poured into the moulds.

SHROPSHIRE

BRIDGNORTH
Severn Valley Railway

*£££ return fare; All year weekends,
summer daily; The Railway Station; Tel:
01299 403816; Website: www.svr.co.uk*

This preserved railway runs for over
26km (16 miles) to link up with the
main rail network at Kidderminster.
There are a number of features that
help to make this line special. For rail
enthusiasts there is the exceptionally
large and splendid collection of locomotives and rolling stock. Then there
is the line itself, which offers splendid
views of the river valley and includes
one fine bridge across the Severn.
Last but not least is the effort that
has gone in to preserving the stations,
even adding new buildings that fit
smoothly in with the old.

There is also an opportunity to
visit the town's other railway, built in
1892. This is the funicular cliff railway, the only one in Britain that is
not on the coast. Originally, the two
cars worked on a water balance system: water was added to a tank in the
top car so that as it descended it
pulled up its partner. Now they are
worked by electricity.

There is one more reason to visit
the town – to pay homage to two railway pioneers, John Urpeth Rastrick
and Richard Trevithick. A plaque at the
east end of the river bridge marks the
site of the foundry where the world's
first passenger locomotive was built.

**The view of Daniel's Mill is dominated by
the water wheel, the biggest still working
on an English corn mill.**

**The two restored beam engines at Coleham Pumping Station, built in 1897, have only
recently been restored to working order.**

Daniel's Watermill

*£; Easter to end of August Wednesday,
Saturday, Sunday afternoons, September
Wednesday and Sunday afternoons; On
B4555 Highley road, Eardington,
WV16 5JL; Tel: 01746 762753*

The mill still has a railway connection, for it sits in the shadow of the
Oldbury viaduct, but it can at least
claim to have got there first. It has
actually been in the same family for
more than two centuries. The 12m
(39ft) water wheel drives three pairs
of stones, still making flour.

SHREWSBURY
Coleham Pumping Station

*£ special steaming days (information
01743 362947)*

In 1896 a scheme was begun to link
the sewers of Shrewsbury into a ring
main. Two compound beam engines
were supplied by Renshaw of Stoke-
on-Trent and a new engine house
constructed to hold them. The house
looks remarkably like a non-con-
formist chapel, even boasting a small
spire – only the tall chimney rising
above it like an oversized classical
column gives the game away. The
engines have recently been restored
and steamed in public at a re-open-
ing in August 2001. Plans are in
hand for regular openings in the
future.

Shropshire Union Canal

Free; Access to towpath

This was one of the last great efforts of
the canal age, begun in 1835 as the
Birmingham & Liverpool Junction
Canal under the direction of Telford. It
used all the latest technology, taking a
particularly direct line from Aldersley on
the edge of Woverhampton to Nantwich
in Cheshire. It is noted for its very deep
cuttings, often crossed by high arched
bridges, and its high embankments. The
technique of 'cut and fill' can be seen
clearly between Norbury and Knighton,
where the deep Grub Street cutting gives
way to the tall Shebdon embankment,
the material excavated from the one having been used to build up the other.

Snailbeach

Free; Open access

The little village of Snailbeach lies at the
heart of what was once the richest lead
mining area in Europe. The Romans
came here, but it was only in the late
eighteenth century that production grew
to immense proportions. The result was
the extraordinary landscape that has
been left behind, with mountains of
spoil like snowy hills, ruined engine
houses and the remains of the old transport system. This is land devastated by
industry, but somehow its eerie landscape has its own appeal. Visit the village
and explore the area, such a contrast to
the natural beauty of Stiperstones.

STAFFORDSHIRE

The county's prosperity was built from the first on natural resources. The presence of clay in close proximity to a productive coalfield led to the introduction of the pottery industry, which in turn threw up a series of smaller scale industrial plants to provide specialist raw material, such as bone and flint. The excellent spring water of the Trent valley made Burton a brewing centre that lasted from the days of the monasteries to the present. Like all land locked areas, Staffordshire found development slowed as a result of inefficient transport. The situation was not helped by the habit of some local potters satisfying a sudden shortage of clay by digging holes in the roadway outside the works. Early in the eighteenth century an inquest heard how an unfortunate traveller had stepped into a hole on a road filled with water and drowned. These were the first real potholes. The eighteenth-century solution was the canals, and two of the most important of the early routes, the Trent & Mersey and the Staffs & Worcester, pass through the county. The former includes the country's first canal tunnel, which

can best be seen at Kidsgrove, alongside Telford's later replacement. An interesting feature of the area's transport system is the use of a standard design of cast iron milestone on both roads and canals, quite a few of which still survive.

BURTON-UPON-TRENT
The Bass Museum

££; Daily; Horninglow Street, DE14 1YQ; Tel: 01283 511000; Website: www.bass-museum.com

Anyone who thinks of brewing as a minor industry will find this museum a revelation. To give one example of the importance of Bass, when the Midland Railway was opened in 1839, Michael Bass arranged for the cellars under St Pancras Station to be designed to take hogsheads of his beer. By the 1920s Bass had 26km (16 miles) of its own railway track, served by eight locomotives. In an earlier age beer was carried on the adjoining Trent & Mersey Canal, and one old transport tradition survives in the handsome shape of the dray horses. Transport is just one of the stories told in the museum, housed in the former Engineers Department and join-

The two mills that were used for grinding flints for the pottery industry stand by the River Churnet at Cheddleton.

ers shop. Here you get a chance to look back at the history of one of the giants of the brewing world, a history that goes back for over two centuries. Beer enthusiasts will be particularly happy to see that the double Burton Union has been preserved – not a collection of workers, but a system whereby the beer was fermented in a double line of casks and in which the strain of yeast could be preserved to ensure continuity of taste. It was a wonderful sight when it was still in regular use. Sadly, now it sits somewhat incongruously in the open air, its working days over.

CHEDDLETON
Flint Mill

Free; All year weekends and most weekdays; Leek Road, ST13 7HL; Tel: 01782 502907; Website: www.pigpen.demon.co.uk/flint.htm

When I want to show people just how efficiently eighteenth-century industrialists could organise their works, I bring them here. There was a water-powered grain mill here in the seventeenth century, then in the eighteenth century the Caldon Canal was built, linking the site to the potteries of Stoke-on-Trent. One vital ingredient, used to whiten the ware, was powdered flint. The flints were brought to the site by boat, and the first stage was to heat them in kilns to make

In the days before the internal combustion engine, beer was delivered from the brewery by horse-drawn dray: a fine pair of shire horses at The Bass Museum.

them easier to crush. So the kilns were built into the wharf and the flints were loaded directly into the top from the boats. After firing, they were removed at the bottom and taken by plateway to the works, where a second water-powered mill had been added. Here the flints were ground to a slurry that was gradually dried out and the finished product sent back on its way to the canal. The machinery works and is a delight.

Nearby is the Cheddleton Railway Centre, based at the former Cheddleton Station.

LEEK

Brindley Watermill, Mill Street

*£; Easter to September weekend afternoons, some extra days in summer; On A523, Leek to Macclesfield Road;
Tel: 01538 483741*

A pleasant little corn mill of 1752, which owes its fame to the fact that it was built by the famous canal engineer James Brindley, who began his working life as a millwright. As a local man, he had his workshops in Mill Street, Leek. There is a small Brindley museum in the mill.

MILLMEECE

Pumping Station

Free, but small charge when engines in steam most weekend afternoons through the year; On the minor road between Millmeece and Cotes Heath, Nr Eccleshall; Tel: 01782 791339

The old Etruscan Bone and Flint Mill, now home to an industrial museum, took its name from Wedgwood's Etruria pottery.

Steam pumping stations seem so much a part of the Victorian age that it comes as a surprise to find the first engine was installed here in 1914 and the second in 1927. And, unlike most such engines, these are not beam engines but a pair of horizontal, compound engines of the type more usually associated with textile mills. They were powerful beasts, each operating five pumps to supply 5 million gallons of water a day.

SHUGBOROUGH

Shugborough estate

NT and Staffordshire County Council; ££ farm (extra charges for house and museum); March to September daily except Monday, October Sunday only; Milford, Nr Stafford, ST17 0XB; Tel: 01889 881388

In 1805 a corn mill was built as part of a 'model estate', where all the latest ideas on agricultural improvement were incorporated into the Park Farm. The farm is now an agricultural museum and rare breeds centre. The gardens, which are separate, are famous for their classical monuments – and for one of Britain's odder railway bridges. The Trent Valley Railway had to cross the Lichfield Drive to the estate, and the Earl of Lichfield demanded that it was in keeping with the grandeur of its surroundings. So here it is, laden with carving, supported by classical pillars and with plinths bearing a seahorse at one end, a lion at the other and the coat of arms in the centre.

STOKE-ON-TRENT

The city is made up of the six towns of the Potteries – Tunstall, Burslem, Hanley, Stoke, Longton and Fenton – not five as Arnold Bennett had it. The great firms are still here, and many have visitor centres and museums. Among these are Spode in Church Street, Stoke, the oldest works still on its original site but very modern in its day. Josiah Spode was the first to turn to steam power, as early as 1779. Royal Doulton in Nile Street, Burslem has a visitor centre with a collection of 1500 figures. For anyone interested in the products of the area, the collection of ceramics in The Potteries Museum and Art Gallery, Bethesda Street, Hanley is outstanding. All these concentrate on the finished product, but the area also has museums that look more closely at the processes of manufacturing.

The statue of Josiah Wedgwood outside the ornate station hotel in Stoke.

Etruria Industrial Museum

£; Wednesday to Sunday, in steam first weekend of month April to December; Etruria Vale Road, ST4 7AF; Tel: 01782 233144; Website: www.stoke.gov.uk/museums

Tucked into an angle between the Trent & Mersey and Caldon Canals, this was the Etruscan Bone and Flint Mill, established around 1820. The date on the gable end, 1857, records the arrival of a new steam engine, which is still there and in full working order. Inside is a fascinating array of kilns, grinders and wash tubs, used in the long process of preparing the raw materials for the potteries. It all makes for a very interesting comparison with the water-powered equivalent at nearby Cheddleton.

Gladstone Pottery Museum

££; Daily; Uttoxeter Road, Longton, ST3 1PQ; Tel: 01782 319232; Website: www.stoke.gov.uk/gladstone

Paradoxically, the great virtue of this pottery is its very ordinariness, which makes it an ideal representative of the working life of the area. At its heart are the shapely bottle ovens, which must rank among the most sinuously beautiful of all industrial structures. In effect, they are just giant kilns; once there were hundreds of them dominating the Stoke skyline. The whole site seems haphazard and ramshackle, yet there is logic and order here, as the ware proceeded through the different stages of being moulded and assembled before being packed into the saggars for firing in the furnace. As well as providing regular demonstrations of pot making, the museum provides an opportunity to see manufacturing techniques of different ages and the end products from decorative tiles to ornate Victorian toilets.

Railway Station, Winton Square

Built in 1848 by the North Staffordshire Railway the style is Jacobean, with a façade dominated by shaped gables. The entire square was planned by the company, who built their railway hotel opposite.

STRETTON
Claymills Pumping Station

Free when static, £ in steam; Saturdays throughout year and some summer weekends; Tel: 01283 509929

This is an especially big and important sewage pumping works, serving Burton-upon-Trent – big because it had to deal with the vast quantities of water discharged from the local breweries. There are two engine houses, built in 1885, each holding two compound beam engines. These machines are so big that a separate small steam engine was added just to turn over the 24-ton flywheels for starting. Steam was supplied from five Lancashire boilers. The site also contains a blacksmith's forge and period workshop.

JOSIAH WEDGWOOD AND THE POTTERIES

Wedgwood was born in the heart of the potteries at Burslem in 1730. It was a world of craftsmen who made individual pieces. When he died in 1795, this world had been transformed, and ware was being made in factories on what was in effect a production line system. His success depended on more than one factor. Firstly, he was fortunate enough to enter into partnership with Thomas Bentley, a man who understood public taste. The result was the famous cream ware, which was earthenware but with a far lighter coloured body than was usual at the time. This meant that thin glazes could be used, giving it a true elegance. It became very popular, and when Wedgwood made a service for Queen Charlotte, it was renamed Queen's ware, a public relations coup which any modern adman would have been proud of.

Wedgwood realised that his empire could only grow if it was served by a good transport system, and he became one of the leading promoters of the Trent & Mersey Canal. He built his new factory, which he dignified with a suitably classical name, Etruria, on a canalside site – and had a new house, Etruria Hall, looking down on it all. The factory has long since been moved to a new site at Barlaston. All that remains of the original is a little round building by the canal road bridge. Etruria Hall still stands but is no longer a home. However, a few of the

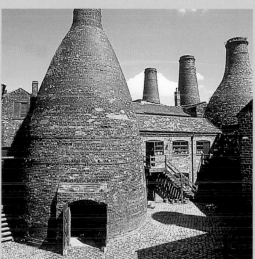

Shapely bottle kilns once dominated the Potteries skyline. These at Gladstone Pottery Museum are among the rare survivors.

Vase celebrating the opening of the Etruria Pottery.

houses that made up the new village of Etruria can still be found. It was at Etruria that he worked out the system of a series of workshops, arranged in logical order that was to be copied in works throughout the area. He was an enthusiastic amateur scientist, and his best known achievement was the design of a high temperature thermometer. This served a real practical purpose: for the first time a potter could accurately measure kiln temperatures and reproduce the conditions time and again to ensure uniformity in the ware.

The name Wedgwood lives on because the classical simplicity of the designs has never fallen out of favour, and the blue jasper ware is still on sale today, which is not a bad record for ware that first went into production in 1775. Wedgwood's achievement was twofold. He refined the end product of the Staffordshire potteries so that it found a new market among the increasingly wealthy middle classes, and he brought modern technology to bear on an age-old craft. The story is told at the new visitor centre at the modern works at Barlaston.

Wedgwood Visitor Centre

££; Open daily; Barlaston, ST12 9ES; Tel: 01782 204141; Website: www.wedgwood.co.uk

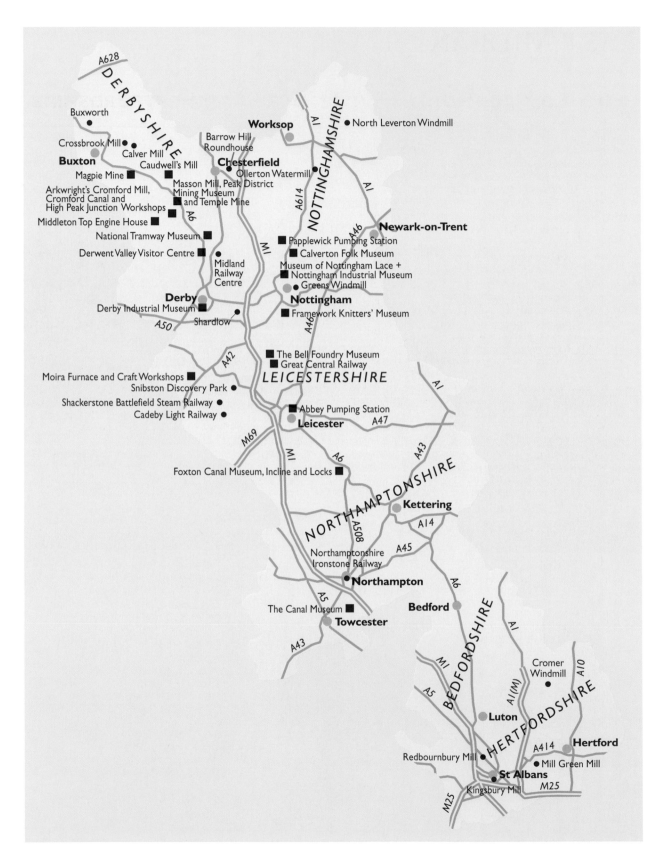

East Midlands

Bedfordshire, Northamptonshire and Hertfordshire

Moving eastward across the Midlands, the landscape changes and the importance of industry appears to dwindle. Two industries that have left their mark, however, are brickmaking and ironstone mining. Bedfordshire in particular was dominated by brick making, and the tall chimneys of the works are often the highest features to be seen for miles around. A book published in 1974 recorded 111 brickworks chimneys in the county, though I must confess I have not checked to see how many still stand. But to make bricks you need to dig big holes for the clay, and many have been left and adapted to new uses. What is now the Stewartby Lake Country Park in Bedfordshire is based on old clay pits, and the town itself was created as a model village for London Brick Company workers and named after a former chairman, Sir Hailey Stewart. Ironstone mines and quarries are less obvious, but the ironstone itself can be seen as a building material, especially in Northamptonshire, where it gives a rich, reddish gold colour to many of the older houses.

The Canal Museum at Stoke Bruerne on the Grand Union Canal, with the fore cabin of the narrowboat *Northolt* in the foreground.

Stoke Bruerne
The Canal Museum

££; Easter to October daily, November to Easter Tuesday to Sunday; Towcester, NN12 7SE; Tel: 01604 862229; Website: www.thewaterwaystrust.co.uk

An excellent small museum that gains immensely from its setting. It is housed in a former corn mill beside the Grand Union canal. Alongside are old canal cottages, and opposite is the pub much frequented by boating families and a welcome stop in the days before motors when boats were legged through nearby Blisworth tunnel. After moving a loaded boat for 2.8km (1¾ miles) by pushing on the tunnel sides with your feet, a pint must have been more than welcome. Locks crossed by a particularly handsome bridge complete the scene. Inside is a wide range of exhibits, including a narrow boat cabin, showing the extraordinary organising skill of the families who spent their lives in such constricted quarters.

See Also

Cromer Windmill, Ardley, Herts
£; Mid-May to mid-September 2nd and 4th Sunday afternoons, Tel: 01438 861662
A weather-boarded post mill of 1740.

Kingsbury Mill, St Michael's Street, St Albans, Herts
£; All day Monday to Saturday, Sunday afternoon; Tel: 01727 853502
Watermill with museum of eighteenth- and nineteenth-century farm equipment.

Mill Green Mill, Hatfield
Free; Open all year all day Tuesday to Friday, weekend afternoons; Tel: 01707 271362; Website: www.welhat.gov.uk
A working mill with breast shot water wheel, grinding three days a week. Local history museum attached.

Northamptonshire Ironstone Railway, Hunsbury Hill Country Park, Northampton
Free (££ steam ride); Museum open daily, train service timetables vary; Tel: 01604 702031
Both a museum of the local ironstone mining industry and an industrial locomotive collection, with rides on 3.2km (2 miles) of track.

Redbournburys Mill, Redbourn, Herts
£; Sunday afternoons; Tel: 01582 792874
An eighteenth-century mill with three pairs of stones, still milling. Auxiliary Crossley oil engine.

LEICESTERSHIRE

Leicestershire has had, like many areas, an interesting working past, but the evidence is not always there to see, or at least is not presented in a form designed to attract visitors. This was an important area for the development of the early cotton industry, and a number of old mills can be seen along the River Soar in Leicester. There was at least one event that deserves to be remembered. The very first rail excursion train ran from Leicester to Loughborough in 1841, organised by a young gentleman called Thomas Cook. The old Cook building can still be seen in Leicester, with a bas relief frieze showing landmarks in the package tour business: the first excursion, a train to the Crystal Palace for the Great Exhibition and a paddle steamer on the Nile.

One of the beam engines in the Victorian splendour of Abbey Pumping Station.

FOXTON
Canal Museum, Incline and Locks

£; Museum open daily except Monday and Tuesday in winter; Open access to locks and incline; Middle Lock, Gumley Road; Tel: 0116 279 2657

The locks on the Leicester Arm of the Grand Union Canal were opened in 1812 and consist of two five-lock staircases, a system where the locks run straight into each other with no stretch of water in between. By 1898 the hold ups had become so severe, with boats queuing to use the locks, that engineers built the remarkable inclined plane. Caissons like giant bathtubs on wheels ran up and down the slope on a railed track with the narrow boats floating inside them. After just ten years, the system was proving uneconomic and was closed down. Now it is being restored. The whole story is told in the museum created in the former boiler house of the old winding engine.

LEICESTER
Abbey Pumping Station

Free (££ when engine in steam); April to September daily, October to March Monday to Saturday and Sunday afternoon; Corporation Road, LE4 5PX; Tel: 0116 299 5111

Like so many Victorian local authorities, when Leicester's representatives installed new engines to pump the city's sewage, they set them in an engine house of great grandeur. There are four beam engines here, built in 1890 by the local firm of Gimson & Co., and like all beam engines they are seen at their best when one is set in motion on special steam days. In their working days they pumped the sewage to a treatment centre 2.4km (1¹/₂ miles) away. They form the splendid centrepiece for a new museum dealing with public health, and this is probably the only place where you can see what happens to your waste products once they have been flushed down the loo. The faeces may be artificial, but it is an interesting rather than a beautiful sight. The museum spreads outside the buildings for some of the exhibits, which include an immense Ruston Bucyrus steam excavator.

A little Bagnall locomotive en fete at Shackerstone on the Battlefield Steam Railway; it is about to be given a new name, *King*.

LOUGHBOROUGH
Great Central Railway

££££ (££ museum only); May to October, November to April weekends; Great Central Road, LE11 1RW; Tel: 01509 230726

Britain's last important main line just sneaked in an opening before the end of the nineteenth century. The aim is to recreate the main line experience, with long trains headed by big locomotives from many different regions.

MOIRA
Furnace and Craft Workshops

££; April to September afternoons weekdays and all day weekends but closed Monday, winter Wednesday to Sunday afternoons, weekdays and all day weekends; Furnace Lane, DE12 6AT; Tel: 01283 224667; Website: www.nwleicestershire.gov.uk

This immense stone blast furnace rears up above the Ashby Canal. It was built around 1800 for the Moira iron works and has now been restored. Interactive displays explain the operations to the visitors. The craft workshops and other attractions have all been recently added, but at least they do nothing to detract from the grandeur of an important industrial monument.

See Also

Cadeby Light Railway, The Old Rectory, Cadeby

Free occasional openings, usually 2nd Saturday in the month; Tel: 01455 290462
No one can pretend that this is a major preserved line, but it is gloriously eccentric, as indeed was its originator, that great enthusiast the Reverend Teddy Boston. Real narrow gauge engines on a tiny rectory line, enormous fun – even if I can no longer shoot off down the country lanes with Teddy on his traction engine.

Snibston Discovery Park, Coalville

££; Open daily; Ashby Road, Coalville, LE67 3LN; Tel: 01530 510851
One of the new generation of interactive science theme parks and very good fun, as well as educational. It is, however, based on the former colliery.

Shackerstone Battlefield Steam Railway

££ return fare; March to October weekends, July to August Wednesdays; Shackerstone Station, CV13 6NW; Tel: 01827 880754; Website: www.battlefield-line-railway.co.uk
Steam trains run to Bosworth Battlefield Centre. The station has a delightful small museum.

LOUGHBOROUGH
The Bell Foundry Museum

£; Tuesday to Friday, Saturdays in summer; Freehold Street, LE11 1AR; Tel: 01509 233414; Website: www.taylorbells.co.uk

This museum is mainly the story of the Taylor family, who have been casting bells in the area since 1784. Their most famous bell is Great Paul, the 17-tonne monster cast for St Paul's Cathedral in 1881. At the other end of the scale they also produce small chimes and handbells. Once cast, a bell has to be tuned by skilled removal of metal from inside the bell. All this is explained in the museum, but for a small extra fee visitors can see the real thing in a tour of the works. These do have to be booked in advance, as numbers are strictly limited.

Two big bells being cast at the Loughborough Bell Foundry. The metal is being poured into the mould for the smaller bell and poled with a willow branch.

NOTTINGHAMSHIRE

Nottinghamshire has a lot in common with neighbouring Leicestershire, in that both have a rich and varied industrial history but one that is no longer immediately obvious. Two important elements are still well represented – hosiery and lace – but museums only tell a part of the story. The factory age brought impressive buildings to the area round Nottingham, great factories at places like Beeston, some of which are quite elaborate in their architecture. The coalfield which was once so important has left few reminders, apart from the spoil heaps, though the cottage where one of the best known chroniclers of mining life, D.H. Lawrence, was born has been preserved in Eastwood. One hugely important event did take place in the county. In June 1785 the Robinson family, cotton spinners of Papplewick, wrote to Boulton & Watt to ask them to build a steam engine to power the machinery of their mill. It was to be the first mill engine, and its success revolutionised the factory world. There may not be much left to recall the event, but appropriately Papplewick Pumping Station has survived as one of the grandest of all the great Victorian pumping stations, the splendid engines constructed by James Watt & Co. They are described below.

The robust machinery contrasts with the delicate material it makes: an exhibit at the Museum of Nottingham Lace.

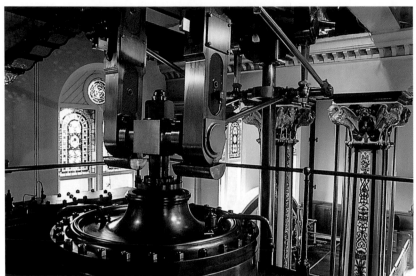

Of all the great Victorian pumping stations, Papplewick is by far the most ornate, a superb setting for the powerful steam engines.

CALVERTON
Calverton Folk Museum, Windles Square

£; April to September last Sunday afternoon in month; Tel: 0115 965 4843

This is just the place to come to find out about the hosiery industry, for it was right here in 1589 that Rev William Lee invented a machine for knitting stockings. Queen Elizabeth I came to take a look but lost interest when she discovered it could only be used for wool not silk. The cottages of Windles Square have typically large windows to ensure good light for the workspace where the simple stocking frames were used. It all looks almost quaint now, but there were some 20,000 frames in use in the area by the end of the eighteenth century. This is a fascinating, and little known, side of domestic industry.

NOTTINGHAM
Museum of Nottingham Lace

Free; All year; 3–5 High Pavement, The Lace Market, NG1 1HF; Tel: 0115 989 7365; Website: www.nottinghamlace.org

The museum tells the story of lace making from the early years when bobbin lace was made in homes all round the region, through the huge expansion that began in the 1820s with the introduction of machines that did the job far more cheaply. There are regular demonstrations of hand working and machine working.

For such a beautiful material, the factories where it was made are generally distinctly drab. There is one exception, worth a detour, the extravagant Anglo-Scotian mill in Wollaton Road, Beeston.

RAVENSHEAD
Papplewick Pumping Station

££; Summer weekends; Off Longdale Lane, NG15 9AJ, between Ravenshead and Nottingham (map ref. 120/5852); Tel: 0115 963 2938; Website: www.papplewickpumpingstation.co.uk

If you ever thought pumping water to supply city needs was boring, visit Papplewick and you'll never think so again. In 1884 the Nottingham Water Department purchased a pair of massive beam steam engines from James Watt & Co. They then built an engine house and boiler house, and there was no need to provide anything especially grand as only a few workmen would ever see them. But they were proud of their new engines and built them a palace. From the outside it is rather glum Gothic but inside is a riot of decoration. Bright work

Nottingham Industrial Museum

Free weekdays, £ weekends; April to September daily, special steaming days in winter; Wollaton Park, NG8 2AE;
Tel: 0115 915 3190

The setting is unlikely – the old stable block of Wollaton Hall, not quite the spot one associates with coal mines and steam engines. Nevertheless, this is a good, no nonsense museum, covering all aspects of the local scene, including such often neglected areas as pharmaceuticals. The assortment of steam engines, including a beam engine, are regularly steamed. The main emphasis is on textiles, particularly the lace and hosiery industries. Nottingham was also one of the first centres to develop bicycle manufacturing in the

1860s, which was later to develop into a much bigger motor cycle manufacturing centre. Locals will tell you that the Borough was the Rolls-Royce of the two-wheel motoring world. It is not easy to do much about the other important industry, coal mining, in such a space, but out in the courtyard is the old horse gin from Pinxton colliery. The horse walked round and round a circular track, turning a drum that allowed men and materials to be moved up and down the shaft.

A colliery horse gin. The horse walked round the circular track, turning the central drum, from which rope or cable was taken over the pulley on the right to the shaft.

fishes swim up columns topped with capitals of ibis and lily; stained glass windows continue the watery theme. And in among them the great engines bob up and down with stately solemnity and a faint hiss of steam. Outside you can get an idea of the prodigious work that was done, for you can see the pump rods that dragged water up from a reservoir 60m (200ft) below ground.

RUDDINGTON

Framework Knitters' Museum

£; Easter to January Monday, Tuesday, Sunday morning; Chapel Street, NG11 6HE; Tel: 0115 984 6914

This is framework knitting on the semi-industrial scale, with workshops

as well as cottages. As at Calverton, there are typical knitting frames but more modern machines as well. The circular knitting machine – which makes sense for knitting what are basically tubes – was first patented by Marc Brunel in 1816 and was improved throughout the nineteenth century. All the machines are regularly demonstrated.

See Also

North Leverton Windmill
Free; Sunday afternoons;
Tel: 01427 880573
A working tower mill with ornate ogee cap. Still worked commercially. Museum.

Green's Windmill, Sneinton, Nottingham
Free; All year Wednesday to Sunday;
Tel: 0115 9156878
Working tower mill named after physicist George Green. Appropriately, there is also a hands-on science centre.

Ollerton Watermill
£; Easter to September Sunday afternoons;
Tel: 01623 822469 / 824094
Three-storey mill built in 1713.

DERBYSHIRE

There are few areas which have more fascinating and exciting remains of the early industrial world than Derbyshire. Several places have proclaimed themselves 'Birthplace of the Industrial Revolution' and Derbyshire has a much better claim to the title than most. But industrial history began here long before the eighteenth century. Lead mining goes back at least as far as Roman times, and by the medieval age it was flourishing. It is difficult to identify the oldest mines, simply because they were likely to have been opened up again and reworked at a later date. The simplest to identify are the 'rakes': great gashes in the land where the miners followed the veins down through the rock. They can be found throughout the limestone region, though they are seldom signposted or awarded any recognition. One of the most striking can be seen on the moors between Castleton and Bradwell. The Dirtlow Rake (map ref. 110/1481) is a deep, narrow, rocky chasm. The men who opened up the first mines were known to later generations as 'T'owd men', and one of these medieval miners can be seen in effigy as a carving in Wirksworth church. The other great survivors from the period of extensive mining are the drainage adits or soughs, some of which extended literally for miles deep underground. The exploration of these remains is fascinating but is not for the inexperienced. The importance of Derbyshire to the development of the textile industry, for the hugely important change from work in the home to work in the factory, is now generally recognised. The most important sites are listed below. It is

A Glasgow tram of 1922 runs underneath the Bowes-Lyon Bridge, built in 1844 for an estate in Hertfordshire and re-erected at Crich.

astonishing just how much there is to see – and how much probably remains to be discovered – in Derbyshire. The importance of the Derwent Valley received official recognition in 2001 when it was pronounced a World Heritage site.

CRICH

National Tramway Museum

£££; Summer daily, January to March Sundays and Mondays, November to January weekends and Mondays; Tel: 01773 852565; Website: www.tramway.co.uk

This one just sneaks into the book, because although most of the trams date from the early twentieth century, there are a few splendid nineteenth-century examples here as well. In any case,

it's just too good to leave out. The first thing you see on entering the site is the recreated street scene and the indoor exhibits. The real appeal, however, lies with the constant stream of trams carrying visitors up and down the line. The lines are laid out along the hillside, offering splendid views; visitors can ride up and down and try as many different vehicles as they choose with no extra payments. There are trams from all over Britain and even examples from Prague and Vienna for comparison. It might seem odd to find trams, those essentially urban vehicles, in a quarry setting, but at least it is at one with historic tramway connections. The limestone quarries were worked by no less a person than George Stephenson, who built the first horse-drawn tramway on the site to shift the stone to the lime kilns in the valley.

BELPER
Derwent Valley Visitor Centre, North Mill

£; Easter to September afternoons, October to Easter afternoons Thursday to Sunday; Tel: 01773 880474

This is one of the most important industrial buildings in Britain. Jebediah Strutt began constructing cotton mills in Derbyshire in 1778. North Mill, like the rest, was constructed on a wooden frame, but was burned to the ground in 1803. Strutt was determined it would not happen again, so he built the present fireproof mill. Down in the basement it is like a cathedral crypt, with gloomy arches and great stone pyramids acting as the base for an iron frame of pillars, beams and ties. Brick arches fill the spaces and support the floor. The machinery was originally driven by a water wheel, now gone, though the impressive weir that controlled the water supply can be seen outside. The attic was once used by Strutt as a Sunday School for the mill children. Strutt was a benevolent employer but even he feared the reaction of the old hand workers who threatened to destroy his works. A bridge crosses the road, joining the main mill buildings, and here one can still see gun embrasures cut for the defence of the mill against the mob that never came.

It is well worth walking up into Belper to see the handsome stone houses in Long Row, built by Strutt for the mill workers.

The original North Mill at Belper built for Jebediah Strutt is the small L-shaped building. It has been dwarfed by the Victorian mill behind it.

ARKWRIGHT AND STRUTT

Richard Arkwright started off in life as a barber and wig maker but he worked in the heart of the Lancashire textile districts, where all the talk was of finding new ways to spin cotton. Quite how much of his best-known invention was his own work and how much he borrowed from others is still uncertain, but what is absolutely clear is that he was the man who put his machines to practical and highly profitable use. New inventions were by no means always welcomed by those who earned their living in the old cottage industries, so Arkwright took himself down to Nottinghamshire. There he met two men who were to become partners in his enterprise, Samuel Need of Derby and Jebediah Strutt of Belper. Strutt in particular was open to new ideas, for he had himself invented a machine for making ribbed stockings. He was also interested in anything that would increase the supply of yarn and lower his costs.

Arkwright's spinning machine was quite unlike earlier devices, in that it was not adaptable for use in the home. It relied on the power of the water wheel – hence its name, the water frame. The cotton fibres were straightened by a carding engine, then passed to the frame where they were pulled out by rollers travelling at different speeds and then twisted together. Once the first experiments had proved a success, Arkwright looked for a site on which to build his first mill. He settled on what was then the hamlet of Cromford in Derbyshire, having a good water supply and far enough removed from the traditional textile areas for there to be no threat from rioters and machine breakers. But its very isolation created a new problem. He would have to recruit a work force – and the work force would need somewhere to live. So he set out to build a new village, which can still be seen at the heart of the modern town.

The houses were good, solid terraces – very different from the jerry built slums of later textile towns and villages. The best can be seen in North Street. They look very roomy, with three stories, but

Masson Mill represents the finest surviving example of one of Arkwright's cotton mills. It now houses a textile museum, with machinery from different periods. Here we can see the older style of power looms, driven by belts from overhead line shafting. The weaving shed is a later addition to the old spinning mill.

this is deceptive: the top floor was not living space but a loom shop. It was here that the men worked as weavers at handlooms. The job of running the new machines went to women and young children. Over the years he added a market and built the rather grand Greyhound Inn. This was very much his town, and by 1789 he had purchased the Lordship of the Manor and built himself a splendid mansion, Willersley Castle, on the edge of town, a building designed as much to make an impression as to provide a comfortable home. Arkwright added other mills in the region, of which Masson Mill at nearby Matlock Bath is the outstanding example. He allowed others to use his machines under licence. One who did so was David Dale, following Arkwright's lead in opting for a country site, but this time in Scotland. It was destined to become famous under the direction of his son in law, Robert Owen. Dale's village was near Lanark and was simply named New Lanark.

A hand-operated model of the Arkwright water frame in the Lewis Textile Museum. The cotton passes through the rollers at the top, which draw it out, then passes to rotating 'fliers' at the bottom, which impart the twist.

All these activities brought Arkwright a knighthood and a fortune – at his death he was estimated to be worth half a million, a huge amount in those days. He remained, however, an overbearing and irascible man, and never more so than in the period from 1781 to 1783, when the courts overthrew all his patents. He was notoriously mean, not least in the treatment of his workforce. Nevertheless, he expected those workers to revere him, and on the yearly fete day they were required literally to sing his praises. In his lifetime he took textile manufacture out of the home and brought it into the factory. Women and children worked long hours in the new mills for little pay and often with disastrous results for their health. He was not perhaps excessively harsh by the standards of the day, but he was certainly not generous. Yet he did provide living conditions that were far better than those that many of the families had come from, and were certainly better than those of later mill towns. His partner Jebediah Strutt had a very different character.

Although Strutt had begun his life as a wheelwright, he was an educated man and his surviving letters to Elizabeth Woollett who was to become his wife are touchingly romantic. He soon established his own mills at nearby Belper. Here he, too, built houses, but his benevolence was of a different order from Arkwright's. His housing in Long Row and The Clusters is both sturdy and has added extra features, such as small front gardens. His wife established a cottage hospital by the bridge over the Derwent, while he established a Sunday School and built a Unitarian Chapel in 1788. He was a man of simple tastes, and his house near Milford Mills was as austere as Arkwright's was flamboyant.

The contribution the two men made to the development of the cotton industry, and to the whole course of the Industrial Revolution, was immense, and they complemented each other well. Indeed, their contribution was not limited to Britain. Among the apprentices who came to work in Strutt's office around 1782 was fourteen-year-old Samuel Slater. By 1789 he was on his way to America, taking the secrets of textile machinery with him. He was soon helping to establish a mill at Pawtucket, Rhode Island. Slatersville was to become America's Belper. To walk around the two towns of Cromford and Belper is to walk through places where the modern age was born, to see the factory age in its first infancy.

See Also

There are two outstanding examples of early cotton mills, though only viewable from the outside: Cressbrook begun in 1779 and extended in 1815, and Calver of 1803.

Leawood pumping station stands at the far end of an aqueduct carrying the Cromford Canal across the River Derwent.

CROMFORD
Arkwright's Cromford Mill

Mill site free, guided tour £; Open daily; Mill Lane, Cromford, DE4 3RQ; Tel: 01629 824297; Website: www.cromfordmill.co.uk

Sadly, little remains of the pioneering water-powered cotton mill of 1771: much has gone or been overwhelmed by later additions. Restoration work has begun, and this is really a place of pilgrimage for anyone interested in the origins of the Industrial Revolution. It is only a part of the story, however, and the rest of the sites are described in the short piece on Arkwright and Strutt.

Cromford Canal, High Peak Junction Workshops

£; Easter to end of October daily, winter weekends; Tel: 01629 822831

The canal begins at a wharf close to the Arkwright mill. The workshops are 1.6km (1 mile) away, accessible from the minor road to Crich or by walking the towpath. In 1825 the decision was taken to link this canal to the Peak Forest Canal that lay on the far side of the hills. So the Cromford & High Peak Railway was built, on which horses pulled trucks along the level sections and steam engines coped with the steep inclines. This is the workshop, preserved much as it was in the working days, and apart from being of interest in its own

right, it also shows film of this extraordinary railway in the days when steam locomotives took over from horses.

A short walk further down the towpath brings you to the wharf and the warehouse where boats were unloaded and where the tracks head off to the hills. Beyond that again is the aqueduct across the river and Leawood Pumping Station. This houses a Cornish beam engine, which supplied the canal with water and is occasionally steamed. Information on open days is available at the workshops or at the local tourist office. See also Middleton.

DERBY
Industrial Museum, The Silk Mill

Free; All day weekdays, afternoons weekends all year; Silk Mill Lane, DE1 3AR; Tel: 01332 255308; Website: www.derby.gov.uk/museums

This can reasonably claim to be the site of Britain's first ever textile factory, for it was here in the 1720s that Thomas Lombe installed water-powered machinery for winding and twisting silk threads. Most of the original buildings have gone, but this gives some idea of how it once looked. Inside, the whole story of Derby's industrial past is told, from the work of lead miners to the manufacture of aero engines.

MATLOCK BATH
Masson Mill

£; Open daily; Tel: 01629 760208; Website: www.massonmills.co.uk

The building is immensely impressive and provides perhaps the best example that we have of an eighteenth-century cotton mill. Although it was begun in 1783 by Richard Arkwright, it was greatly extended over the years. Now it is home to a 'shopping village', but that at least has meant that the building has been saved. Happily, space has been found for a working textile museum, and it is a vital part of the Arkwright story. The machinery is all more modern than it would have been in Arkwright's day, and a new use for water power has been found that he could never have dreamed of: the water wheel has gone, replaced by a turbine, now generating electricity for the national grid. No doubt he would have been equally impressed by the introduction of steam power.

Peak District Mining Museum and Temple Mine

££; Open daily; Temple Mine, afternoons only; The Pavilion, DE4 3NR; Tel: 01629 583834; Website: www.peakmines.co.uk

There are two parts to this complex. The first is a traditional museum, housed in

It is difficult to imagine anything looking less like an industrial museum, but this handsome pavilion is home to the Peak District Mining Museum.

Middleton Top Engine House. Conventional locomotives ran on part of the Cromford & High Peak Railway, but immense engines such as this were needed to haul trains up the inclines.

the unlikely setting of a domed spa building. This tells the important story of local lead mining, but it is the former Temple Mine that provides the opportunity to see the real underground world.

MIDDLETON-BY-WIRKSWORTH

Middleton Top Engine House

*£; Easter to October weekends;
Tel: 01629 823204*

I have been coming here for years and never tire of it, for it really is unique. This is part of the Cromford & High Peak Railway story (see p.78 under Cromford). The engine house stands at the top of a long incline. Inside is the magnificent beam engine that was used to haul trains of wagons – and for a time passenger coaches – up and down the incline. As the beam nods, three massive overlapping wheels turn with a steady rhythm, controlling the continuous cable to which trucks were hitched. It is possible to explore more of this astonishing railway from here, as the old track bed is now a footpath and cycle track.

It is worth seeing the other end of the line at Whaley Bridge, where there is an unusual interchange warehouse. The railway lines come in at one end of the building and boats float in from the Peak Forest Canal at the other.

ROWSLEY

Caudwell's Mill

££; March to October daily, winter weekends only; Tel: 01629 734374

This is quite different from the familiar watermill for grinding grain. This is Victorian modern – water turbines take the place of the old wheel, and rollers do the work once done by grindstones. There is also a craft centre.

SHELDON

Magpie Mine

Free; Open access; South of the village (map ref. 119/173682)

This is the best preserved of all the old lead mining sites in the region. There are remains of two engine houses, one for a pumping engine and the other for the winding engine. The manager's house, maintenance buildings and a small gunpowder store can also be seen. The wild, open setting gives this spot its special atmosphere.

See Also

Barrow Hill Roundhouse, Staveley, Chesterfield
£; Weekends
Actually a square house, but all locomotive sheds where engines are grouped round a turntable are known as roundhouses. Built in 1870, this is the last to survive in working condition and has a large collection of locomotives on show.

Buxworth
Free; Open access
Extensive restored remains of old Peak Forest Canal basins and tramway connections.

Midland Railway Centre, Ripley
£££; Open daily; Butterley Station, Ripley, DE5 3QZ; Tel: 01773 570140
A major railway museum complex, with locomotives and rolling stock on display and under restoration. Steam rides.

Shardlow
Free; Open access
A town that developed in the eighteenth century at the junction of the River Trent and the Trent & Mersey Canal. An interesting array of houses and warehouses.

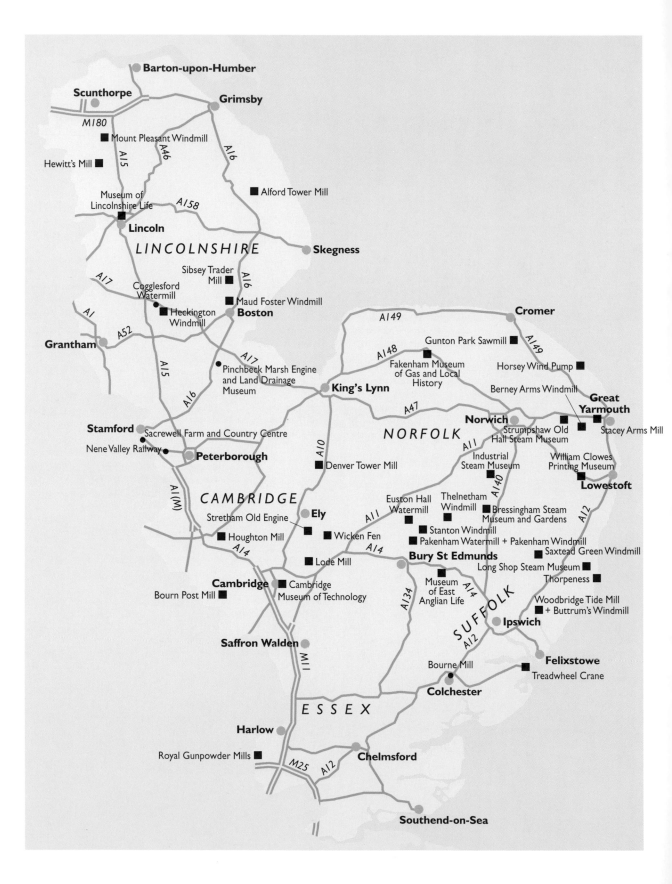

Barton-upon-Humber

Scunthorpe

Grimsby

M180

Mount Pleasant Windmill

A15 A46 A16

Hewitt's Mill

Alford Tower Mill

Museum of Lincolnshire Life

A158

Lincoln

LINCOLNSHIRE

Skegness

Sibsey Trader Mill

A16

A17

Cogglesford Watermill

Maud Foster Windmill

A1

Heckington Windmill

Boston

Grantham

A52

A17

Pinchbeck Marsh Engine and Land Drainage Museum

A149

Cromer

A149

A15

A148

Gunton Park Sawmill

A16

Fakenham Museum of Gas and Local History

Horsey Wind Pump

King's Lynn

Berney Arms Windmill

Great Yarmouth

Stamford

Sacrewell Farm and Country Centre

A47

NORFOLK

Norwich

Nene Valley Railway

Peterborough

A10

Strumpshaw Old Hall Steam Museum

Stacey Arms Mill

Denver Tower Mill

A11

Industrial Steam Museum

William Clowes Printing Museum

A1(M)

CAMBRIDGE

A140

Lowestoft

Stretham Old Engine

Ely

A11

Euston Hall Watermill

Thelnetham Windmill

Bressingham Steam Museum and Gardens

A12

Houghton Mill

Wicken Fen

A14

Stanton Windmill

Lode Mill

A14

Bury St Edmunds

Pakenham Watermill + Pakenham Windmill

Saxtead Green Windmill

Long Shop Steam Museum

Cambridge

Cambridge Museum of Technology

A134

Museum of East Anglian Life

A14

Thorpeness

Bourn Post Mill

SUFFOLK

Woodbridge Tide Mill + Buttrum's Windmill

A12

Ipswich

Saffron Walden

M11

Bourne Mill

Felixstowe

Treadwheel Crane

Colchester

ESSEX

Harlow

Royal Gunpowder Mills

M25 A12

Chelmsford

Southend-on-Sea

EASTERN ENGLAND

ESSEX AND CAMBRIDGESHIRE

One of the dominating factors in determining the history of the area has always been the balance between water and land. The drainage of the Fens was probably begun under the Romans, and the best preserved of the drainage schemes is the Car Dyke, a wide waterway, much of which can still be seen running from the Cam at Waterbeach for 11km (7 miles) to the Old West River. Generations of engineers followed in the Romans' footsteps, harnessing the power of windmill and water wheel to work pumps, moving on to the power of steam and criss-crossing the region with dykes. As the waters receded, agriculturalists moved in; the grain mill has become one of the best known and most appreciated reminders of the working past.

HARWICH

Treadwheel Crane, Harwich Green

Free; Open access

This is a true rarity. The crane was built in 1667 for the Naval Yard. There are two 4.9m (16ft) diameter wheels, and men walked inside them to provide the power for the 5.5m (18ft) jib that projects out from the building. Alarmingly, the crane has no braking system.

Harwich has other interesting sites, including the High and Low Lighthouses, built in 1818 by John Rennie. The former houses a radio museum, the latter a maritime museum. The Ha'penny Pier Visitor Centre was once a waiting room for paddle steamer passengers and is now home to a display on the Pilgrim Fathers. And, although it really lies outside the scope of this book, I cannot resist mentioning the Electric Palace cinema of 1911, still in use.

HOUGHTON

Houghton Mill

NT; ££; June to October afternoons but closed Thursday and Friday, March to June and October Sunday afternoons; Tel: 01480 301494

The watermill occupies a splendid site on an artificial island in the Great Ouse. It was built in the seventeenth century and is an unusually big building for the time. Built of brick and timber it rises for four floors, the upper levels being clad in weather-boarding. Originally it was powered by three water wheels, working ten pairs of stones. One wheel has now been reinstated, and the mill has been brought back to life, once again producing flour. It is regularly worked on all open days.

LODE

Lode Mill, Anglesey Abbey

NT; ££ gardens and mill only; July and August daily, April to July and September closed Monday and Tuesday, winter weekends only; Tel: 01223 811200

The watermill stands on Bottisham Lode, the waterway that links the mill to the River Cam. Built in the eighteenth century, it is an attractive weather-boarded building, with a projecting lucam on the fourth floor. The stones, driven by a breast shot wheel, are again being used for grinding flour, though in its latter days under private ownership it was used for grinding cement. The mill is now part of the grounds of the abbey; the admission price also gives access to the gardens and arboretum.

Houghton Mill. Three water wheels drove ten pairs of millstones and operated the sack hoists and other machinery.

CAMBRIDGE Museum of Technology

£ (££ in steam); Easter to October Sunday and Wednesday afternoons, the rest of the year first Sunday in month; Cheddars Lane, CB5 8LD; Tel: 01223 368650

The former sewage pumping station was equipped with what was in its day the very latest technology. In place of the familiar beam engines of other Victorian sites, this has a pair of massive tandem compound engines, with high pressure cylinder and low pressure cylinder in line. They were installed in 1894 and are regularly steamed The engines are by Hawthorn Davey, and enthusiasts will come to stare at the unique valve gear – and non-enthusiasts can simply be quite happy marvelling at the display of silky precision and power. These are not the only attractions: the original boiler feed pump for the two 1895 boilers is still in place, and there are two splendid gas engines. The other area, which has nothing whatsoever to do with pumping sewage, is the print room with a variety of old printing machines – a chance to see a technology which has been all but swept away in the electronic revolution of recent years.

A magnificent engine built at the end of the nineteenth century, which could raise 150 gallons of water from a 12.2m (40ft) well at every stroke.

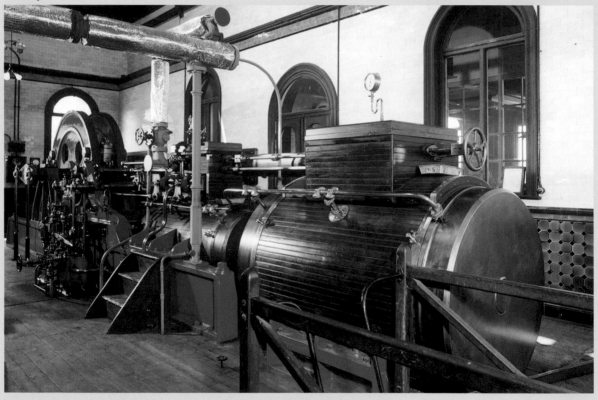

Stretham Old Engine

£; Easter to September second Sunday of each month; Tel: 01353 649210; Website: www.ely.org.uk/soe/index.html

Although opening hours are limited, this is an important site – even the exterior is worth a detour to see. Situated beside the Old West River to the south of the village, this is a rare survivor of more than ninety engines that were once used for land drainage in the Fens. The beam engine, built at Butterley in Derbyshire, was installed as a brand new example of the latest technology in 1831 and worked right through to 1925. It drove an 11m (37ft) diameter scoop wheel, which turned at a leisurely 4 revolutions a minute but lifted 30 tons at every turn. It is now worked by electricity rather than steam. Its work was taken over by a diesel-operated pump, also on show, but that too has been replaced by a modern electric pump at a different location. Land drainage has come a long way since the early 1800s, when the work was carried out by some 800 windmills.

WALTHAM ABBEY
Royal Gunpowder Mills

£££; March to October daily; Powdermill Lane, EN9 1BN; Tel: 01992 767022; Website: www.royalgunpowdermills.com

Gunpowder has been made here since the 1660s and was taken over by the Crown in 1787. The Ministry of Defence left in 1981 and twenty years later it was open to visitors, so this is all very new and restoration work is still continuing. It is an immense site, with a complex canal system for the powder barges. Although many buildings remain, almost all the machinery has gone, so everything has to be viewed using a good deal of imagination, helped by the interpretative displays in the exhibition centre. The name is also slightly misleading, as no actual gunpowder mills survive on site, having been replaced by cordite manufacture in the twentieth century.

Wicken Fen

NT; ££; Open daily; Wicken Fen National Nature Reserve, Lode Lane, Wicken, CB7 3XP; Tel: 01353 720274; Website: www.wicken.org.uk

The site is best known as a nature reserve, a last remnant of the old undrained Fens. It is not, however, an entirely natural habitat. Man has

The semi-circular arched bridge allowed gunpowder barges with high-covered tops to pass down the canal at Waltham Abbey.

exploited it for all kinds of uses, from reeds for thatching to clay for brick-making. Water levels have to be maintained and the work goes to a tiny windpump, moved here from neighbouring Adventurers' Fen. It works a scoop wheel and is the last survivor of the many wooden wind-pumps that once turned throughout The Fens. It is ironic that a pump designed to remove water from the Fens is now used to pump it in again, just to preserve this last remnant of an ancient landscape.

See Also
Bourne mill
NT; £; June to August Sunday and Tuesday afternoons; Bourne Road, Colchester, Essex, CO2 8RT; Tel: 01206 572422
An odd little watermill that began life in 1591 as a rather ornate fishing lodge.

Sacrewell Farm and Country Centre, Thornhaugh
££; Open daily; Tel: 01780 782254
Eighteenth-century watermill with pitchback wheel as the centrepiece of a country park with working farm.

Nene Valley Railway, Wansford
£ site only, £££ site and ride; Closed Monday; Wansford Station, Stibbington, Cambs, PE8 6LR; Tel: 01780 784404; Website: www.nvr.org.aol.com
A steam railway with a difference: here there is a strong emphasis on locomotives and rolling stock from overseas, ten countries represented in all. Return trip to Peterborough.

The pinnacled gables date from 1591 when Sir Thomas Lucas built his fishing lodge, but the weather-boarded sack hoist marks the conversion to Bourne Mill.

SUFFOLK

From medieval times Suffolk and neighbouring Norfolk were famous for their woollen industries. Very little in the way of physical remains has survived. This is not surprising, as the clothiers handed out the work to spinners and weavers throughout the area. Industrialisation failed to have any impact on the industry, which withered and died as other regions prospered. There is, however, ample evidence of former wealth in the famous wool towns and in particular in the magnificent churches endowed by the merchants. Much of the superb building seen in Lavenham church, for example, was paid for by Thomas Spryng, known as 'The Rich Clothier', in the late fifteenth and early sixteenth centuries. In his will he also endowed some 130 other churches in East Anglia. Such was the wealth of the trade in renaissance East Anglia.

The pride of the William Clowes collection of old printing machines is, rather appropriately, the Lion Press of 1866.

BECCLES

William Clowes Printing Museum

Free; Weekday afternoons; Newgate, NR34 9QE; Tel: 01502 712884

The modern computer systems of printing are hugely efficient but lack the grandeur of an age that has not long past. Clowes was founded in London in 1803 and moved to Beccles in 1870. They have kept their old machines, and it is a truly remarkable collection. One can view machines, such as the 1838 pivotal type caster, from the days of 'hot metal' printing and compositors' frames, including one with over 6000 Chinese characters. The real stars, however, are the presses, masterpieces of ornate ironwork dating back to 1834. There are displays on all aspects of book manufacture, from wood engravings to binding. This is not just for those interested in printing technology, it is a joy for anyone who has ever enjoyed a good book.

Euston Hall Watermill

££, entrance to grounds including mill; June to October Thursday afternoons; Tel: 01842 766366

The mill was built in the 1660s for Lord Arlington, and rebuilding over the years included the supply of a new cast iron axle from Burrell of Thetford, a company best known as a manufacturer of traction engines. As well as being a conventional corn mill, the mill also pumped water for the estate. The water tower sits incongruously on the roof, giving the mill the look of a rather tiny church.

LEISTON

Long Shop Steam Museum

££; From end of March to end of October daily; Main Street, IP16 4ES; Tel: 01728 832189

The name of Leiston might not be familiar but the name of the man who set up the works is known to traction engine enthusiasts throughout the world – Richard Garrett. The Garretts were among the first to apply steam

The fact that Euston Hall watermill looks like a small church is no accident: it helped a mundane pump fit the grand surroundings of a formal park.

power to threshing, and went on to build traction engines, steam tractors, rollers and stationary steam engines. In 1851 Richard Garrett III visited America to study production line assembly, and on his return he built the Long Shop, so that portable engines could be built under one roof in a continuous process. It was known locally as 'the cathedral' and it does look the part. There are many examples of Garrett engines on display but historically it is the great building itself that is of the highest importance. There are many steam engines on display in Britain, though nowhere quite like this.

PAKENHAM

This is one of the few places that can boast both a working watermill and a windmill.

STOWMARKET
Museum of East Anglian Life

££; Start of April to end of October daily; Tel: 01449 612229

As the name suggests, this town centre museum covers all aspects of life in the area, and the industrial past certainly gets its fair share of attention. Alton watermill has been re-erected on site, and is unusual in having an internal overshot wheel. The machinery has been restored and still grinds flour on special days. Alongside are the mill house, complete with two-seater privy, and the cart lodge. Wind power is represented by a small smock mill, originally built for land drainage. It operates a single pump through a crank. Steam comes in many forms, from a small stationary engine to big traction engines. One of the great attractions is to see the engines at work, including a pair of ploughing engines. These are unlike the familiar traction engines, in that they are situated at opposite sides of the field and the plough is pulled between them by cable. As each furrow is completed, the engines move forward for the next run. Farm life, domestic life and industrial work are all represented on a site that may start in the town but reaches out into the countryside.

The Thetford firm of Charles Burrell was one of the leading makers of steam traction engines. This example is *The Empress of Britain*, and is regularly used at the open-air museum.

Watermill

£; Easter to September Wednesday, Saturday, Sunday afternoons; (map ref. 155/937694); Tel: 01359 270570

Built in 1814, the mill incorporates part of an earlier structure. Power comes from a breastshot wheel, and there are three pairs of stones and a rare example of a 'Midget' roller mill. A Blackstone oil engine is the nearest it has come to modernisation.

Windmill

Free; Open all year when working; Tel: 01359 230277

It is impossible to miss the five-storey mill on the minor road from Pakenham to Ixworth. It has only recently been fully restored and has a strikingly handsome cap and fantail. It is unusual in having been in the ownership of the same family for well over a century.

SAXTEAD GREEN
Windmill

EH; £; April to October Monday to Saturday; Tel: 01728 685789

This is just about the most spectacular post mill in Britain. The buck perches above a two-storey roundhouse and is reached via a vertiginous ladder – not for the faint-hearted. The buck is moved by means of a fantail mounted on the steps. The mill

The humble water tower that became 'House in the Clouds'.

was probably built in the eighteenth century, was last worked commercially in 1947 and still has its machinery intact.

THORPENESS

Free; Open Access

This is a most remarkable place. Work began in 1910 to create an olde worlde holiday village – but olde worlde with modern amenities. That meant providing running water. The job of pumping went to a suitably picturesque windmill. Two large iron water towers, however, had to be disguised. One was hidden away in a stone tower, the other was given a much more imaginative treatment – it became the House in the Clouds. The result was an oversized mushroom of a house. The actual tank was given a pitched roof, surrounded by weather-boarding and given false windows complete with curtains. The lower part is real, and genuinely habitable. Extraordinary!

WOODBRIDGE
Tide Mill, Tide Mill Way

£; Summer daily, winter weekends; Tel: 01473 626618

One of Britain's few surviving examples of this type of mill. The mill pond is filled by the rising tide, then the water is released to turn a wooden undershot wheel. The machinery still works but whether you will see it at work is entirely dependant on the tide. In general, the mill would have worked for little more than four hours a tide, or eight hours a day. It is worth seeing in any case. It is a fine building of 1793, and there are interesting displays on tide mills.

Buttrum's Windmill, Burkitt Road

£; May to September weekend afternoons; Tel: 01473 583352

This is a six-storey tower mill, built in the 1830s and restored in the 1980s.

NORFOLK

BERNEY ARMS
Windmill

EH; £; April to October daily; (map ref. 134/465051); Tel: 01493 700605

This one is a bit of a challenge. You have two choices – walk from Berney Arms station or come by boat. It is worth the effort to see the biggest of all the Broads windmills. A seven-storey high tower mill, it was used to grind clinker for cement until 1880 and then converted for drainage.

FAKENHAM

Museum of Gas and Local History, Hempton Road

Free; Thursdays; Tel: 01328 863150

Once a commonplace all over the country, the advent of North Sea gas saw the disappearance of the town gas plant; this is a lonely survivor. The gas was made by burning coal in horizontal retorts, producing gas and tar and leaving coke behind. The gas was stored in the gas holder, now over a century old. This fascinating structure rises and falls as the gas enters and leaves within the confines of its ornate iron frame.

FORNCETT ST MARY

Industrial Steam Museum, Low Road

££; May to November first Sunday in month; Low Road, NR16 1JJ; Tel: 01508 488277; Website: www.oldenginehouse.demon.co.uk

A fine collection of steam engines of all type: beam engines, compound mill engines and a splendid vertical triple expansion engine from the very end of the steam era – only installed at the Dover waterworks in 1954. Enthusiasts will be particularly interested in the Hick Hargreaves engine, the oldest in the collection and one of the very first British engines to be fitted with the American Corliss valve gear – which is literally revolutionary. There is even one of the famous engines from London's Tower Bridge.

GUNTON PARK
Sawmill

£; April to September 4th Sunday in month; Tel: 01603 222705

What an extraordinary watermill this is! The building itself looks at first sight like a big, thatched barn that has

The Berney Arms tower mill, tallest of the many mills that rise above the Norfolk Broads.

mysteriously acquired a pair of water wheels. This is, in fact, a saw mill serving the estate of Gunton Hall. One wheel powers a giant reciprocating frame saw, installed in the 1820s and almost certainly the oldest mechanical saw in Britain. Its action is similar to that of the two-man saw of the saw pit, and it was able to handle tree trunks up to 6m (20ft) long and 76cm (2½ft) wide. The second wheel worked a (now incomplete) circular saw. The system of working the saw itself and the moving timber carriage through a complex system of belts, pulleys, gears and ratchets is a mechanical delight.

STRUMPSHAW

Strumpshaw Old Hall Steam Museum

££; July to October; Tel: 01603 713392

There are some places that specialise in stationary steam engines, others that concentrate on those that move. Here you get both. The stationary engines include a beam engine from Croydon and a large horizontal engine, with an imposing Ruston diesel to bring the collection up to date. To add to this is the impressive array of traction engine and steam rollers, more than twenty in all. The engines are only in steam once a month, usually at weekends, so if you want to see them in action, it is as well to check in advance.

BRESSINGHAM

Steam Museum and Gardens

£££–££££, depending on what is in steam; April to October daily; Tel: 01379 688585; Website: www.bressingham.co.uk

This represents one man's dream realised. Alan Bloom, rather appropriately, is a passionate gardener and set about creating superb gardens in the 89-hectare (220-acre) estate at Bressingham Hall. He is equally enthusiastic about steam. What began with just one traction engine grew and grew, until he has what must be one of the finest private collections in the world. He began small, with a miniature steam railway, added industrial narrow gauge and finally moved up to standard gauge. Now he has some spectacular exhibits, including a standard gauge Beyer Garratt, with its articulated chassis, so that it is rather like two engines fastened together, sharing just one cab. More conventional exhibits include the magnificent L.M.S. locomotive *Royal Scot* and the Norwegian engine *King Haaken 7*. His first love, the traction engine, has certainly not been neglected, and steam wagons have also been added. There is a display of stationary engines and just for fun there is a wonderful fairground ride, a set of steam gallopers. It is difficult to imagine any aspect of steam power that is not represented here.

Just two of Bressingham's many engines: the 5-ton Garrett tractor *Bunty* is on the left, overshadowed by the 16-ton Burrell road locomotive *President*.

DRAINING THE FENS

The area known as The Fens stretches from Lincoln almost down to Cambridge, and acts as the great sump of England: something like one-eighth of all the water that falls on the land drains out to the sea through The Fens. Left to their own devices, the rivers wound through the countryside, first through the bogs and pools of a landscape of deep peat deposits. Then the silt that had collected along the way built up to form high banks, and finally the sea was reached through the salt marshes.

The first drainage efforts were undertaken by the Romans, who farmed the rich peat land. They built a complex of drainage channels, of which the best preserved survivor is the Car Dyke of Cambridgeshire, which might also have been used for transport – making it Britain's first navigable canal. Not much more happened until the seventeenth century, when the Earl of Bedford brought over the Dutch engineer Cornelius Vermuyden, who created the Bedford Levels. The wandering rivers were straightened and enclosed between high banks, fed by a complex system of drainage channels. The scheme was successful in the short term, but as the land dried out, so the peat shrank. Soon, much of the peat fen was lower than the rivers, and water could no longer drain away. There is an impressive measure of just how far the land has fallen at Holme on the edge of the former Whittlesey Fen in Cambridgeshire. A cast iron column was driven

Wicken Fen has been preserved as one of the last remaining areas of unimproved fen, and is a haven for wildlife. The little wind pump, which drives a scoop wheel, began its working life on nearby Adventurers' Fen.

flush with the ground at the start of drainage in 1852. A century and a half later it rises 4m (13ft) into the air. Drainage itself was not enough to keep The Fens dry.

The solution came from Holland – wind-powered pumps. The great majority of the windmills were smock mills, driving simple scoop wheels to lift the water into the drainage channels. Only one survives intact, at Wicken Fen (p.83). This was built in 1908 to drain the Adventurers' Fen and removed to the National Trust site at Wicken Fen in 1955. It is ironic that this, the last area of fenland to be preserved, now stands proud of the surrounding countryside and has to have water pumped into it to retain its old character.

Inevitably, the windmill gave way to the steam engine. The first was installed at Sutton St Edmund in 1817 and a number have survived. The most impressive example is the Stretham Old Engine (p.82), which, like the windmills, drives a scoop wheel. The reign of the steam engines was short, and from the late nineteenth century onwards they were replaced by oil engines. Because these ran at a higher speed than steam engines, they could be used with more efficient rotary pumps. Today, the work of drainage has been taken over by electric pumps, but there are still memories of the old days, when wind and steam kept the fenlands dry.

LINCOLNSHIRE

BOSTON
Maud Foster Windmill

£; All year Wednesdays, Saturdays and Sundays, July and August plus Thursday and Friday; Willoughby Road; Tel: 01205 352188; Website: www.lincolnshire.net/travel/windmills

There are several good reasons for giving this windmill an entry of its own: it is the tallest working windmill in Britain, seven storeys high. It is unusual in having five sails, and as well as the stones, it has a full complement of flour dressing machinery. But what makes it especially appealing is its setting on the Boston waterfront, surrounded by old warehouses.

HECKINGTON
Windmill

£; Easter to mid-July afternoons Thursday to Sunday, July to September afternoons daily, September to October weekend

afternoons, November to Easter Sundays only; Tel: 01529 461919; Website: as above

The last surviving eight-sailed tower mill in Britain. It has been fully restored and put back to work. There is a craft centre on the site.

LINCOLN
Museum of Lincolnshire Life

£; Open daily; Burton Road, LN1 3LY; Tel: 01522 528448; Windmill, Tel: 01522 523870; Website: as above

This is a typical collection, covering all aspects of life in the county, including its industrial life, though inevitably there is a large emphasis on agriculture. It has the advantage of being very close to Ellis's windmill, built in 1798 and now back in full working order. It is a simple tower mill, mainly distinguished by the very large fantail on the cap.

Ellis's windmill would be just another East Anglian mill if it were not for its shapely ogee cap.

See Also

Pinchbeck Marsh Engine and Land Drainage Museum
Free; April to October daily; Off West Marsh Road; Tel: 01775 725468
The name almost says it all: the engine is an 1833 beam engine, driving a scoop wheel. It has been fully restored and is now the centrepiece of a small museum on land drainage.

Cogglesford Watermill, Sleaford
Free; April to September daily; Tel: 07966 400634
A working mill with an internal wheel, built around 1750.

WINDMILLS

The windmill seems to have arrived in Britain several centuries after the watermill, and the earliest record is of a long vanished mill in Yorkshire described in a document of 1185. We do, however, have a number of illustrations of medieval mills, and we can still see mills that conform very closely to this early type. These are post mills. The basic mechanism of all mills is the same. The sails are blown round by the wind. In the earliest mills there were four sails, consisting of canvas spread over a wooden frame. Just as in a ship, the sails could be reefed in high winds, usually by pulling the cloths diagonally across the frame. The sails will only rotate, however, if they face the wind. The machinery of a post mill is housed in a wooden structure, known as the buck, which pivots on the central post. A long pole, the tailpole, leads from the back of the buck, and this can be used manually to haul the entire buck round to face in the appropriate direction. The stairs giving access to the buck are generally pulled up clear of the ground to allow it to swing. Later mills have more sophisticated systems. The mill at Avoncroft Museum (see p.50), for example, has a tailpole ending in a wheel that moves around a circular track with the aid of a winch. Saxtead Green Mill (p.85) goes one better. Here a fantail is mounted at the foot of the steps. When the mill is correctly positioned, it is shielded from the wind, but when the wind shifts, the fantail begins to turn, acting like a propeller to drive the buck round. Bourn Mill represents the post mill at its simplest, with the whole frame exposed. Most later mills enclosed the

Saxtead Green is a large post mill, though the post itself is out of sight inside the roundhouse. The buck is turned automatically through a fantail mounted on the steps.

post by a roundhouse, which both protects the timbers and acts as a useful store.

The obvious disadvantage of the post mill was that it was limited in size. It was eventually realised that it made little sense to move the entire mill, when all you needed to do was to position the sails. A new generation of mills appeared, where the sails were mounted on a movable cap at the top of the structure. Where the main mill is built of brick or stone it is known as a tower mill; if it is timber, it is a smock mill. As at Saxtead Green, the sails are moved by means of a fantail, but this time mounted on the cap. There were also improvements to the sails. Instead of being covered in cloth, they were shuttered, rather like a Venetian blind, and the speed of the sails could be adjusted by opening and closing the shutters. Access to the sails is usually from an outdoor gallery. The bigger mills were sometimes supplied with more than the usual four sails, and the grandest surviving example must be eight-sailed Heckington mill.

The machinery inside the windmill is much the same for all types. A large gearwheel, the brake wheel, is mounted on the rotating wind shaft, and this engages with a smaller wheel, the wallower, mounted on a vertical shaft to turn the stones. Ancillary machinery can also be added, including sack hoists and flour dressing machines. Not all mills were used for grinding, particularly in East Anglia, where they were used extensively for land drainage. There are many examples of all the main types of mills in this area – not surprising for a flat, windy region – and one with close associations with Holland. The following are some of the area's best examples, though a few can also be found as separate entries under the individual counties. The majority of the mills are only open a few days a week but all are worth seeing for the exteriors alone: charges are either non-existent or modest.

Alford, Lincs
£; July to September daily, November to March Tuesday and Saturday, February and March plus Sunday afternoons, April to June plus Friday; Tel: 01507 462136; Website: www.lincolnshire.net/ travel/windmills
A very imposing six-storey tower mill with five sails. It is one of the few still worked commercially, producing flour and cereals and complete with its own large oven.

Bourn, Cambs
Exterior view
Located off the minor road from Bourn to Caxton, this is probably Britain's oldest mill. With its pitched roof and open trestle, the tiny mill is the closest we have to a medieval post mill. It is open only a few days a year but is worth a diversion to see on any day.

Denver, Norfolk
££; Daily; Tel: 01366 384009
The six-storey tower mill has been fully restored in recent years, and has a visitor centre and guided tours.

Hewitt's Mill, Heapham, near Gainsborough, Lincs
£; End of March to end of October Saturdays; Tel: 01427 838230
A typical tower mill of 1876, it was struck by lightning in 1956 and fully rebuilt.

Horsey Wind Pump, Norfolk
NT; £; April to October daily; Tel: 01493 393904
Just south of the village on the edge of Horsey Mere, this is a charming little drainage mill with a boat cap.

Mount Pleasant, Kirton in Lindsey, Lincs
£; Friday, Saturday, Sunday, plus August weekdays; Tel: 01652 640177; Website: www.lincolnshire.net/travel/windmills
Although I swore that after twelve weeks square bashing at the nearby airfield I would never come back, I made an exception in order to see this fine brick tower mill with its shapely ogee cap, not least because it is still at work producing flour.

Horsey wind pump is a small tower windmill with a boat-shaped cap – very appropriate for its setting on the Norfolk Broads.

Sibsey Trader Mill, Lincs
EH; £; Easter to August 2nd and 4th Sundays; Tel: 01205 820065; Website: www.josrival.demon.co.uk
A fine big mill with six sails mounted on an ogee cap, with milling demonstrations on open days.

Stanton Windmill, Suffolk
£; Open when milling; Tel: 01359 250622; Website: www.stantonwindmill. members.beeb.net
A post mill of 1751, moved to this site in 1818: surprisingly, perhaps, it was quite common for mills to be taken apart and erected on a fresh site. It is still in use and has a photographic display of British mills.

Stracey Arms Mill, A47 between Acle and Great Yarmouth, Norfolk
£; Easter to September daily; Tel: 01603 222705
Surrounded by the marshland it was once used to drain, this brick drainage mill houses an interesting exhibition on drainage mills.

Thelnetham, Suffolk, on the minor road to Blo' Norton
£; July to September Sunday; Tel: 01395 250622; Website. www.thelnetham.freeserve.co.uk
A small tower mill by East Anglian standards, but still at work.

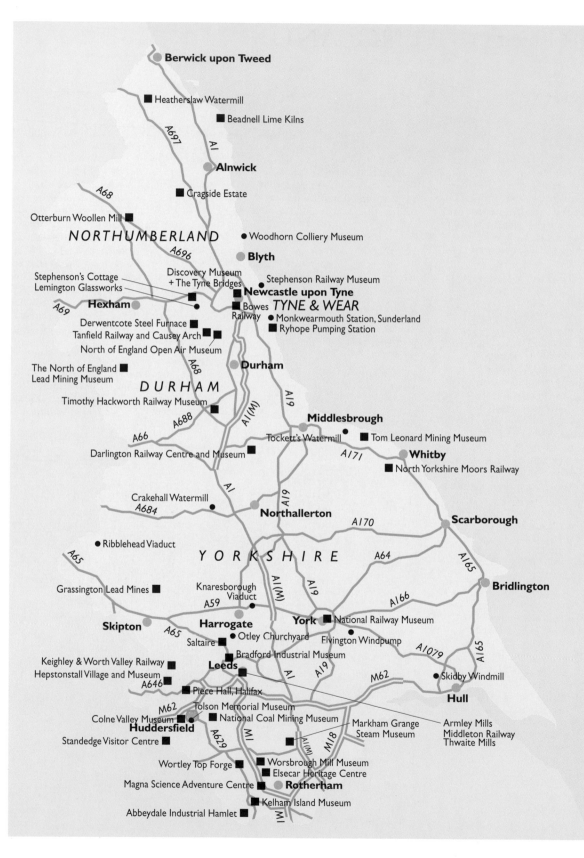

Berwick upon Tweed

■ Heatherslaw Watermill

■ Beadnell Lime Kilns

Alnwick

■ Cragside Estate

Otterburn Woollen Mill ■

NORTHUMBERLAND   ● Woodhorn Colliery Museum

                                    Blyth

Discovery Museum   Stephenson Railway Museum
Stephenson's Cottage   + The Tyne Bridges
Lemington Glassworks   Newcastle upon Tyne
Hexham   ■ Bowes   TYNE & WEAR
                                 Railway   ● Monkwearmouth Station, Sunderland
Derwentcote Steel Furnace ■   ● Ryhope Pumping Station
Tanfield Railway and Causey Arch ■
North of England Open Air Museum ■

The North of England ■   Durham
Lead Mining Museum
                DURHAM
Timothy Hackworth Railway Museum ■

                                          Middlesbrough
                          Tockett's Watermill
                                    ■ Tom Leonard Mining Museum
Darlington Railway Centre and Museum ■
                                       Whitby
Crakehall Watermill   ■ North Yorkshire Moors Railway

                                  Northallerton
                                                    Scarborough

● Ribblehead Viaduct   Y O R K S H I R E

Grassington Lead Mines ■
                        Knaresborough
                        Viaduct   Bridlington
Skipton   Harrogate   York
                                        ■ National Railway Museum
                    Saltaire ● Otley Churchyard   ● Elvington Windpump
Keighley & Worth Valley Railway ■   Bradford Industrial Museum
Hepstonstall Village and Museum ■ Leeds   ● Skidby Windmill
                                                      Armley Mills
        ■ Piece Hall, Halifax   Hull   Middleton Railway
        Tolson Memorial Museum   Thwaite Mills
Colne Valley Museum ■   National Coal Mining Museum   Markham Grange
Huddersfield   Steam Museum
Standedge Visitor Centre ■
Wortley Top Forge ■   ■ Worsbrough Mill Museum
                          ■ Elsecar Heritage Centre
Magna Science Adventure Centre ■   Rotherham
                          ■ Kelham Island Museum
Abbeydale Industrial Hamlet ■

NORTH EAST ENGLAND

YORKSHIRE

Yorkshire has now been split up into separate units – north, south, east and west, with York stuck in as an extra in the middle. As a Yorkshireman born and bred, the best I am prepared to allow is that there are three divisions, and those are the Ridings – South Riding only occurs as the title of a novel. Anything else is just Whitehall and can be ignored. But even the most xenophobic Tyke has to concede that there are real differences between the different parts of the county. The south is the land of coal, iron and steel. The former West Riding was the bustling heart of the woollen industry. The north means The Dales and moors and sheep, but a good deal else besides, and in particular the metal mines that have left their mark on so much of the countryside. In the former West Riding you see the evidence of the past everywhere, in the stern rows of weavers' cottages with their long windows and their dark walls of millstone grit, and in the woollen mills that seem to pop up in almost every town and village. Often the mills themselves are quite small and could almost be mistaken for large houses if it were not for the tall chimney at one end. You can see the changes that time has brought in many valleys, but one of the best is the Colne Valley, stretching eastwards from Huddersfield until it is brought to a halt by the looming bulk of Standedge Fell. Up on the brows of the hills and scattered over the hillsides are the isolated cottages and some small workshops. Down in the valley floor, the mills crowd in, clumping ever closer together until they seem almost to touch on the outskirts of Huddersfield.

Finding reminders of the mining past is slightly more difficult, and often you have to make your way high up on the moors. Anyone who wants a really romantic setting for a mining landscape cannot do better than to follow the path down the east bank of the Swale as it dashes down over waterfalls on its way from Keld. You will come to the unmistakable signs of spoil and ruins and the wonderful, mysterious deep valley of Swinner Gill with the bizarrely named Crackpot Hall at the entrance. It is a good walk from the nearest road but well worth the effort (map ref. 91/9000).

South Yorkshire is now well represented by some of the country's finest industrial museums, listed below.

BRODSWORTH

Markham Grange Steam Museum, Markham Grange Nurseries

Free; Open weekdays, steaming on Wednesdays and Bank Holidays; Longlands Lane; Tel: 01302 330430; Website: www.mgsteam.btinternet.co.uk

Here in the unlikely setting of a garden centre is a major collection of steam engines, eleven in all – though the owners have certainly not stopped collecting. The big engines include a tandem compound mill engine and a compound marine engine, while the smaller engines are regularly set to work on steam days, driving a variety of machinery.

ELSECAR

Heritage Centre

Free access to site, £££ for full range of attractions; Site open daily; Wath Road, S74 8HJ; Tel: 01226 740203; Website: www.barnsley.gov.uk

When I first visited here some twenty-five years ago, this was a working village with a still active colliery. That has all gone, but a familiar hotchpotch of hands-on, interactive exhibits has moved into the old buildings, and at its heart is a genuinely unique steam engine. The colliery and ironworks were owned by Earl Fitzwilliam and in 1795 he installed a Newcomen engine for pumping. It has been modified over the years but is still the only atmospheric engine still standing in its original engine house, a solid affair of local gritstone. Restoration work is in hand, and it will certainly be a fine sight to see the great beam engine move again. It stands among the houses of the old village. An added attraction is the little steam railway offering rides on the old private branch line – the Earl had his own private station.

The Elsecar engine house contains the only surviving Newcomen type atmospheric steam engine still to be seen on its original site. The end of the beam can be seen at the top of the wall.

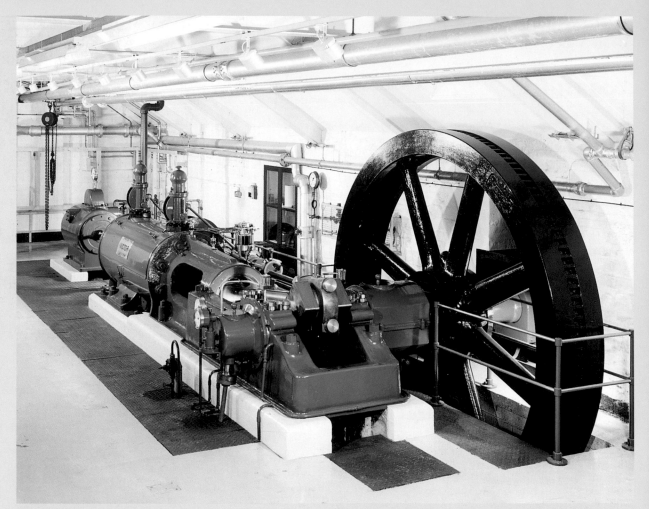

This mighty engine comes from the very end of the age of steam. It was built in 1921 and was used at Linton Mill, Grassington, both to drive machinery and to generate electricity. This is a particularly efficient type of steam engine, first developed in 1827, known as the 'uniflow'.

BRADFORD
Bradford Industrial Museum, Moorside Mills

Free; All year but closed Mondays and Sunday mornings; Moorside Road, Eccleshill, BD2 3HP; Tel: 01274 631756; Website: www.bradford.gov.uk

Perhaps the best recommendation I can make is to record the fact that I have made four long visits here in the last three years and I still don't feel that I have exhausted my enthusiasm. The setting, a former woollen mill, is just right and it still has an appealing raw edge to it so that you get a real sense of what it once was. The main exhibits are obviously the textile machines, and visitors have a chance to follow through the main processes from raw wool coming in to weaving, with regular demonstrations. These are big, noisy and sometimes very complex machines, yet it is still quite easy to see just what they are doing and how each fits into the steady progression towards the finished product. There is an extensive section on power, and not just steam engines but also some truly magnificent gas engines are on show. There is a small but interesting transport collection inside the main building, and outside there are heavy horses that are put through their paces. Managers' and workers' houses complete the display.

The city itself still has memories of the days when wool ruled and brought prosperity. There are fine warehouses in the area known as Little Germany, the gothic splendour of City Hall, and the flamboyant Wool Exchange, where once merchants traded, now houses a book shop and is well worth seeing.

GOLCAR
Colne Valley Museum

£; Weekend afternoons and public holidays;
Cliffe Ash, HD7 4PY; Tel: 01484 659762

A row of old weavers' cottages stands on the rim of the Colne valley. Like many in the area, the looms were kept on the top floor and the family lived downstairs, but these are slightly different. Because they are built against the hillside, the workshops have a separate entrance from the upper road – originally there was no internal connection. The cottages have been restored, looms are back in place and there are demonstrations of spinning and carding on the lower floor and weaving up above, together with a spinning jenny. I cannot think of anywhere that gives a better picture of this type of domestic industry.

GRASSINGTON
Lead mines

Free; Open Access; Map ref. 98/0165

Lead mining was hugely important in the area, and this is simply the best place to see the physical remains – and enjoy some tremendous Dales scenery at the same time. The area is approached via the dead end road leading up the moors from Grassington, then turning off onto the broad track. At first sight there is a jumble of decayed buildings, humps and hollows and a solitary chimney marking the end of the old smelting cupola. There are information boards everywhere and you can even go down a dripping tunnel to reach the well-guarded top of a 110m (360ft) deep shaft. If you want to go further, there is a terrific walk that follows the stream back down to Hebden with more remains along the way.

GROSMONT
North Yorkshire Moors Railway

£££ return fare; April to November daily;
Tel: 01751 472508;
Website: www.nymr.demon.co.uk

A beautiful line running through the heart of wild moorland, linking Pickering and Grosmont, and offering 29km (18 miles) of travel by steam. It is also a line of considerable historical interest. Built in 1833 as the Whitby and Pickering Railway, it was worked entirely by horses for nine years – even though the man in charge was George Stephenson. At Grosmont you can still find traces of the old line, including a tunnel with castellated portals now used by pedestrians.

HALIFAX
Piece Hall

Free, Open Access

In 1775 the wool merchants of Halifax built themselves this magnificent trading centre in the middle of the town. There is a grand entrance through

Piece Hall, Halifax shows in its style and elegance just how rich the woollen trade was in eighteenth-century Yorkshire.

ornate iron gates to the open courtyard surrounded by galleries where the traders had their offices. It is all stylishly classical, though today the market sells anything rather than simply trading in wool, and the offices have become shops and an art gallery.

HEPTONSTALL
Village and Museum

£ Museum weekend afternoons, free access
for village; Tel: 01422 358087; Website:
www.calderdale.gov.uk

The hilltop village seems the model of a quiet backwater, with its old houses and cobbled streets. However, it was once an important centre of the woollen industry. It had its own wool hall and lay at the heart of a web of packhorse routes. One of these is a cobbled way, The Buttress, leading down to the bridge built c.1500, which gives Hebden Bridge its name. The wealth enabled the locals to build a grammar school, now housing the excellent small museum. There are weavers' cottages, the best just behind the octagonal Wesleyan Chapel. This is a place to walk round and delight in – and from its heights you can look down on the industrial town of Hebden Bridge, where the mills crowd round river and canal.

The A2 Pacific *Blue Peter* storming along the North Yorkshire Moors Railway with a trainload of enthusiasts.

LEEDS

Armley Mills, Leeds Industrial Museum

£; Open daily; Canal Road, LS12 2QF; Tel: 0113 263 7861; Website: www.leeds.gov.uk/tourinfo

The site alone makes this worth a visit. Set beside the River Aire, the mill complex was built in 1788 and was then the biggest woollen mill in the world. It was rebuilt, rather belatedly, as a fireproof mill when the original burned down in 1805. This is the grand setting for the museum. Inevitably textiles dominate, and the changes are traced from the first water wheel-powered machinery to that driven by the mill's steam engine. The other side of the woollen trade is not forgotten: the manufacture of ready-made clothes. There is a lot more to see, including a recreated silent cinema, with regular shows.

Middleton Railway

£; April to Christmas weekends; The Station, Moor Road, Hunslet, LS10 2JQ; Tel: 0113 271 0320; Website: www.middletonrailway.org.uk

No one could pretend that this is Britain's grandest preserved railway, but historically it is probably the most important of the lot. It was here in 1812 that the world's first commercial steam railway opened for business. It was unusual in working on a rack and pinion system to reduce the load on fragile rails. It was also the first standard gauge railway to be taken over by volunteers. Unfortunately, little remains of the original line, though some of the old stone sleeper blocks can be spotted around the site, with the give-away central hole into which rails were spiked.

Thwaite Mills

£; All year weekends, on school holidays Tuesday to Friday; Thwaite Lane, Stourton, LS10 1RP; Tel: 0113 249 6453; Website: www.leeds.gov.uk/tourinfo

Tell someone you are going to visit a putty mill and they might well think you are a bit deranged, but this is actually a really wonderful site. The mill was built by the Aire & Calder Navigation Co. in the 1820s and converted to a stone-crushing mill half a century later, eventually turning to putty manufacture. Power comes from two big water wheels, supplemented by aged diesel engines. The process involved pumping, crushing and mixing the raw ingredients, using an amazing array of machinery that seems to fill every inch of space as it trundles and grumbles away like one of the more eccentric inventions of Heath Robinson.

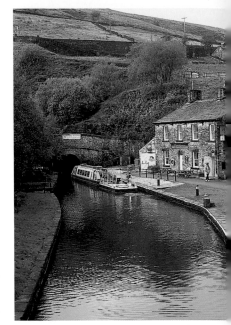

The Marsden end of Standedge tunnel on the Huddersfield Canal, with the trip boat from the Visitor Centre.

Leeds is an interesting city to explore, and it does have one truly original factory: Marshall's Flax Mill in Marshall Street, built in the early nineteenth century. The flax was processed for linen manufacture and the building was designed to look like an Egyptian temple. It was even stranger in its working days. To provide insulation the roof was covered with soil; to stop that blowing away it was planted with grass; to keep that under control a flock of sheep grazed on this Leeds rooftop.

MARSDEN

Standedge Visitor Centre, Waters Road

££; May to November daily; Tel: 01484 844298; Website: www.standedge.co.uk

The Huddersfield Narrow Canal was reopened in 2001. This amazing canal cuts right through the Pennines with 186 locks in just 110km (68 miles) and contains Britain's longest canal tunnel, around 5km (3 miles) of it. The story is told in a visitor centre, housed in the old maintenance yard buildings, and from here there are trips into the tunnel but only far enough to get an impression of what it was like in the days when boats were legged all the way through.

The Armley Mills Industrial Museum complex seen from the towpath of the Leeds & Liverpool Canal.

OVERTON

National Coal Mining Museum

£££; Open daily; New Road, WF4 4RH; Tel: 01924 848806

This museum is based on the former Caphouse Colliery and mercifully it has not been tidied up and prettified for visitors. No museum could recreate the actuality of a working mine, with its dark low galleries, ear-drumming noise and the perpetual showers of dust – and probably no one would want it. This does, however, give a real impression of underground life, beginning with a stomach-churning drop down the 137m (450ft) shaft to the gloomy workings. Above ground there is just as much to see, from the pit ponies to the 1876 steam winding engine. A word of warning: you may not emerge as dust caked as a real miner, but this is not a site at which to wear your Sunday best.

OXENHOPE

Keighley & Worth Valley Railway

££; June to September and school holidays daily; Tel: 01535 647777

Apart from passing through splendid scenery, having an excellent stock of steam locomotives and vintage carriages, there is something else that makes this line special: it is complete. The modern line covers the whole of the original branch line and all the stations are immaculately preserved – right down to gas lighting.

SALTAIRE

Free; Open access; Tourist Office Tel: 01274 774993

There was nothing much here until Sir Titus Salt decided to build a new mill to manufacture alpaca and mohair. In 1849 cholera hit Bradford, so he moved to this site beside the River Aire. Over the next quarter of a century the mill and the village grew together. Salt settled on an Italian style for everything, from mill to houses. He built schools, church, almshouses, infirmary and even provided a park. He did not, however, build a pub and refused to allow anyone else to do so either. Although his regime was authoritarian, it must have seemed heaven after the filth and disease of nineteenth-century Bradford. Parts of the mill buildings are open, with shops and the David Hockney Gallery. A walk round Saltaire is always interesting, but do try to join one of the weekend guided walks that start from the tourist office and experience the enthusiasm of the local guides. Saltaire was designated a World Heritage site in 2001.

ROTHERHAM
Magna Science Adventure Centre

£££; Open daily; Sheffield Road, Templeborough, S60 1DX; Tel: 01709 720002; Website: www.magnatrust.org.uk

Much as you might expect, this is a state of the art, interactive, all systems go sort of place, opened in 2001 – and very good it is too, although that is not why it is included here. Firstly, there's the main building, originally part of the great Templeborough steel works that dominated Rotherham; it is absolutely huge – over 0.4km (½ mile) long, a vast cavernous space that dwarfs the pavilions containing the different exhibits. Secondly, there is a spectacular recreation in sight and sound of the working life of the great 'E' furnace. This does not pretend to be an industrial museum, pure and simple, but it is wonderfully impressive and imaginatively conceived. Its ingenious combination of old industrial building and new specially designed units earned it the Building of the Year Award in 2001.

The old building of Templeborough steel works is itself the most awesome exhibit.

SHEFFIELD
Abbeydale Industrial Hamlet

*££; April to October Monday to Thursday
and Sunday; Abbeydale Road South,
S7 2QW; Tel: 0114 236 7731;
Website: www.simt.co.uk*

This is a very special site, for you see a
complete industrial cycle from raw
materials to finished product. Some
time in the late eighteenth century the
works was set up to make scythes.
Water power was used, the wheels supplied from a big mill pond. The first
step was to make steel by what was
then the very new Huntsman crucible
process. The crucibles were made on
site, then filled with a carefully measured mixture of blister steel and lime.
Following this, they were heated in the
furnace and after melting, the steel was
poured out or 'teemed' into moulds to
make ingots. Now manufacture of the
blades could begin by forging the crucible steel between two pieces of
wrought iron, done under the blows of
the great water-powered tilt hammers.
The blades were ground to give an
edge, bored for fastening to the handles
and finished. The work continued here
up to the 1930s. Workers and manager
all had houses on the site, which are
also open to the public.

**An exhibit showing hand working and
loading in the drift mine at the Tom
Leonard Mining Museum.**

**The rough wooden construction of hand crane and water-powered hammer at Wortley
were still at work in the railway age.**

Kelham Island Museum

*££; All year but closed Friday and Saturday;
Alma Street, S3 8RY; Tel: 0114 272 2106;
Website: www.simt.co.uk*

The site is interesting: it began as a
foundry on an artificial island in the
River Don, which was then demolished to make way for a power station
in 1899 to supply electricity for the
new city trams. Now it is a good
museum, with a wide variety of
things to see and do, and one really
spectacular exhibit. The 'River Don
Engine' was built in 1905 to drive an
armour plate rolling mill, and could
handle plate up to 41cm (16 inches)
thick, weighing up to 50 tons. It is
said to be the biggest working engine
in the world. It may well be, but I can
say that it is the only thing I have
ever come across that has silenced my
eldest grandson!

The other industrial site of interest
in Whiteley Woods is off Hangingwater
Road. Shepherd Wheel is a survivor of
what were once water-powered grinding
shops. The outside can always be seen
in the park but open days are rare.

SKINNINGROVE
Tom Leonard Mining Museum, Deepdale

*££; April to October afternoons, July and
August Monday to Saturday plus
Sundays; Tel: 01287 642877; Website:
www.ironstonemuseum.co.uk*

Not a coal mine but an ironstone
mine, one of a number that once
flourished in the Cleveland area.
Visitors are given a very full guided
tour, lasting over an hour, which
includes an underground visit to one
of the drift mines.

WORSBROUGH
Worsbrough Mill Museum

*£; All year Wednesday to Sunday; Tel:
01226 774527*

This is not one mill but two working
together. The earliest part, the water-
powered grain mill, was built around
1625. Then in 1843, with the growing industrialisation of the region, a
second mill was tacked on, powered

by steam engine. In the 1920s the mill was turned over to grinding animal feed and the steam engine was replaced by a 1911 Horsby hot bulb diesel engine. So just this one site gives you a potted history of almost four centuries of milling, all in the attractive setting of a country park.

WORTLEY
Top Forge

£; February to end of November open Sundays; Map ref. 110/294999, Tel: 0114 281 7991

Superficially, this is similar to Abbeydale in nearby Sheffield. Once again, giant hammers are powered by water wheels to shape metal. The end product, however, was very different. The forge was first set to work in the early seventeenth century and it looks old, open to the elements and far from the nearest village. But this forge survived to have an important job in the nineteenth century. A puddling furnace and rolling mills for wrought iron were introduced, and it began turning out railway axles. There is a sense of time having stopped here; even the venerable jib cranes look ready for work.

YORK
National Railway Museum

Free; Open daily; Leeman Road, YO26 4XJ; Tel: 01904 621261; Website: www.nrm.org.uk

What to say about such a place? This is one of the great national museums. I was lucky enough to come here and spend several days before it was opened to the public, and I have been coming back ever since, seeing it get better and better, as well as bigger and bigger. The setting is perfect in old railway buildings, the exhibits covering a huge range of material, from the dawn of the railways right up to the present. Everyone has their favourites, whether the Victorian elegance of the Stirling single locomotive or the streamlined power of the speed record-breaking *Mallard*. And the emphasis is not just on locomotives. There is an equally splendid collection of rolling stock. The story has now been brought right up to date with the arrival of a Japanese 'bullet' car for exhibition. If you are a railway enthusiast, you will need no encouragement from me; if you are not, come anyway. It really is quite splendid.

One of the very popular exhibits at the National Railway Museum is the coach built for Queen Victoria's use in 1869. It was her favourite railway carriage, and was not replaced until after her death.

See Also

Crakehall Watermill
£; Easter to September closed Monday and Friday; Tel: 01677 423240
A seventeenth-century mill building with older machinery; also a collection of agricultural implements.

Elvington Windpump
Free; Open access; Open daily; On minor road between Elvington and Wheldrake; Tel: 01904 608255
A small nineteenth-century windmill used for pumping out clay pits at the brickworks.

Tockett's Watermill, Guisborough
£; Sunday afternoons, Spring Bank Holiday to September
A particularly fine mill with pitchback wheel and mill house.

Tolson Memorial Museum, Huddersfield
Free; All day weekdays, afternoons weekends; Ravensknowle Park, Wakefield Road, HD5 8DJ; Tel: 01484 223830
The former wool magnate's home provides an appropriate setting for an important collection of textile machinery.

Knaresborough Viaduct
Free; Open access
A very picturesque example of a viaduct given an architectural treatment to fit it to its setting. Here the railway crosses the River Nidd close by the castle keep, so the bridge has battlements, arrow slits and turrets.

Otley Churchyard
Free; Open access
A reminder that there was a human price paid for railway building. Shaped as a replica of nearby Bramhope tunnel, there is a memorial to the navvies who died during its construction.

Ribblehead Viaduct
Free; Open access
A splendid stone viaduct in a wild moorland setting. Built for the Settle & Carlisle Railway, it is still in use; the line remains one of the great scenic routes in Britain.

Skidby Windmill
£; Weekends, summer plus Wednesday to Friday; Tel: 01482 884971
Recently renovated tower mill of 1821 with modern roller plant.

DURHAM

To the industrial historian the name Durham is synonymous with coal. The task of getting that coal from the pithead to the customer gave rise to a complex transport system, which made this an important area for the early development of railways.

DARLINGTON
Railway Centre and Museum

£; Open daily; North Road Station, DL3 6ST; Tel: 01325 460532; Website: www.drcm.org.uk

This is a site of special interest in railway history. The Stockton & Darlington was the first public railway to use steam locomotives, but that was for freight only. Passengers had to make do with horse-drawn coaches fitted with flanged wheels. It was only in 1842 that this system was scrapped and Darlington got a real station. It is now a museum, and prize exhibits include the original *Locomotion*, a chance for comparison with the Beamish replica, and an example of the kind of locomotive that would have used the station when it opened: the *Derwent* of 1845. There are many other exhibits and occasional short steam runs.

A North Eastern Railway 2-4-0 locomotive of 1875 on display at the old Darlington Railway Station.

HAMSTERLEY
Derwentcote Steel Furnace

EH; Free; End March to end September daily, all year1st and 3rd Sunday; Off the A694, between Hamsterley and Rowland's Gill; Tel: 01207 562573

When I first came here it was a semi-ruin all but lost in the undergrowth. Happily, English Heritage has recognised its importance and restored the furnace. This is Britain's oldest surviving steel furnace, built in the early eighteenth century to produce blister steel by heating wrought iron and charcoal in sealed containers. It was steel from furnaces such as this that was sent down to Abbeydale (p.98) for manufacturing high quality crucible steel. It is an imposing conical structure of rough stone blocks.

KILLHOPE
The North of England Lead Mining Museum

££; April to September daily, October weekends; On A689 between Stanhope and Alston; Nr Cowshill, Upper Weardale, DL13 1AR; Tel: 01388 537505

There is no chance of missing the site, dominated by the 10.3m (34ft) diameter overshot water wheel installed in the 1870s to work the lead mill. Before the ore, galena, could be separated from the stone, the material had to be crushed. Then it was agitated with water, when the heavy ore separated out. Separation could also be done by hand at the recently restored washing rake. Visitors can visit the mine itself, which involves a sort of Groucho Marx crouch in the constricted space. The mine is wet and uncomfortable but the effort is rewarded by the sight of a fascinating survivor. Water wheels have been used to operate pumps to de-water mines since Roman times, but I know of few places in Britain where one can be seen working underground. You can straighten out afterwards with a walk through the woods to see more mining remains.

SHILDON
Timothy Hackworth Railway Museum

£; Easter to end of October closed Monday and Tuesday; Tel: 01388 777999

The museum is based on Hackworth's old home. He is one of the unjustly neglected pioneers of steam locomotion, having designed a number of powerful engines for the infant Stockton & Darlington Railway. He is, however, best known as designer of *Sans Pareil*, the engine beaten in the Rainhill Trials by Stephenson's *Rocket*. A replica built for the 150th anniversary of the trials is generally in steam at the museum, but may be out on loan to other lines.

STANLEY
Tanfield Railway and Causey Arch

Free; The arch has free access from A6076, Stanley to Sunniside road (map ref. 88/201559); Railway: Marley Hill Engine Shed, NE16 5ET; Tel: 0191 3887545

There are two reasons to come here. The first is to see the world's oldest railway bridge, a handsome structure that spans a deep gorge in a single arch. It was built to carry the wooden rails of the Tanfield tramway of 1727. Around 1835 the old horse-drawn line was replaced by iron rails and the power of steam. That is the second reason for calling in, for the railway has been brought back to life as a preserved line from Marley Hill.

BEAMISH
North of England Open Air Museum

££££ (prices reduced in winter); April to October daily, winter closed Mondays and Fridays; Tel: 01207 231811; Website: www.beamish.org.uk

There is nothing quite like this anywhere else in Britain. It has some of the characteristics of a museum of buildings, such as Avoncroft, but on a much larger scale. It is also arranged in quite distinct areas: the town, the colliery and colliery village, the working farm and the manor, all linked together by railway and tramway. The colliery is the nearest thing to a very local industry, for the unique vertical steam winding engine spent its working life at the Beamish colliery, before being moved up the road to the museum site. Now it is part of a major, and brilliantly executed, reconstruction of a nineteenth-century colliery. Even a local drift mine has been reopened for underground visits. It is linked to the village by a railway on which a replica of George Stephenson's *Locomotion* runs. The original engine was built for the Stockton &

Darlington Railway in 1825, and it is well worth watching in operation, if only to see just how complicated it is to reverse. The main railway is built around the former Rowley station, steam trains running on a regular service. The transport collection is wide ranging, and as well as the trams that link the various parts of the site together, there is also an immense steam navvy by Ruston Bucyrus. The 1920s town includes the splendid Co-op and an item without which no self-respecting northern town would be complete – a cast iron bandstand. There is a great deal more to see, and the farm is particularly interesting for, like several other farms in the region, it introduced a steam engine for threshing in the nineteenth century. If there was a competition for best industrial museum in Britain, Beamish would go straight onto the short list.

Pit cottages built in the 1860s by the Hetton Coal Company at Hetton-le-Hole. The gardens provided valuable food, but were also used for growing prize leeks.

TYNE AND WEAR

In this region the story of coal and railways that began in Durham is continued. A new element, however, is added – shipbuilding. The Tyne is one of the few areas in Britain where the industry survives, and anyone who feels they want an overview of two millennia of history can go down to Wallsend, where Hadrian's Wall ended and where a new museum tells the story of the Wall and its forts. From an observation tower, visitors can look down on the excavated fort of Segedunum and out over the cranes of the Swan Hunter yard, which in 1906 saw the launching of the *Mauretania*, the biggest ship ever built on the Tyne. Just across the road are the excavated remains of Wallsend Colliery, so famous and productive in its day that Grand Duke Nicholas of Russia turned up for a visit in 1816, looked down one of the shafts, declared it looked like 'the mouth of Hell' and left.

NEWCASTLE UPON TYNE
The Tyne Bridges

Free; Open access

Walking along the Newcastle river front is rather like taking a seminar in engineering design. The oldest bridge is in many ways the most daring. Robert Stephenson's High Level Bridge, begun in 1846, carries road and rail traffic in two tiers. Bowstring arches of cast iron are tied together by wrought iron chains. Cast iron columns from the ribs support the upper rail deck. The swing road bridge was opened in 1876, moved by hydraulic machinery provided by the Armstrong works a little way up the river at Elswick. The Tyne Bridge, an elegant bowstring bridge, was added in the 1920s. Other later arrivals were comparatively nondescript, until the delicate Millennium footbridge was built to show that the twenty-first century had its own ways of working with grace and artistry.

While in the area, there is one other 'must see' example of Victorian design at its best – Central Station, with its spectacular curved roof.

NORTH SHIELDS
Stephenson Railway Museum

Free, £ for steam rides; May to September Tuesday to Thursday and weekends; Middle Engine Lane, NE29 8DX; Tel: 0191 200 7146

The main attraction for enthusiasts is the presence of one of Stephenson's Killingworth engines and, moving ahead a hundred years, the 1909 electric locomotive. Displays tell the history of railway development in the area, and there are steam rides to Percy Main Village.

RYHOPE, SUNDERLAND
Ryhope Pumping Station

£; Easter to end of December Sunday afternoons; Tel: 0191 521 0235; Website: www.g3wte.demon.co.uk

It is hard to imagine quite what the architects had in mind when they designed this elaborately gabled water pumping station in the 1860s, but it is certainly unforgettable. The cooling ponds and reservoir in the park-like grounds give it something of the air of a miniature Versailles. Inside, however, all is workmanlike, with two massive compound beam engines and a range of three Lancashire boilers. They are regularly steamed.

SPRINGWELL
Bowes Railway

Free, £ steam days; Centre open daily; Springwell Village, NE9 7QJ; Tel: 0191 416 1847; Website: www.bowesrailway.co.uk

This offers a trip back to the earliest days of the railway age, when hills were conquered by hauling trucks up and down inclines by means of stationary steam engines. The Bowes railway was a typical colliery line opened in 1826 and extended over the years, with seven inclines in all. Two of these inclines, still worked just as they were in Stephenson's day, are demonstrated on open days, and visitors can travel to the site by steam train from Springwell. The site with its interpretative centre can be visited at all times.

The Tyne Bridge rises high above the little cupola on top of the operator's cabin at the centre of the swing bridge.

The pioneering steam turbine vessel that astonished the world by reaching the previously undreamed of speed of 34 knots. Its designer, Charles Parsons, at once received orders for fast ships for the Royal Navy, and soon turbines were installed in ocean liners.

NEWCASTLE UPON TYNE
Discovery Museum

Free; Monday to Saturday, Sunday afternoon; Blandford Square, NE1 4JA; Tel: 0191 232 6789

This is a museum in the making, with a development programme that is not due for completion until 2004. By then there will be extensive displays, covering all aspects of Tyneside industry. At the time of writing the main interest in this area lies in the pioneering steam turbine vessel *Turbinia*. This extraordinary craft, little more than an engine with a sleek hull built to contain it, is worth the visit for itself alone. A science section is also up and running.

See Also

Monkwearmouth Station, Sunderland

Free; Open daily; North Bridge Street, SR5 1AP; Tel: 0191 567 7075

A small station built in an imposing classical style, restored to look as it would have done in 1900.

Lemington Glassworks, Lemington, Newcastle

Free; Open access, exterior only; Map ref. 88/184646

The glass cone is a prominent landmark, standing 36m (120ft) high. The factory was established in 1787, and of four cones, this is the only unit to have survived. It was restored in 1993 and is now preserved as a monument to what was once one of the major industries of the area.

ROTHBURY

Cragside Estate

NT; ££ (grounds only), £££ (to include house); April to November daily but closed Mondays, November to mid-December closed Monday and Tuesday; Off B6341, north of Rothbury; Tel: 01669 620333

Although stately homes don't make many appearances in this book, this one is different. It was the home of William Armstrong, armaments manufacturer and pioneer of hydraulic machinery. He applied his technical expertise to his new home. He set up his own hydro-electric plant to provide power for the house, the first to be used for any private home, and he installed hydraulic machinery to work all kinds of machinery, from a lift to the kitchen spit. The lakes, which are such a feature of the grounds, are artificial, created for the hydro-electric plant.

When Cragside was built in 1864–66, starting off as a very modest weekend retreat, Armstrong was one of the most powerful industrialists in Britain. He had started life as a solicitor but his real interest was in engineering and he soon abandoned the law to develop his own inventions. In 1847 he had established W.G. Armstrong and Co. on the banks of the Tyne in Elswick (p.102). Here he began manufacturing hydraulic machinery, and having established a hugely successful business, he turned his attention to armaments; his breach loading 18-pound gun was considered the finest of the age. The government rewarded his efforts with a peerage in 1859. Eventually, the ordnance factory and engineering works were merged, and by the end of his life he had added a yard building warships to the Elswick complex. Sadly, little remains to be seen of this great enterprise, but at least in the house one has a glimpse of his ingenuity and design skills.

The Cragside Estate is an extraordinary example of landscape gardening on a grand scale. The pleasure grounds cover 1700 acres and were given a suitably Romantic air by blasting away hillsides to create crags and by importing plants from around the world. The artificial lakes also had a practical use, damming water for the hydro-electric plant.

NORTHUMBERLAND

The eighteenth-century Beadnell lime kilns are now useful stores for lobster pots.

BEADNELL
Lime Kilns

NT; Free; Open access

Down at the harbour is a group of four well-preserved eighteenth-century lime kilns. Lime kilns are not uncommon, but such large groups are rare, and each of these kilns is very large, with either three or four archways for extracting the burned lime, which could then be loaded on to boats for export down the coast. This is an interesting group in a very attractive setting.

FORD
Heatherslaw Watermill

£; April to October daily; Cornhill-on-Tweed, TD12 4TJ; Tel: 01890 820338; Website: www.secretkingdom.com

Ford is a good example of a model village, with its own mill of *c*.1830. It is unusual in that there are actually two independent mills within the same building, each with its own water wheel. The flour goes to the estate bakery. There is also a narrow gauge railway, offering steam and diesel rides up the attractive Till valley.

OTTERBURN
Woollen Mill

Free; Open daily; Tel: 01830 520225

This mill, close to the Scottish border, not surprisingly specialises in tweed. It was built in 1812 and extended in 1895. One can see all the changes in power supply, from water wheel through diesel engine to electricity. It remains at work, and little seems to have changed over the years. Line and shaft are still used to transmit power, and the old machinery includes such rarities as fulling stocks and a gig mill set with teazles to raise the nap of the cloth. It is a rare pleasure to see a cloth mill such as this being worked commercially rather than for occasional demonstrations.

WYLAM
Stephenson's Cottage

NT; £; April to November Thursday, Saturday and Sunday; Access along riverside, west of Wylam (map ref. 88/126650); Tel: 01661 853457

It was here in the most modest of surroundings that George Stephenson was born in 1781. It has been refurnished as it might have been at that time. Outside the door is the trackbed of the Wylam Waggonway, laid down with wooden rails in 1813. It was along this line that one of the pioneers of steam, William Hedley, ran his first locomotive in 1813, a year before Stephenson's own first locomotive. The story of these early years is told in the Wylam Railway Museum.

See Also
Woodhorn Colliery Museum, Queen Elizabeth II Country Park
Free; Wednesday to Sunday; Tel: 01670 856968
Former colliery buildings with mining exhibition. The park has other attractions, including a narrow gauge railway.

George Stephenson's birthplace is a modest cottage, but the Stephensons shared the building with another family.

BIRTH OF THE RAILWAYS

The railway age began before the invention of the steam locomotive in the age of tramways. The first systems were introduced into Shropshire and Nottinghamshire at the end of the seventeenth century. They were both designed in the same way and for the same purpose: wooden rails linked a colliery to a navigable river. Loaded trucks descended under gravity and were hauled back empty by horses. The system soon spread to other industrial regions and became an important part of the transport system of the north-east of England, where a complex system of lines developed around the Tyne. The oldest surviving structure from these days is the Causey Arch, an impressive bridge crossing a deep valley in a single 31.4m (103ft) span (see p.100). An important change came in the 1760s, when the Darby works at Coalbrookdale began casting iron rails instead of timber. Often, however, all that remains of these early railways is an obvious trackbed and the tell-tale stone sleeper blocks. Because the work was done by horses, the area between the rails had to be kept clear for their hooves. So rather than the familiar wooden sleepers of later years, square stone blocks were laid in parallel rows, each with a hole in the centre that was plugged to take a spike to hold the rail. One place where these can be seen is on the line of the Penydarren tramway in South Wales (p.125). It was here in 1804 that Richard Trevithick gave the first public demonstration of the steam locomotive. He had already built a road locomotive in 1801, which made a triumphant run up Camborne Hill in Cornwall three years earlier. A replica of this little engine was built for the bicentenary, and now makes regular appearances at steam events. Trevithick built a trial engine at Coalbrookdale in 1803 and he then went on to the Penydarren trial. Although the locomotive was a success, it proved too heavy for the brittle cast iron rails,

The replica of Richard Trevithick's very first locomotive, the road engine of 1801, being tested before the bicentenary celebrations in Cornwall.

and shortly after this Trevithick abandoned locomotive building; the next phase of development took place in the north-east of England.

In 1812 war in Europe had resulted in a steep increase in the price of fodder. John Blenkinsop, manager of the Middleton Colliery near Leeds, took a fresh look at Trevithick's locomotive. His colliery had been joined by a tramway to the Aire and Calder Navigation in 1758, and he looked for a way of using the engine without smashing the rails. He decided to ease the problem by using a rack and pinion system, with a third, toothed rail engaging with a toothed cog on the engine. The locomotive was designed and built by a local engineer, John Murray, and proved a success. In June 1812 the first regular, commercial steam railway went into business. Steam locomotives still run on the old line but with conventional engines and rails (see p.96).

It was improvement in rails that brought the Blenkinsop-Murray experiment to an end; the scene now shifted to Tyneside. Trevithick had sent an engine to Gateshead but it had never been used for transport. Interest was reborn. Engineers came down to Leeds to see what was being done, including among their number a young George Stephenson. There were now several engineers looking at steam locomotives. The first real success came in 1813, when William Hedley of the Wylam colliery built an engine to run on the local tramway, the *Wylam Dilly*. It is curious looking, with two vertical cylinders and oscillating beams, like a pair of stationary engines strapped to the side of a boiler. It was followed by another engine, *Puffing Billy*.

Now it was George Stephenson's turn. He began with an engine for the Killingworth colliery, *Blucher*. It was not notably different from Hedley's engines, though it was the first to have flanged wheels, a device rapidly adopted for later locomotives. Over the next few years Stephenson concentrated on building and improving locomotives. From 1815 to 1825 he was the only man in Britain building locomotives of any kind and a tireless protagonist of railway construction. His first great achievement was to be appointed chief engineer to a public railway that would be worked by steam. This was the Stockton & Darlington, opened in 1825, with Stephenson's own engine, *Locomotion*, leading the triumphant procession. The gauge chosen was that of the local tramways that he knew, an arbitrary 1.44m (4ft 8½in.), and he was to use this on every railway that he built, so that what began as the 'Stephenson' gauge eventually became a standard throughout the British rail system.

From Stockton, Stephenson moved to an even grander scheme: the first inter-city line, joining the manufacturing centre of Manchester to the port of Liverpool. There were still sceptics who were unconvinced by the steam locomotive, and in 1829 a trial was set up along the line at Rainhill to see if the locomotive was up to the task of running a main line service at speed on a regular basis. There were three main contenders, John Ericsson's lightweight *Novelty*, Timothy Hackworth's *Sans Pareil* (a powerful version of the type of engine already in use on the Stockton & Darlington) and Robert Stephenson's *Rocket*. It was the last that carried the day,

containing important new features: a multi-tube boiler, an exhaust blast turning up the chimney, and cylinders that were inclined at an angle. After the trials, the future of the steam locomotive's place was assured. The features introduced on *Rocket* were to prove the elements on which all further steam engine development was to be based until Britain's last steam locomotive, *Evening Star*, rolled out of the Swindon Works in 1960.

Where to see the old locomotives:

Darlington Railway Centre – *Locomotion*

Ironbridge Gorge Museum – Working replica of Trevithick's 1803 engine

National Railway Museum, York – replicas of *Rocket* and Trevithick Penydarren engine – though both are frequently out on loan and at work

North of England Open Air Museum, Beamish – Working replica of *Locomotion*

Royal Museum of Scotland, Edinburgh – *Wylam Dilly*

Science Museum, London – *Puffing Billy*, *Rocket* and a model of the Blenkinsop-Murray engine

Stephenson Museum, North Shields – Killingworth engine

Timothy Hackworth Museum – *Sans Pareil*

The end of the line: *Evening Star* was the very last steam locomotive to be built for British Railways and is seen here in service on the North Yorkshire Moors Railway.

Carlisle

A69

A596

M6

A686

Little Salkeld Mill

Printing House ● A66

Quarry and
Mining
Museum

A66

Penrith

Acorn Bank Garden

Pencil Museum

Wetheriggs
Country
Pottery

A66

Whitehaven

Haig Colliery

CUMBRIA

A685

Florence Mine

A595

A591

Eskdale
Watermill

Ravenglass & Eskdale Railway
+ Muncaster Mill

Bobbin Mill

Kendal

Lakeside and
Haverthwaite Railway

Heron Corn Mill

A590

Millom ●

A590

A65

Barrow-in-Furness

Gleaston Watermill

Lune Aqueduct

A588

M6

A682

Bancroft Mill Engine, Barnoldswick

LANCASHIRE

M55

Queen St Mill

Blackpool

M65

Leeds and Liverpool Canal

Windmill Museum

Preston

Blackburn

Lewis Textile Museum

Oswaldtwistle Mills

Helmshore Textile Museum

A59

Cheeseden

M62

East Lancashire Railway

M66

Ellenroad Engine House

Hall I' th' Wood

M61

M60

M58

Wigan Pier

Bridgewater Canal

Colliery Museum, Astley Green

Manchester

M57

St Helens

Barton Swing
Aqueduct

Museum of Science and Industry

The World of Glass

M62

Marple

Liverpool

Hat Works

Shore Road Pumping Station

Dunham Massey Sawmill

M60

Quarry Bank Mill

Port Sunlight Heritage Centre

Anderton
Lift

Nether Alderley Watermill

M53

M56

M6

A34

Macclesfield

Ellesmere Port Boat Museum

The Salt Museum

Silk Museum

Chester

CHESHIRE

Bunbury Mill

Railway Age

Stretton Watermill ●

A41

Nantwich

NORTH WEST ENGLAND

CHESHIRE

The image of Cheshire is of a rather rich agricultural area, home to a famous cheese, yet it has an extraordinary industrial diversity.

CREWE
Railway Age

£ weekdays, ££ weekends; Mid-February to November daily; Vernon Way

Unlike most railway museums, the emphasis here is on later railway developments, with diesel and electric locomotives stepping into the limelight. The other important element is the story of Crewe itself. The Grand Junction Railway opened their engineering works here in 1843. The tiny village grew into a town, and the works became famous, not least because of the great British locomotive builders who worked here, starting with the founding engineer Francis Trevithick, son of the great railway pioneer. As well as the works, Crewe developed as an important junction, with lines radiating in all directions. The town itself shows railway influence wherever one looks, from the formal park to the ruined railway church which appears to be solidly built of stone. Tap one of the columns, however, and it produces a metallic ring, for it is actually iron, cast at the engineering works.

ELLESMERE PORT
Boat Museum

£££; Summer all day, winter closed Thursday and Friday; South Pier Road, CH65 4FW; Tel: 0151 355 5017; Website: www.boatmuseum.org.co.uk

Ellesmere Port was a creation of the canal age. When the Ellesmere Canal, later incorporated into the Shropshire Union, was built at the end of the eighteenth century, the port developed at the junction of the canal and the Mersey. A huge dock and warehouse complex was constructed, designed by Thomas Telford, though sadly much was destroyed in a fire in the twentieth century. A lot still remains, now being home to the boat museum. It comes in two parts, the boats out on the water and exhibits inside the former warehouse. The locks and basins have changed little and are still in use, and there is a rich variety of traditional craft to look at, as well as boat trips either round the basin or up and down the canal. Inside are the exhibits telling the story of the life of the waterways. Among them is the old narrow boat *Friendship*, which was the livelihood and floating home of the last of the old independent boating families, Joe and Rosie Skinner – a horse-drawn boat to the last, though the Skinners generally preferred mules to horses. It is this kind of reminder of the working past that brings this museum alive.

MACCLESFIELD
Silk Museum, Roe Street and Paradise Mill, Park Lane

£ each museum, reduced priced ticket for two; Open daily, but Paradise Mill closed Monday; Silk Museum Tel: 01625 613210; Paradise Mill Tel: 01625 618228; Website: www.silk-macclesfield.org

These two museums complement each other. Macclesfield became Britain's most important centre for silk, and Paradise Mill has been restored to show working conditions, and has a fine array of looms, many being Jacquard looms worked by punched card to create intricate and delicate patterns. The Silk Museum is the interpretative centre, housed in the former Sunday School of 1813, where silk mill children were educated. Here you see the finished product both as cloth and made up in costumes.

Paradise Mill: on the left are warping machines for preparing the warp for the loom; on the right are jacquard looms.

NETHER ALDERLEY
Watermill

NT; £; June to September afternoons, except Monday, April, May and October Wednesday and Sunday afternoons; Tel: 01625 523012

The mill is an interesting mixture of the very old and, in watermill terms, the comparatively modern. It was originally built in the sixteenth century, and from the outside it looks its age, with a sweep of stone-tiled roof almost reaching the ground and an interior of oak timbers. The machinery, however, is Victorian. This is a constricted site, so water from the mill pond passes to two overshot wheels set in tandem. There are regular demonstrations.

NORTHWICH
Anderton Lift

Free; Open access; Map ref. 118/648752

This strange looking device is a boat lift, used for moving narrow boats between the Trent & Mersey Canal at the top of the hill and the Weaver Navigation down below. The boats are floated into two caissons – overgrown bathtubs – which are hauled

The Anderton boat lift links the Trent & Mersey Canal at the top to the River Weaver at the bottom.

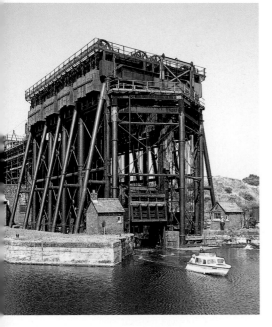

The wooden shoe supplies grain to the eye of the upper grindstone or runner stone at Nether Alderley mill.

up and down vertically. When it opened in 1875, the two caissons were counterbalanced; they now work independently by electric motor. It has recently been restored to full working order.

The Salt Museum

£; All year, closed Monday and weekend mornings; 162 London Road, CW9 8AB; Tel: 01606 41331

The 'wich' in Northwich indicates a salt town, and it is surrounded by old salt mines, some begun by the Romans. This is the story the museum has to tell in a building that looks at first glance like some stately home but was actually the town workhouse.

STOCKPORT
Hat Works

££; Open daily; Wellington Road South, SK3 0EU; Tel: 0161 355 7770; Website: www.stockportmbc.gov.uk/heritage

Hat making seems as if it ought to be a craft – or even an art – not an industrial activity. Yet in the nineteenth century there were over 4000 hatters working in Stockport, many in factories such as this. Here you can see the numerous and complex processes used in the old hat mill, which happily does not include a live demonstration of the use of the planking kettle for felting. This employed mercury, and the fumes had a disastrous effect on the workers, hence the phrase 'mad as a hatter'. There is also an impressive display of the hats themselves.

See Also
Bunbury Mill
£; Easter to September Sunday and Wednesday afternoons; Tel: 01829 261422
An 1850 watermill producing flour. Nearby on the Chester, now Shropshire Union, Canal is a two-lock staircase with attractive stable block.

Marple
A flight of sixteen locks on the Peak Forest Canal leads down to a splendid three-arched aqueduct over the River Goyt.

Stretton Watermill, near Farndon
£; May to August afternoons Tuesday to Sunday; April and September weekends only; Tel: 01606 41331
An unusual mill with two wheels, one overshot and one breastshot.

STYAL
Quarry Bank Mill

NT; ££; Open daily, closed Monday, October to March; Tel: 01625 527468; Website: www.mplc.co.uk/orgs.quarrybankmill

For once the old cliché word 'unique' is justified: there really is nothing quite like this anywhere else. There is, it seems, no hint of dark Satanic mills here, just a beautiful country park centred on the Bollin valley. At the heart of the site is a surprisingly elegant, brick-built cotton mill, its ownership proclaimed over the door 'Built by Samuel Greg Esquire of Belfast Ireland Anno Domini 1784'. At this date there was only one likely source of power – water – and a water wheel still turns, all 50 tons of it, right in the centre of the mill. Inevitably there have been changes through the years, and the tall chimney at one end of the building proclaims the arrival of steam. Sure enough, there is a beam engine built in 1830 to which a horizontal mill engine has recently been added and is regularly steamed. Inside the mill is all the machinery that takes the process through from raw cotton to cloth, and nothing is quite as impressive as the spinning mules. These machines with their whirring spindles fastened to a carriage that trundles backwards and forwards, spinning and winding, spinning and winding, are mechanically ingenious and a joy to watch. But when enjoying the sight from behind the safety rails, it is worth pausing to think of the scene when all this was new. Children as young as ten were crawling in among the working parts, repairing broken threads, clearing away waste. It is the social story that Styal has to tell that is every bit as important as its engineering marvels.

Outside the mill is the overseer's house and, though not open to the public, the far grander house where the

This close-up shows the end of a Hattersley power loom. The machinery looks intricate but basically imitates the action of the hand loom weaver.

Gregs lived. A short way up the road is another fine house, not as big as the Gregs', but handsome and well appointed. This was no family home but the Apprentice House, home to as many as a hundred pauper children. We know a lot about them. We know what they ate, that they slept two to a bed and got a clean shirt once a week. And we know that they worked up to twelve hours a day in the mill, six days a week – and on the Sunday they had to attend church and school. Yet the children of Styal were considered lucky: there were far, far worse mills with far harsher conditions.

Samuel Greg came to an agricultural area to build his mill, and he had to find homes for his adult workers. So he built the village of Styal, neat terraces of attractive cottages with vegetable gardens and a village shop – owned, of course, by Greg himself, so that the wages he paid out soon came back again. It seems an attractive place to us and so it did to the villagers of the eighteenth century, who preferred to take low wages and live here rather than opt for higher pay and the filth and squalor of a Manchester slum. That is what makes Styal so special: the chance to see a whole social system, all the buildings preserved, everything appearing much as it did two centuries ago. Except that, happily, children no longer crawl across the mill floor or suffer the fate of thirteen-year-old Thomas Priestley, who ran away after having a finger torn off in one of those whirring machines. This is a place to marvel at the ingenuity of eighteenth-century technology and to get at least a notion of the human price that was paid in the name of progress.

LANCASHIRE, GREATER MANCHESTER AND MERSEYSIDE

Crossing the Pennines from Yorkshire, wool is left behind in favour of cotton. It is not the only industry established here but it became dominant; by the nineteenth century Lancashire cotton was being sent out around the world. The reasons are not difficult to find. In the early years there was an ample supply of water to turn the wheels for power, and when steam power appeared at the end of the eighteenth century, Lancashire could use coal from nearby coalfields. These conditions existed in other regions but Lancashire had the advantage of being on the right side of the country for importing the raw material, first from India then America. Cotton helped Liverpool to grow into a major port and Manchester to develop into a major commercial centre. Huge numbers of mills survive, some out in the country, others in the middle of the mill towns that grew up around them. A whole transport system developed to meet the needs of the new town. Britain's first wholly artificial canal brought coal to Manchester; the world's first inter-city railway linked Manchester and Liverpool. All these developments are well represented in the museums and preserved sites of the region.

The Bancroft Mill Engine: 'James' is the name of the high pressure cylinder, the low pressure is 'Mary Jane'.

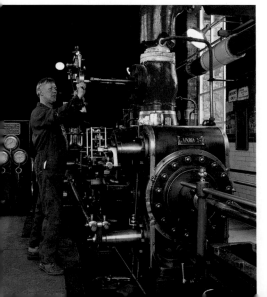

Hall i' th' Wood, the home of the inventor of the spinning jenny, is a fine example of an elaborate timber-framed house.

ASTLEY GREEN
Colliery Museum

Free; Sunday, Tuesday, Thursday afternoon; Higher Green Lane, M29 7JB; Tel: 01942 828121

It seems not very long ago that there were working collieries in this area but now only the museum survives to tell the tale. The tall headstock still rears up to the sky and a steam engine, the biggest colliery winding engine in Britain, has been restored. This monster could raise over 300 tons of coal an hour from a depth of over 900m (3000ft). Other engines are preserved on site, there is a narrow gauge railway and displays on the history of mining in the area.

BARNOLDSWICK
Bancroft Mill Engine, Gillians Lane

£; Saturdays, steamed on selected Sundays and Bank Holidays; Tel: 01282 813751

As a Yorkshireman I would once have claimed this one with pride, but misguided authorities moved the town into Lancashire! This whole site was almost lost until enthusiasts managed to preserve the mighty engine and part of the mill. James Nutter began weaving cotton cloth here in the 1870s, though the mill only dates back to 1914. The engine that drove over a thousand looms is back at work. Many engines were given names, but this one has two: 'James' for the high pressure cylinder and 'Mary Jane' for the low pressure. Despite only a few looms being left, those that remain are still put to work producing tea towels.

BARTON UPON IRWELL
Barton Swing Aqueduct

Free; Open access

This is the site of Britain's first canal aqueduct, carrying the Bridgewater Canal across the Irwell. Then along came the Manchester Ship Canal in the 1890s, swallowing up the river. The old aqueduct was demolished and in its place the engineer Edward Leader Williams built a new aqueduct, which could be swung sideways to allow ships to pass by. Today, few vessels of any size use the ship canal so it remains closed. Nonetheless, it still represents an outstanding engineering feature.

BIRKENHEAD
Shore Road Pumping Station

Free; Summer afternoons Tuesday to Sunday, winter afternoons weekends; Tel: 0151 650 1182

A very imposing red brick building stands close by the ferry terminal for boats across the Mersey to Liverpool. Other transport systems go under the river, including the Mersey Railway, completed in 1886. There was an obvious need to pump water out of the workings while the tunnellers were making their way under the river, so in 1884 a steam engine was ordered from Andrew Barclay of Kilmarnock. It was still needed to keep everything dry after the openings, and it kept on puffing away, though only as a standby in its latter days, right through to 1959. Modern pumps still do the job, and the old engine only steams again for demonstrations. But it is a wonderful sight. It is a beam engine of an unusual type known as a grasshopper engine, and you soon see why when you get there. The beam pivots at one end and the resulting movement looks a bit like the rear leg of a bouncing grasshopper.

BOLTON
Hall i' th' Wood

££; April to October closed Monday; Crompton Way, BL1 8UA; Tel: 01204 332370

This is an amazing fifteenth-century hall house, largely timber framed and added to piecemeal over the years so that it looks as if it has been put together like a jigsaw. Its claim for inclusion here is that it was once the home of Samuel Crompton and it is in this house that he invented the spinning mule in the 1770s.

BURNLEY
Queen Street Mill, Harle Syke

£; May to September Tuesday to Saturday, April and October Tuesday to Friday afternoons, March and November Tuesday to Thursday afternoons; Tel: 01282 412555

There were once so many mills like this, yet now it is a lone example of a nineteenth-century cotton-weaving mill. There were never spinning machines here, but at its peak there were over 1000 looms. Today there are still 300, powered as they always have been by belts from overhead line shafting turned by a compound steam engine of 1895, rather charmingly called *Peace*.

HELMSHORE
Helmshore Textile Museum

££; April to October Monday to Friday and Sunday afternoons, closed in winter; Holcombe Road, Rossendale, BB4 4NP; Tel: 01706 226459

This is an important and serious museum. Anyone with any interest at all in the textile industry should come here. There are two quite different mills on the same site. The story began in the 1780s when the Turner family built the Higher Mill. This is a fulling mill for finishing woollen cloth from the local weavers. The cloth was scoured, then pounded under giant hammers or fulling stocks to shrink the fibres and matt the surface. Power comes from the large water wheel, fed from the mill pond. Other machines used in cloth finishing can also be seen.

newly invented spinning mules. When I first visited this site, mules were still at work and now are part of the museum. Things have changed very little in the intervening years.

The fulling stocks at Helmshore, originally powered by the water wheel seen in the background.

If this were all, it would still be a place to come and see, but there is a good deal more. For here you can find an exceptional array of historic machinery, including water frames, the first powered cotton spinning machines invented by Richard Arkwright. This is how early machines are seen at their best, in the right context, in a building of the right period. It helps that it is also a very attractive site and the buildings have a reassuring solidity which suggests that they will stand for a few centuries yet.

The next stage of development began shortly afterwards, as the Turners decided to get their share of the rapidly growing cotton industry. Soon the buildings were being extended to take Crompton's

Part of the textile display with machines involved in the production of cotton yarn. In the background is a variety of carding engines, which align the fibres and compress them into slivers. These eventually go for spinning on the ring frame, seen in the foreground.

MANCHESTER
Museum of Science and Industry in Manchester

Free; Open every day; Liverpool Road, Castlefield, M3 4FP; Tel: 0161 832 1380; Website: www.msim.org.uk

This is a big museum with purpose-built display halls added on to a historic site. The site is of the world's first main line railway station, the terminus of the Liverpool & Manchester Railway in 1830, though the line was later extended and the station itself has been altered over the years. An interesting feature is the fact that it has two separate entrances – first class and the rest. Also on site are the cotton warehouse of 1830 and a later goods shed. The railway, with its short jaunts by steam, is just one aspect of the museum. The power hall containing its big stationary engines sitting alongside grand locomotives is one of the impressive features, and the transport story is brought up to date as it moves into the area of flight and even space exploration. A new element has appeared in recent years, with interactive science displays and special exhibitions that are changed on a regular basis. There is always a danger that with the urge to be completely up to date, the historic nature of an important site can be swamped: it has not yet happened here.

DUNHAM MASSEY
Dunham Massey Sawmill

NT; ££; Altrincham, WA1 4SJ;
Tel: 0161 928 4351

Details of opening hours are not
known at the time of writing as the
mill is undergoing extensive restoration, which is expected to be completed during 2002. This is a mill with
a history. The building was originally
part of the Tudor Hall, reconstructed
in the eighteenth century. It became a
grmill and was then refitted as a
sawmill and estate workshop, powered
by an overshot wheel, around 1860.
Some nineteenth-century machinery
has survived.

MILNROW
Ellenroad Engine House, New Hey

£; Sunday afternoons, steaming on first
Sunday of month; Elizabethan Way,
OL16 4LG; Tel: 01706 848 1952;
Website: www.ellenroad.org.uk

This is one of the grandest of mill
engines, technically a horizontal double compound of 1892, which can be
thought of as two horizontal compound engines, working together to
turn a drum that had forty-four ropes
taking the drive to machinery throughout the mill.

**One of the old saws, worked by water
power, at Dunham Massey. Original line
shafting can be seen in the background.**

The Lyceum at Port Sunlight, built in the 1890s to serve both as a village school and a church.

PORT SUNLIGHT
Heritage Centre

£; Open daily; 95 Greendale Road,
CH62 4XE; Tel: 0151 644 4800;
Website: www.nmgn.org.uk

This is a pleasantly unassuming little
museum, which does just what is
needed – tells the story of the village
and the works, through models, architect drawings and displays. Port
Sunlight itself is a nineteenth-century
garden village built by William
Hesketh Lever for the workers in his
soap factory. It is the rural ideal
realised in suburbia, with none of the
mess and smells of a genuine agricultural village. It has to be said, however, that it has immense charm,
accommodating more facilities than
many a large town, and some very
Victorian touches, including the separate dining halls for male and female
workers. The village trail is available
from the Centre.

WIGAN
Wigan Pier, Wallgate

LL; All year, closed Fridays; Tel: 01942
323666; Website: www.wiganpier.net

Not just a music hall joke or a George
Orwell book, for there really was a pier
on the Leeds & Liverpool Canal, used
for passenger boats in the eighteenth
century. The site itself is based on a
number of buildings, canal warehouses
and the Trencherfield cotton mill,
linked across the canal by footbridges
or water bus. The warehouses themselves are of considerable interest. The
main row flanking the canal is a mixture of brick and stone, with canopies
and covered hoists over the wharf,
while another, at the end of a short
arm, has arches or boat holes, which
allow vessels to float in under the
building for loading and unloading in
the dry. This does not set out to be a
traditional museum but has a bit of
everything, from jolly seaside fun to a
Variety Theatre, Victorian schoolroom
with mock lessons to a drama telling
Wigan stories, performed by a resident
theatre company. In among the
razzmatazz are a number of industrial
exhibits and one absolutely not to be
missed attraction: the Trencherfield
mill engine. It is huge, a four cylinder
triple expansion giant, working an
8.2m (27ft) diameter fly wheel. It is in
steam every day, so there is no need to
rely on special visits.

THE COTTON KINGDOM

The north-west of England, and Lancashire in particular, was the ideal region for the development of the cotton industry. The climate is moist; in the early days there was ample water supply to turn the wheels, and as steam power took over, there was fuel available from local coalfields. The raw material that came first from India but was rapidly taken over by supplies from America could be brought in through the rapidly growing port of Liverpool. In the seventeenth century cotton was little used, and then only as an inferior fabric. It was the import of colourful, easily cleaned cloth from India that created the demand, which inventors worked to meet. The first successful spinning factory was built by Richard Arkwright in Derbyshire (p.72), and he soon began introducing his machines into Lancashire. He built his first mill at Chorley, but the local domestic spinners and weavers were outraged and in 1779 they marched on the mill and burned it to the ground. They could not, however, fight against a growing demand and the wish of mill owners to profit from it. Inventions flowed throughout the eighteenth century, culminating in machinery that could take over all the tasks that once fell to the handworkers, from carding to weaving. Samuel Crompton, working away in the Tudor splendour of Hall i' th' Wood, began developing his spinning mule at just the time that the rioters were marching through Lancashire destroying mills and machinery. Although he had to be cautious, once the riots died down, mill building was recommenced with fresh enthusiasm, and the mule became one of the most powerful engines for change. Water power was the main requirement: one stream could be harnessed to turn the wheels for a succession of mills. The result was that mills were often built well away from the nearest settlements, so that workers had to trudge miles to and from work every day. Then the steam engine was brought to the mills and everything changed. Now the requirement was to be near a colliery or, if that was not possible, close to a good means of transport. You can still see the results. The country mills went into decline. Follow the valley of the Cheesden Brook, south from Cheesden, and you come across a whole series of small mill ponds and the decayed remains of the mills. It is difficult to imagine where the workers came from to attend the machines in this wild and remote valley.

One of Arkwright's original water frames preserved at Helmshore. This is a double frame, with power supplied from the water wheel to the large gear in the centre.

The four-cylinder Trencherfield mill engine at Wigan. Ropes round the revolving grooved flywheel took power to every floor of the mill.

There is no better way to see the other side of the picture than to travel down the Leeds & Liverpool Canal. Boats brought in coal and cotton and took out the finished product, and every town along the route in Lancashire has its warehouses and mills.

The steady development of the steam mill led to a new generation of mill towns. Unlike the attractive villages, such as Styal, these consisted of mean terraces, huddling right up against the factory walls. The worst of the jerry built houses have gone, not in many cases deliberately destroyed but collapsed from their own mediocrity. Nevertheless, something of the old style can still be seen in towns such as Rawtenstall, which, ironically, was the scene of some of the most ferocious rioting against the factory system in 1826. The commercial heartland of the cotton kingdom was Manchester, a town that grew into a city, crammed with mills, offices and warehouses. There are grand public buildings, such as the Cotton Exchange, now a theatre, and the gothic splendour of the Town Hall. Even warehouses were built to impress, and so splendid were they that they can now be adapted to other uses without the least

sense of incongruity. Who would imagine that the sumptuous Britannia Hotel once held bales of cotton instead of pampered guests? Enthusiasts for the Industrial Revolution loved to quote statistics – however dubious – to show the world just how mighty the cotton industry had become. Edward Baines writing in 1835 declared that the yarn spun in Britain would, if fastened together as a single thread, go round the equator 203,775 times. The figures are remarkable, and it had all happened in little more than half a century, thanks, as Baines put it, to 'the genius of a few humble mechanics'.

There is ample evidence of the changes brought by the revolution in cotton manufacture throughout Lancashire and further afield, and a number of excellent museums exist that explore the whole dramatic story. The earliest machines, however, are comparatively rare. The best collection is no longer open to the general public. The Lewis Textile Museum in Blackburn covers the whole range from early spinning wheels and looms onwards. Anyone with a serious interest in the subject can arrange a visit by appointment through the Blackburn Museum and Art Gallery.

St Helens
The World of Glass

££; Open daily; Chalon Way East, WA10 1BX; Tel: 08707 444777; Website: www.worldofglass.com

Glass making was begun on this site by the British Plate Glass Company in 1773, by the side of the St Helens Canal, then known as the Sankey Brook. The industry has continued here ever since. The main historical feature is the glass cone of 1887. At the centre of the cone was the furnace where silica, soda and other ingredients were fused into molten glass. The men working inside the cone, around the furnace, removed globules of the glass, which they blew into bubbles. These could be shaped for ornamental ware or split and opened out to make flat sheets of glass. The glass was then slowly cooled in annealing hearths at the edge of the cone. The cone itself acted both as a cover and a giant chimney. The present museum opened in 2000, and as one would expect, uses all the latest display techniques, while at the same time letting visitors see the old craft technology of glass blowing.

The site may be old but the presentation is modern. This is the interactive Glass Roots gallery, telling the history of glass from prehistory to the present.

See Also

Leeds & Liverpool Canal, Burnley
Free; Open access
The towpath crosses the huge embankment, then swings round past an array of mills and warehouses, with a small museum on the wharf.

East Lancashire Railway, Bury
£££ return fare; Weekends, plus Fridays, July, August; Bolton Street Station, BL9 0EY; Tel: 0161 764 7790
A preserved steam line to Rawtenstall that gives splendid views over the Irwell valley and a mill landscape.

Lune Aqueduct, Lancaster
Free; Open access
The aqueduct carrying the Lancaster Canal over the river is one of the most impressive masonry aqueducts in Britain and is the work of John Rennie.

The Lune aqueduct shows that John Rennie, as well as being a fine engineer, was also an excellent architect.

Windmill Museum, Lytham St Anne's
Free; Easter Holiday, May Bank Holiday to September daily except Monday and Friday; Tel: 01253 794879; Website: www.visitor.uk.com
A tower mill of 1805, housing an exhibition.

Oswaldtwistle Mills, Moscow Mill, Oswaldtwistle
£; Open daily; Tel: 01254 871025
The mill now houses a shopping village and a textile museum. It tells the story of textiles, with special emphasis on James Hargreaves, and has a spinning jenny. Also power looms.

Bridgewater Canal, Worsley, Manchester
Free; Open access
The starting point of the historic canal. The canal emerges from underground mines, and goes under the main road to a basin with Packet House, used by passengers on the packet boats.

CUMBRIA

Looking back over the ages, one could say that this has one of the oldest industrial sites in the whole country. There was an 'axe factory' at Pike of Stickle in the Langdale Pikes some 5000 years ago, when axe heads were fashioned from the local rock and traded as far away as Cornwall. Quarrying and mining were actually widespread in a region which we now think of as the 'unspoiled' Lake District.

BOOT

Eskdale Watermill

£; April to October but closed Mondays; Tel: 019467 23335

Not the usual English grain mill, this one looks north of the border and has a feature common in Scotland: an oatmeal kiln. It is also unusual in having two overshot wheels. A working mill, it produces animal feeds. The nearby Dalgarth station is the terminus of the Ravenglass & Eskdale Railway (see under Ravenglass).

CLIFTON DYKES

Wetheriggs Country Pottery

Free; Easter to October all day except Tuesday; the rest of the year closed Tuesday and Wednesday; Tel: 01768 892733; Website: www.wetheriggs-pottery.co.uk

When I first came here, it was simply a working pottery. It has now been reborn as an all-singing, all-dancing family entertainment centre. But the essentials are still here to be enjoyed, and if the extras are needed to keep it going, then so be it. It is certainly worth preserving. This is quite exceptional, for although there are many potteries around Britain, this is the only one I know where you can see the whole process from digging out the clay to finishing the pots. This is a miniature industrial unit, where steam power was used for a variety of processes. The stationary engine hauls trucks of clay along a narrow gauge track, works the blunger, the plug mill and the ball mill for preparing the clay and, in the latter stages, was even used to turn the potter's wheel. At the heart

Wetheriggs Country Pottery boasts one of the very few surviving examples of a beehive kiln for firing the ware.

The headstock gear at Haig Colliery rises high above the sea on the cliffs near Whitehaven.

of it all is the beehive kiln where the pots are fired. Today, the old system is preserved but the special character that came from having the engine and machines in daily use for everyday manufacture has gone.

EGREMONT
Florence Mine

£ Heritage Centre, £££ Underground tours; March to November, underground tours weekends and Bank Holidays only; Tel: 01946 820683

Despite the first view of the site suggesting a colliery with prominent headstock gear, there was no coal here. This is an iron ore mine, and what is brought up from the depths is the distinctive red mineral haematite, a name which can be roughly translated as bloodstone. Deep mining in the region began in the 1830s, but Florence mine was first cut in 1914 and finished working in 1980. The underground workings are far more cavernous than one would find in most coal mines but are no less dirty – so be prepared for a fascinating but mucky experience.

RAVENGLASS
Muncaster Mill

£; Easter to October daily; November to March weekends only; Tel: 01229 717232; Website: www.muncaster.co.uk

The grain mill is basically a building of c.1700, though the machinery is Victorian. There are three pairs of stones powered by an overshot water wheel, now producing organic flour.

Ravenglass & Eskdale Railway

£££ return fare; April to November; Ravenglass Station, CA18 1SW; Tel: 01229 717171; Website: www.ravenglass-railway.co.uk

This is a line with a strange history. It began quite conventionally as a narrow gauge industrial line, bringing iron ore from Eskdale down to the port at Ravenglass. Trade declined and it closed, but the old line was bought up by model railway builder W.J. Bassett-Lowke, who had the brilliant idea of using miniature locomotives to provide a genuine passenger service. For a time it even found a commercial role serving the Beckfoot quarries. Now it has returned to a purely passenger line, and a very scenic one at that. One can travel behind perfect miniature steam locomotives, either specially designed for the line or copies of famous, mightier engines. It is a much loved line, even if its popular nickname, 'The Ratty', does not sound especially endearing.

THRELKELD
Quarry and Mining Museum

£ (££ with mine visit); March to November daily; Nr Keswick, CA12 4TT; Tel: 017687 79747; Website: www.golakes.co.uk

Based on a former granite quarry, this is a museum in two parts. At the surface there is a collection of mining equipment, including a unique array of mechanical navvies. Different parts of the site are linked by a narrow gauge steam railway. The underground section takes visitors through modern mine workings and on to a section worked since Tudor times. You get to see the workings as the miners saw them, by lamplight and, in the oldest parts, by candle.

WHITEHAVEN
Haig Colliery

Free; Daily except Wednesday; Solway Road, Kells CA28 9BG; Tel: 01946 599949; Website: www.haigpit.com

There was a time when Whitehaven was a hugely important industrial centre, developed as a port for sending out coal from the local mines. There was an undersea pit here in the 1720s and the area once boasted the world's deepest pit. Haig Pit remains as a representative of the past. The museum covers the story of mining in the whole region, and there are two winding engines, built in the 1920s, one of which has been restored and operates daily. This is a new museum and still developing, so by the time these words are read there could be even more to see. It is also possible to take a guided tour from the site to visit other remains in this fascinating area, including the ruins of Saltom Pit, which was extended out under the sea in 1729.

The entrance to the old ore mine at Threlkeld, where visitors also begin their underground visit.

FINSTHWAITE
Stott Park Bobbin Mill

EH; ££; April to October daily; Tel: 01539 531087

Raise a glass and drink a toast to whoever it was at English Heritage who decided to leave this site just as it was in its working days. Instead of interactive displays and wordy panels, you get enthusiastic guides who actually know, love and understand the old mill. The works were begun in 1835 and the power source changed over the years, from water wheel to turbine, steam and finally electricity, but the fundamentals remain unchanged. Machines are still worked by an array of shafts and whizzing belts. Probably no one knows just how many thousands, or more likely millions, of wooden bobbins were turned here and sent down to the cotton mills of Lancashire, but we can see precisely how they were made on a grand array of old machines.

A splendid example of a workshop in the days before electricity. The overhead shafts turned, the pulleys whirred and the belts took the drive down to individual machines.

See Also

Heron Corn Mill, Beetham
£; April to October Tuesday to Sunday;
Tel: 01539 565027
Eighteenth-century watermill, with adjoining museum on papermaking.

Printing House, Cockermouth
££; Easter to Christmas Monday to Saturday; 102 Main Street;
Tel: 01900 824984
A working print museum with a very good collection of old presses.

Gleaston Watermill
£; Easter to October Tuesday to Sunday, winter weekends; Tel: 01229 869244;
Website: www.ourworld.compuserve.com/ homepages/watermill
A three-storey mill with breastshot wheel and wooden gearing.

Pencil Museum, Keswick
£; Easter to November daily;
Tel: 017687 73626
An excellent museum, not just explaining how pencils are manufactured, but also dealing with local graphite mining.

Lakeside and Haverthwaite Railway
££ return fare; April to October daily; Haverthwaite Station, LA12 8AL;
Tel: 015395 31594
The line links with the old Windermere steamer station and runs past a cotton mill and the former Backbarrow Ironworks.

Millom
Tel: 01229 779423 (site being moved)
The seawall to the south of the town was built to preserve the old Hodbarrow ironstone mines. There are extensive remains alongside what is now a bird sanctuary. The story is told in the local Folk Museum.

Little Salkeld Mill
£; March to October Monday, Tuesday and Thursday; Tel: 01768 881523; Website: www.cumbria.com/watermill
Working watermill with two overshot wheels.

Acorn Bank Garden, Temple Sowerby
NT; £ for gardens and mill; April to November daily; Tel: 017683 61893
Three-wheeled watermill with granary and kiln currently under restoration.

SOUTH WALES

As the area has now been allocated to a number of small counties, it seems to be more sensible to group them under one heading. This section contains entries for the following new counties: *Blaenau Gwent, Bridgend, Caerphilly, Cardiff, Merthyr Tydfil, Monmouth, Neath Port Talbot, Newport, Rhondda Cynon Taff, Swansea, Torfaen, Vale of Glamorgan*

The industrial history of South Wales is closely tied to the geology of the region – to the presence of coal and iron. The labyrinthine system of passages and chambers, known as Clearwell Caves, right on the border in the Forest of Dean are known to have been worked for iron ore at least 2000 years ago. Indeed, iron making goes back a very long way, to a time when the woodlands of the river valleys provided charcoal for the blast furnaces. What we now consider picturesque beauty spots were once busy with the sounds of industry. Visitors who come to wander round the ruins of Tintern Abbey are probably not aware that

iron wire was made here in works that were first established right back in the sixteenth century. Unfortunately, so little remains that it can only give a hint of what was happening right up to the nineteenth century. For example, the Royal George Hotel at Tintern was the home of the eighteenth-century lessee of the wire works. The small pond outside the hotel was once much bigger, and its water turned the wheels that powered the wire drawing machinery.

The great period of development of industry in the valleys began in the eighteenth century and depended on the

abundance of good quality coal. It was a valuable commodity in its own right, and the steam coal in particular found a ready market; by the middle of the nineteenth century literally millions of tons were being exported every year. But it was the change from the charcoal blast furnaces to the coke fired furnaces in the iron industry that brought a sudden surge of development. Great iron works appeared alongside the collieries, and the landscape of the valleys was transformed by the spoil heaps of mining, the slag of the furnaces and the ever present sights and sounds of heavy industry.

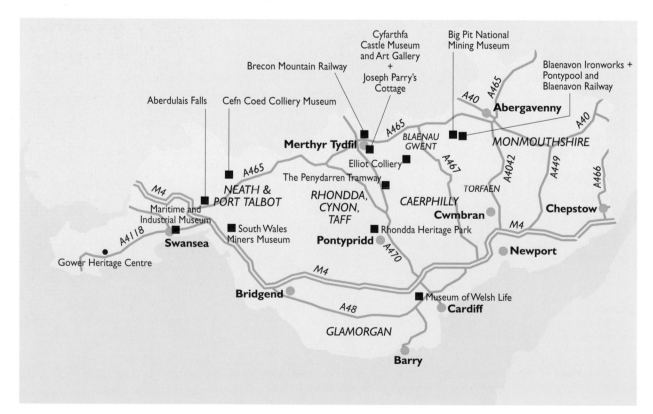

The overshot water wheel at Aberdulais Falls. In the background is a chimney, a survivor from the tinplate works.

ABERDULAIS
Aberdulais Falls

NT; ££; March weekends, April to November daily; Tel: 01639 636674

The falls are mainly visited because this is a famous beauty spot, but the tumbling water has been used for industry for more than four centuries. Copper smelting began here in the 1580s, replaced by iron working in the seventeenth century, and a hundred years later a grain mill was added. The final stage of development came with the establishment of a tinplate works. Today there are remains of old rolling mill pits, and the water wheel still turns, now generating electricity.

BLAENAVON

How times change! When I first came here, it was possible to wander around what seemed to be an almost derelict industrial landscape, forgotten and unloved. Now this is a World Heritage Site, and it richly deserves the honour. South Wales had ample supplies of iron ore, and once coke became available as a fuel, the presence of coal made large-scale development very attractive. Add to that limestone, an essential flux, for use in the furnaces, and it is easy to see why iron masters in England should look on the area with considerable interest. Thomas Hill of Stafford and his associates arrived in 1789, built blast furnaces and opened up a coal mine to feed them. The town grew up dominated by iron – you can even find iron 'gravestones' covering the inhabitants of the local graveyard. A complex of tramways was built, leading out to limestone quarries and on to the Brecon & Abergavenny Canal (see p.130), and they can still be traced winding round and over the local hills. There are now two important sites here, and a day at Blaenavon is as good an introduction to the Industrial Revolution as you will find.

Blaenavon Ironworks

CADW; £; Easter to October daily; North Street, NP4 9RQ; Tel: 01495 792615

This is without doubt the finest example of an eighteenth-century ironworks to survive in Britain. It has the majesty of some great fortress, with the gaunt towers of the furnaces themselves set against the hillside. Dominating everything is the water balance tower. It was used to move material between the upper and lower levels of the site, and is in effect a giant lift. It consisted of a pair of linked containers; when water was added to the one at the top of the tower, it would descend, raising the other. In the casting house, the molten metal from a furnace was run into a central channel in the floor with side channels running away from it. It was fancifully thought to resemble a sow feeding her offspring, hence the term 'pig iron'. There is a social story here as well, for workers lived in cottages literally in the shadow of the furnaces. A reminder of the later phase of iron making and forging can be seen in the giant steam hammer.

Big Pit National Mining Museum

£££; March to November daily; Tel: 01495 790311; Website: www.nmgw.ac.uk

This is the National Mining Museum of Wales, based on a colliery that was working right up to 1900. The great attraction is undoubtedly the visit underground, which lasts about an hour, starting just as it did in working days with a descent by cage. A mine to the uninitiated is a bit like a three-dimensional maze, with a complex ventilation system and its own transport. It is perhaps surprising to see how much mine there is for what seems a surprisingly small coal face. There was also iron ore mining in a section that was opened up in 1840. The surface remains are extensive, and as well as the familiar winding gear and winding engine house, there are pit head baths, the essential lamp room, workshops and a reconstructed miner's cottage. Because it closed comparatively recently, there are still men around who worked here, and they now act as guides – and it is difficult to think of a better guide than a man who knew the real life of the mine.

Pontypool and Blaenavon Railway

Part of the former colliery line is now run as a preserved railway with, appropriately, the emphasis on industrial locomotives and rolling stock.

The water balance tower at Blaenavon iron works, used to move material between the upper and lower levels of the site.

CRYNANT
Cefn Coed Colliery Museum
Free; April to October daily; Tel: 01639 750556

This is one of the latecomers to the valleys. Two shafts were sunk in 1926; when mining began in 1930, this was the deepest anthracite coal mine in the world. Conditions below the surface were so grim, with gas always a threat and occasional roof falls, that it was known locally as the 'slaughterhouse'. It closed in 1968 but important machinery was saved, including the 1927 horizontal steam winding engine, the Lancashire boilers and the compressor that supplied underground power. A shallow gallery has been specially created to allow visitors to see underground working methods. It is unusual in that no mining village ever developed around the colliery.

The steam winding engine took the cage up and down the shaft to a maximum depth of 2,400 feet. Coal was whizzed up in 50 seconds, but miners were given a more leisurely ride.

CYNONVILLE
South Wales Miners Museum
£; April to September daily; Afan Argoed Country Park, SA13 3HG; Tel: 01639 850564

The Afan Valley has now become a local beauty spot, the river squeezed in between wooded hills. It was not always like this, for this was a mining valley, serving the vast iron and steel works on the coast at Port Talbot. The last pit closed in 1970 and a museum of mining was created shortly afterwards in the Afan Argoed Country Park. It was designed to tell the story both of mining and the mining communities of South Wales, with mining equipment and a simulated coal face. It was a pioneering effort and is beginning to show its age, but the collection, particularly of early machinery, makes it well worth a visit. There are plans for a major modernisation in the near future.

William Crawshay's Gothic extravaganza, Cyfarthfa Castle, built on the fortune made in his iron works.

MERTHYR TYDFIL

Two sites here offering different viewpoints on the Industrial Revolution – not strictly industrial sites at all, but very much a part of the social history of the region.

Cyfarthfa Castle Museum and Art Gallery

Free; March to October daily, November to April Tuesday to Friday and weekend afternoons; Cyfarthfa Park, Brecon Road, CF47 8RE; Tel: 01685 723112

William Crawshay was among the richest of all Welsh industrialists and owner of the local Cyfarthfa Ironworks. In 1824 he moved away from the smoke and dirt, and built himself a new house surrounded by parkland. It was not a modest house: a riot of battlements and towers, it vividly demonstrates the wealth made by the few.

Joseph Parry's Cottage, 4 Chapel Row

Free; Easter to September Thursday to Sunday afternoons; Tel: 01685 723112

Close to the Cyfarthfa works, of which little remains apart from a large engine house, stands this row of iron workers' cottages, with a chapel at the end. Built by the Crawshays, these are typical two-up-two-down houses. This one was the

birthplace of composer Joseph Parry in 1841. Amazingly, at one time it housed not just the Parrys and their eight children but two lodgers as well. Outside the cottages is one of the few surviving lengths of the Glamorgan Canal and a canal boat. Unlike the boats of the English network, these were completely open and pointed at both ends. There is also a tramway truck

It is appropriate that in the area that saw the first public demonstration of a steam locomotive running on rails, there is now a steam railway to travel just north of the town.

Brecon Mountain Railway

£££; Easter to November; Pant Station, Dowlais, CF48 2UP;
Tel: 01685 722988; Website:
www.breconmountainrailway.co.uk

A narrow gauge railway running north into the Brecon Beacons National Park, with locomotives from Germany and South Africa, as well as more familiar British engines.

NEW TREDEGAR

Elliot Colliery

£; Easter to October afternoons; White Rose Way, NP2 6DF; Tel: 029 2088 0011

This colliery was so important to the life of the community that the area in which it stood is still officially known as Elliot's Town. In its heyday at the end of World War I it employed almost 2500 men underground and another 350 at the surface. When it closed in 1967 its twin-tandem compound winding engine was the last of its kind in South Wales. This giant was built in 1891 by Thornewill and Warham of Burton-on-Trent, and happily the decision was taken to preserve it and its engine house in situ rather than taking the engine off to a museum.

QUAKERS YARD

The Penydarren Tramway

Free; Open access

A track leads away along the River Taff, on the opposite bank from the A470. Follow it north towards Merthyr Vale, and as it passes under the high viaduct built for the Taff Vale Railway, parallel lines of stone blocks can be seen along the path. These are the sleeper blocks into which the rails of the Penydarren tramway were spiked. And it was on this line, in 1804, that Richard Trevithick gave the first public demonstration of a railway locomotive. There may not be much to see, but there is somehow a special thrill in standing on a spot where history was made.

An old tramway wagon stands by a section of the Glamorgan Canal in front of the iron workers' cottages in Chapel Row.

COAL MINING

Coal was acknowledged as a fuel by the Romans but considered of minor importance. After the Romans left, it was largely unknown for a considerable time: there is no mention anywhere in the Domesday Book. Its use as a domestic fuel was limited in an age when most people used wood or peat, and there were comparatively few industrial applications. It was the growth of industries that encouraged development. By the fifteenth century there were a number of mines in South Wales, though they were not mines in the sense that we usually think of them. These were either drift mines, cut into a hillside, or bell pits, workings that spread out from the bottom of a single short shaft. When the space reached a point where it was in danger of caving in, the pit was abandoned and another sunk nearby. Two developments gave a spur to mining: the use of coal for making coke for the iron industry, and the growth of towns, where the citizens no longer had access to wood for fuel. A further impetus came with the development of the steam engine, first for working pumps, then for providing power for factories and eventually for the railways. South Wales was to prove a significant area, for the coal was of high quality and came in three varieties, each of which met a market need. Anthracite is a very slow burning coal,

with little flame; bituminous coal is suitable for coking; and in between these two types is a form of coal that proved so good for raising steam in boilers that it has become known simply as 'steam coal'. By the early nineteenth century the demand was enormous, not just to meet local needs, but to feed a hungry export market as well. Meeting that demand required a new industry based on deep mines and employing a large work force. Because the miners had to locate where coal was found, whole new communities developed – the mining villages of South Wales.

The surface buildings of a colliery are familiar. The most obvious sign is the headstock gear or winding frame. In the nineteenth-century pit, the workings could be many hundreds of feet below the surface, so a steam engine was used for moving men, coal and material up and down the shaft. Wire passed round the rotating drum was fastened to the cage, which could be controlled with great accuracy by the engine man. There were other systems in use, notably the water

The headgear has always been the most distinctive feature of any colliery. This example stands above a shaft at Cefn Coed sunk in 1926. The sheaves at the top of the frame carry the wires attached to the cage, providing access to the underground labyrinth.

balance winding gear, in which two cages were connected by wire passing over a wheel on the surface. Each cage had a water tank underneath. By adding enough water to the cage at the surface, it would drop, raising the other cage at the same time.

At the bottom of the shaft was a second underground world spreading out over an immense area. The work of the miner was highly skilled and arduous. There were two main methods of working. In 'pillar and stall' a heading was driven into the coal, and a number of working places, the stalls, ran off to either side. Often these were so low that a miner had to lie on his side to remove coal from the bottom of the seam, which was propped up at intervals as he advanced. When the stall was big enough, the props were removed and the coal in the roof collapsed in under its own weight. It was then loaded into tubs and taken back to the shaft. Pillars of coal were left between the stalls to avoid a general cave in. The alternative system was 'longwall', where, as the name suggests, the coal was removed in one line, a continuous operation that allowed a number of men to work at the face at the same time. It was less wasteful of coal, as there was no need to leave pillars. As the wall advanced, the space behind it was filled with loose rock and stone. For many years all the work was manual, but in 1863 a patent was taken out for a mechanical coal cutter. It was worked by compressed air and imitated the familiar action of the miner, except that the arm powering the pick was mechanical. An early example can be seen in the National Museum of Wales in Cardiff. It was used in Maesteg, and could cut a length of roughly 150 metres (490ft) in an eight-hour shift.

A major problem in all coal mines is ventilation. In the earlier mines this was mainly accomplished by setting a furnace at the foot of one shaft – the downshaft. Air was sucked in and passed through the

Many of the mining remains of South Wales have been swept away as pits have closed. Machinery has been preserved at the South Wales Miners Museum, but its setting has been transformed into the Afan Argoed Country Park.

workings to emerge at the second shaft – the upshaft. To control the system, and to ensure that the air reached all parts, a series of ventilation doors was used, each manned by a young boy, whose dark, solitary day was spent opening and closing the heavy doors to allow the trams carrying the coal to pass. The dangers from inflammable gas in the mines was partly overcome by the invention of the safety lamp, of which the most commonly used was invented by Sir Humphry Davy in 1815. Yet Robert Galloway, recording accidents in South Wales in the years between 1836 and 1850, recorded 137 mine explosions, of which the worst, at Aberdare in 1849, killed fifty-two miners. The accidents were generally ascribed to miners' carelessness. It has to be remembered, however, that owners were not subject to any regulation until 1850, and even then it did not always work. Despite the South Wales Inspector informing the owners of Cymmer Colliery that the ventilation was bad, nothing was done. The result was an explosion that killed 115 men, yet no action was taken; though at another colliery a miner who was found with an unlit pipe in his pocket was sent to gaol. The winning of coal was hard and dangerous work. Although the many excellent mining museums in the area, which will be found listed in this section, give a good idea of the technology of mining, they cannot and should not reproduce the actual working conditions of the nineteenth century. There was a high price to be paid for the millions of tons of coal that were sent out every year from the valleys of South Wales.

The Esgair Moel Woollen Factory was brought to St Fagans from Llanwrtyd. This is a typical rural mill, built around 1760 to serve the local community: farmers brought in their wool, which was spun into yarn, woven and finished as cloth and blankets for the farmers' families.

ST FAGANS
Museum of Welsh Life

Free; Open daily; Tel: 029 2057 3500; Website: www.nmgw.ac.uk

This has to be just about the best free day's outing in Britain; the title of the museum gives some idea of what to expect. This is all about how the people of Wales lived and worked, even if the setting is that of a very grand country house. St Fagans Castle was built in the late sixteenth century and became home to the Earls of Plymouth, who donated it to the National Museum of Wales. It now looks out over a 40-hectare (100-acre) site where buildings of all types and ages have been gathered together and re-erected. The industrial life of the country is well represented. There are three water-powered mills. One is most unusual, a little gorse mill, which does just what you might expect: it takes the tough gorse shoots and crushes and tears them to make animal food. The second is a more conventional grain mill with an overshot wheel. The third is much more complex and an absolute delight. Here you get a chance to see a woollen mill, built around 1760, with some nineteenth-century updating. The power is transmitted by line shafting to a variety of machines, which deal with all the processes from wool coming in to finished cloth going out. The willey disentangles the wool, the fibres are straightened and aligned by carding and then it goes for spinning, in this case by a very rare spinning-jack. The cloth is woven and then goes for finishing. It is rare to find a mill that has fulling stocks as well as the other processes all in the one building, and this adds greatly to the interest. The cloth is dyed, cut and pressed, ready to be sent on its way. Other industrial buildings include the unusual two-level Ewenny pottery kiln, a tannery and a traditional cider press, worked by a horse. There is a chance to compare the ironworkers' cottages of Merthyr Tydfil with another row, again built by Richard Crawshay around 1800. Each one has been dealt with in a different style, from a recreation of how the house would have been when new, right through to a modernised house of the 1980s.

This is only a small part of the whole collection, and for anyone with even the least interest in vernacular architecture this is a treasure house. Everyone will have their own favourites among the cottages, farmhouses and barns, but I take special delight in the humblest building of them all – the pigsty. It is a round, stone building with a corbelled roof – not so much a pigsty as a little pig palace. Even if nothing was happening, one would still be able to spend hours just looking, but there are regular demonstrations of the work of the buildings so that you can watch craftsmen of all kinds, from coopers to weavers. At the start I described this as a day out simply because you really do need a day to enjoy this to the full.

TREHAFOD
Rhondda Heritage Park

£££; Easter to October daily, winter closed Mondays; Lewis Merthyr Colliery, Coed Cae Road, CF37 7NP; Tel: 01443 682036; Website: www.rhonddaheritagepark.com

The Lewis Merthyr Colliery was just one of many which together made the name Rhondda synonymous with coal – and in particular with high quality steam coal. Now as a heritage centre it has to stand for an industry that did not so much die as fall victim to political homicide. There are museums in South Wales that present the coal story simply and with few frills. This one has gone down the other route with multi-media displays and underground simulations. As a family outing there is enough serious matter to keep the interested adult happy and it's plenty of fun for the kids.

A scene that epitomises the Rhondda of just a few years ago, but Merthyr Main Colliery is now a Heritage Park.

The transit shed was once crowded with cargo when Swansea docks were thriving, and is now part of the museum.

See Also
Gower Heritage Centre, Parkmill, Swansea
Free; Open daily; Tel: 01792 371206; Website: www.gowerheritagemuseum.sagehost.co.uk
A number of craft workshops are clustered round a water-powered grain mill.

SWANSEA
Maritime and Industrial Museum

Free; All year Tuesday to Sunday; Museum Square, Maritime Quarter, SA1 1SN; Tel: 01792 650351; Website: www.swansea.gov.uk

The former docks have become the Maritime Quarter, full of new buildings, and it is hard to imagine it as it was a century or so ago, crammed with ships and covered by a perpetual pall of smoke from the surrounding copper smelters. The maritime part of this museum has its most exciting exhibits where they should be, out on the water. The industrial part is in a former transit shed. A large part of the space is taken up by a working woollen mill, recreated here with working machinery, including a set of spinning mules.

Between the docks and the new leisure centre is an embankment, a survivor of the Swansea & Mumbles Railway of 1804. It was originally used for horse-drawn trucks, linking the Oystermouth quarries to Swansea, but in 1807 a passenger service was begun, the first regular rail passenger service in the world.

CONNECTING LINKS

Industrial growth depends on transport: bringing raw materials in and taking finished products out. In the valleys of South Wales, geography made things very difficult. The valleys run generally in a north-south direction, separated by high ridges and falling steeply towards the sea. The main market for coal and iron was to be found in England or further afield, so the first requirement was a system that would connect to the main ports, Cardiff and Swansea. Then there were connections to be made between the valleys themselves. In the eighteenth century canals were the latest thing in technology, but to complete the connections across the hills would have meant an impossibly large number of locks with all the problems of finding water to fill them. So canals were built where canals could be built and tramways were built to link them. There is no better way to see how it all came together than to look at the Brecon &

Abergavenny Canal as it was known when work began on it in 1793.

The canal runs from a connection with the Monmouthshire Canal at Pontymoile, near Pontypool, for 53km (33 miles) to Brecon. Today it is admired for the beautiful scenery through which it passes, particularly in the east where it curls itself around the hillside of the Blorenge, sliding round the edge of the Brecon Beacons National Park. Travelling by boat or walking the towpath is a pure delight, and it is easy to forget its old role as a servant of industry. There are some unmistakable signs, such as the lime kilns alongside the wharf at Llangattock. What is less obvious is the extent of the tramway connections, over a dozen lines linking into the waterway from quarries, mines and foundries. Perhaps the best place to see this is Llanfoist: not a place to reach by car, best approached by a delightful walk along the towpath

The line of Hill's Tramway can be clearly seen as it hugs the hillside on its way to the quarries on Gilwern Hill. There were connections to the ironworks at Blaenavon, where limestone was brought as a flux for the furnaces, as well as down to the Brecon & Abergavenny Canal.

The Brecon & Abergavenny Canal at Llanfoist. Boats could either tie up at the wharf or float in underneath the warehouse. Trucks were lowered down the incline through the trees of the wooded hillside, to run on tracks behind the warehouse at first-floor level.

from Govilon or along the very minor road leading uphill beside the church in Llanfoist itself. The wharf is the focal point. The first hint of a tramway presence is the flat topped bridge over the canal, which allowed trucks to continue on down the hill, and the pedestrian tunnel under the canal. A handsome wharf house looks down on a warehouse on two levels. A flat track runs behind it, along which trucks passed for unloading, and boats could float in underneath. This now forms part of a hire base for boating holidays. A footpath leads up the hill from the bridge. This is the old tramway incline, where the movements of trucks were controlled by a cable. Those who are feeling energetic can walk up the path, find old sleeper blocks and a platform which once held the brake drum. The very energetic can follow the line out onto the slopes of the Blorenge. Where did it go? The answer lies in the name – Hill's Tramway. It was built for the ironmaster of Blaenavon. One of the clearest sections can be seen rather more easily by taking the B4246 from Govilon to Blaenavon. About half way along, by the hill known as The Tumble, the trackbed can be seen swinging away

towards the quarries to the right of the road. It was this combination of tramway and canal that brought thriving trade. By the 1820s the little canal, which now has a scattering of holiday cruisers, was carrying 30,000 tons of coal, much the same amount of iron and 12,000 tons of limestone every year.

The use of tramway connections to canals was common throughout Wales. The Montgomery Canal, for example, had lines from limestone quarries to wharves at Crickheath and Llanymynech, while the line to Pant ended at an impressive bank of lime kilns. The most famous tramway of them all was the Penydarren. This was used to bypass the heavily locked section of the Glamorgan Canal between Abercynon and Merthyr Tydfil. The canal has virtually vanished at Abercynon itself, though it is remembered on a pub sign, but the line of the tramway can still be seen. The wharf site is now home to the local fire station and outside it is a plaque commemorating Trevithick's famous locomotive runs of 1804 – an event that was soon to see the age of canals and tramways give way to the railway age.

FLEECE TO CLOTH

For centuries, wool lay at the heart of Britain's prosperity: it has been estimated that by 1500 there were three sheep for every human being in the country. And as early as 1300, water-powered machinery was introduced into the manufacturing process in the shape of the fulling mill. Throughout the eighteenth and into the nineteenth centuries, mechanisation spread to all aspects of the processing. The industry in Wales never developed as it did in other regions, such as Yorkshire and the south-west of England, but it has shown great tenacity. Small mills have survived, sometimes still using water power as they did when they were the latest examples of the new technology of the eighteenth century. And being small scale, there was no great incentive to rush to replace old machines, or bring in new power sources when water was free. As a result, it is still possible to see mills either working as museums or even still producing cloth using old equipment and techniques. The following brief description lists the basic processes used by a mill that took in the fleeces from the shearers and sent out fine cloth.

The wool that arrived at a mill was likely to be a tangled mass which needed to be washed and disentangled. Once that was done, the fibres had to be aligned by carding. Originally this was done by hand, drawing the wool through a pair of boards held in the hands, each card covered with wire teeth. This operation was rapidly replaced by a carding engine, where a rotating drum was used. If worsted was being made, the wool was combed – a process just like combing hair – to separate out the necessary long fibres from the short. Other processes were introduced to prepare the fine web of carded wool, and one of the earliest devices brought in was the slubbing billy, drawing out rolls of wool to as much as 1.8m (6ft) from 20–23cm (8–9in.). Few of these survive, and the only one I have ever found in use can be seen in a woollen mill on Islay (p.173) Now the wool is ready for spinning. Since antiquity, this had been done by hand on the spinning wheel, but

machinery first introduced into the cotton industry was soon applied to wool. In the nineteenth-century Welsh mills, mules came into general use, replacing the single spindle of the spinning wheel with the many spindles turned by machine.

The next stage in the process is winding to make it ready to be brought to the loom. Weaving consists of laying out warp threads, which can be alternately raised and lowered, allowing the weft thread, carried by the shuttle, to pass in between. People often get confused over which set of threads is which, and it was an old Welsh weaver who gave this simple aide-memoire: 'the warp goes up and down, the weft goes from weft to wight'. Corny maybe, but you never forget it! Warping is a complex, skilled and painstaking business. The loom proved a far more difficult machine to mechanise than the spinning wheel, and it was not until 1786 that the first patent for a power loom was taken out. The inventor had no experience whatsoever of textiles; he even claimed never to have seen a weaver at work. He was clergyman Dr Edmund Cartwright.

This flannel press is a rare survivor from the early days of the Welsh woollen industry.

The final processes in Welsh mills included fulling, a process already described in an earlier section (p.12). There were certain types of cloth that required special treatment. One speciality of the Welsh mills was flannel, which was compacted by flannel presses, not unlike printing presses. Each cloth required its own treatment. Where a smooth finish was required, cloth was brushed with teazles to raise the nap, then cut smooth by skilled men using shears. These operations were among the last to be mechanised. Teazles were set in a rotating gig mill, and the cloth dressers' shears were replaced by rotating blades. The latter are often remarked upon as being rather like a lawn mower. This is not too surprising, since the inventor of the lawnmower borrowed the idea from the woollen mill in the first place. Today we can see virtually all these processes in older mills and museums, and some of the very best examples are to be found in Wales.

The main entrance to the Dolaucothi gold mine, which has been worked since Roman times. Visitors have the opportunity to explore the underground workings.

PONTERWYD
Llywernog Silver Lead Mine

££; March to October Tuesday to Sunday, July and August open daily; Tel: 01970 890620; Website: www.silverminetours.co.uk

They have been mining here for ores of silver, lead and zinc since 1740, but mostly what is on view dates back to the nineteenth century when water power was used for the various operations involved in separating out the valuable ore, concentrating and then crushing it. The shafts have long been filled in, as work stopped here in 1914, but a drift mine has been recreated to give visitors the underground experience, complete with audio and light displays, to create a working atmosphere. Even if this sort of simulation is not to your taste, there are many other reasons to come here. First of all, the mine has a splendid situation on the flank of a high, wooded hill. The surface remains are extensive, and in particular this is an excellent place to come to see just how adaptable water power could be. Machinery includes jiggers and buddles, both involved in washing the material to allow the heavy ores to settle out, and rock crushers.

PUMSAINT
Dolaucothi Gold Mine

NT; ££ Site, ££ extra charge for underground tour; Mid-April to mid-September daily; Tel: 01558 825146

There are really two elements to this site, one above ground and one below, and in many ways it is the former which is the more interesting. All the oldest workings are to be seen from the surface, and in this case they really are old, for the first mine was opened up by the Romans. One of the fascinations of this site is to see just what lengths the Romans were prepared to go to in order to reach the precious metal. The start was to bring water to the site via an aqueduct which can still be traced as a shallow depression running 11.3km (7 miles) from the River Cothi. It was used to fill reservoirs at the top of the hill. These were used for 'hushing'. Water was released in a deluge that washed away the topsoil to reveal surface traces of the metal, which could then be followed into the hillside in tunnels, drained by adits. The Romans left and nothing much happened for many centuries until the Victorians rediscovered gold and began working the mines again. With their new technology they were able to penetrate far deeper into the hill, and now visitors can again explore the complex of shafts and levels. This is one of the few places where you can see mining history covering a period of some 2000 years.

ST NICHOLAS
Tregwynt Woollen Mill

Free; Monday to Friday all year; Off the A487 on the minor road from Mathry to St Nicholas (map ref. 157/895347)

The mill is old and was originally water-powered, but although the wheel is still in place, weaving is now on modern power looms. This is very much a working mill, and as well as the traditional power looms, there are currently modern shuttleless looms also in use.

WELSHPOOL
Powysland Museum and Canal Centre

£; May to September daily except Wednesday, October to April all day Monday, Tuesday, Thursday and Friday, Saturday afternoons; Canal Wharf, SY21 7AQ; Tel: 01938 554656

The museum is housed in a former warehouse beside the Montgomery Canal, which is currently being restored to navigation. It covers all aspects of local history, but also includes good sections on local transport.

Welshpool & Llanfair Light Railway

£££ return fare; Easter to October daily, Tel: 01938 810441

Work began on this 76cm (2ft 6in.) gauge railway in 1901, and although it officially closed in 1956 it was partially reopened as a preserved steam railway in 1963. It has now been extended, and taking pride of place among the locomotives are two Beyer Peacock engines, *The Earl* and *The Countess*, which have worked the line from the start. Rolling stock, however, has a distinctly foreign air, with coaches from Austria and Africa. As a result, passengers can view the attractive scenery from airy balconies on some of the runs.

See Also
Felin Newydd, Crug-y-bar

£; April to October daily except Tuesday and Wednesday; Llanwrda, SA19 8UE; Tel: 01558 650375
An eighteenth-century working corn mill with an overshot wheel.

Y Felin, St Dogmaels

£; Open daily; Tel: 01239 613999
This is a working watermill, built around the end of the eighteenth century and now producing wholemeal flour. There is also a gas engine on site.

Nant-y-Coy Watermill, Treffgarne

Free; April to October Monday to Saturday, June to August plus Sundays; On the A40 between Treffgarne and Wolf's Castle; Tel: 01437 741671
The nineteenth-century water-powered corn mill and miller's cottage forms the basis for a small museum.

NORTH WALES

Anglesey, Conwy, Denbigh, Flint, Gwynedd, Wrexham

The area has been mined for various minerals from coal to copper, but one activity has dominated the region: mining and quarrying for slate. It is not just that the industry has left behind mountains of waste and scarred many a hillside, it has also given the region one of its most popular tourist attractions – The Great

Little Trains. The building of narrow gauge lines was a direct response to the mountainous terrain, with slopes too steep and curves too sharp for conventional railways. So the tiny railways built to haul slate from quarry and mine now carry passengers on scenic rides through the hills. One exciting ride, however, is no longer offered

to tourists. We think riding the tracks for pleasure is something quite new, but long before the first tourist train ran on the little Talyllyn Railway, locals were able to rent trucks at the top of the line and descend under gravity as if they were on some giant roller coaster. It would turn a modern health and safety official grey overnight!

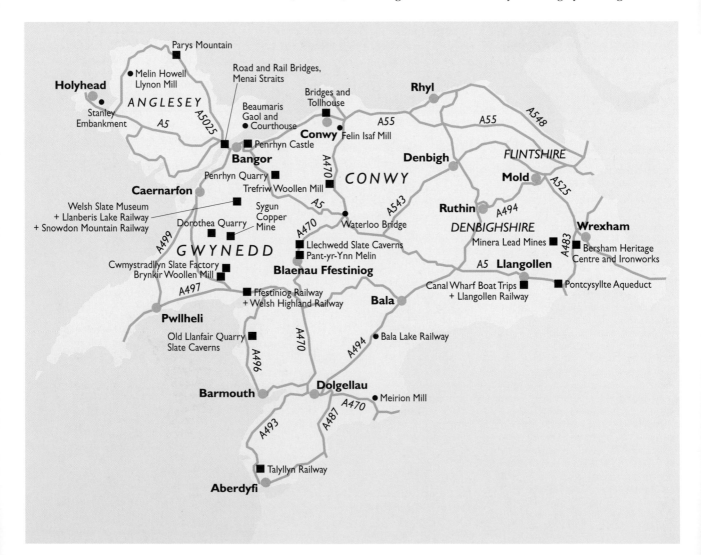

surprise at the end when visitors emerge at the Victoria level above the main site, with a spectacular view out over the mountains of Snowdonia.

The area is full of interest and reminders of the mining past. The energetic who take the walk over the hill behind Sygun, using the path from Llyn Dinas, will find the skeletal remains of an old overhead cableway that once took ore down to the processing plant at Nantmor.

BERSHAM

Bersham Heritage Centre and Ironworks

Free Heritage Centre; Easter to September Monday to Friday all day, weekend afternoons; Ironworks: May to August afternoons only; Tel: 01978 261529; Website: www.wrexham.gov.uk

Bersham has a long history of iron making, with records of a charcoal blast furnace being built in 1719, it was soon converted to using coke, however, almost certainly the first in Wales. The works really achieved fame in the second half of the eighteenth century, when they were taken over by the Wilkinson family. John Wilkinson devised a means of boring cannon with considerable accuracy, and his machines were later adapted for boring cylinders for James Watt's steam engines. The ironworks closed and the water power was used instead for a corn mill that began work in 1828. The

water wheel and gearing have survived. The decayed remains of the blast furnaces can still be seen, and there is an exhibition on the history of the site in one of the surviving buildings. Wilkinson was not the only important iron maker in the area. The Davies Brothers had a forge at Bersham, and they became famous for their decorative wrought iron. An outstanding example can be seen in the gates to Chirk Castle. Their story, and the story of other industrial developments in the area, is told in the Heritage Centre.

BLAENAU FFESTINIOG

There is no escaping slate here: mountains of shattered spoil from mines and quarries rise above the rooftops and working levels scar the hillsides.

Llechwedd Slate Caverns

£££ (price includes one or other of the underground visits); Open daily; Tel: 01766 830306; Website: www.llechwedd.co.uk

There is no doubt what draws the crowds here: the underground visits. There are two options. The Deep Mine begins with a railway ride down a 1:1.8 slope, not exactly a roller coaster experience but remarkable for a passenger-carrying railway. This leads to a walk over 120m (400ft) below ground to visit a series of caverns with light and sound shows, illustrating life in the mines. Also included is a visit to an

A jack roller for hauling up ore stands above a shaft connecting different levels of the Sygun copper mine.

BEDDGELERT
Sygun Copper Mine

££; Open daily; On the A498 Beddgelert to Capel Curig road; Tel: 01766 510101; Website: www.ourworld.compuserve.com/ homepages/snowdoniamine

This is a mine that never quite lived up to the high expectations of the owners from its opening up around 1825 to its closure in 1903. In its last phase the mine was controlled by Alexander Stanley Elmore, and he installed his own patent flotation system for separating out the ore. The system worked on the principle that when pulverised ore and rock are added to a mixture of oil and water, the copper pyrites will adhere to the oil and the rest of the material will sink. The foundations of the system can still be seen. The surface remains at the mine include a set of water-powered stamps for crushing the ore. The real appeal for most visitors, however, is the underground tour through a complex system of shafts and adits leading to different levels of the mine, each of which was distinguished by its own name. At places along the tour the adits open out into man-made caverns, dripping with reddish-brown stalactites, coloured by iron ore. Part of the old underground tramway system has survived, and there is a pleasant

A display of slate splitting at the Llechwedd slate caverns. After splitting, the slate is dressed, cut to a standard size.

It is not difficult to see where Telford drew his inspiration for the Gothic stonework of his bridge, which neatly echoes the towers of Conwy Castle.

CONWY
Bridges and Tollhouse

NT; £ tollhouse, free access to bridges; Tel: 01492 573282

Two bridges stand beneath the walls of Conwy Castle, both designed to link passengers from the mainland to the ferry service at Holyhead. First on the scene was Thomas Telford. He was engineer for the Holyhead Road and work began on the bridge in 1825. This is a suspension bridge given the full medieval treatment to fit in with its surroundings; Telford even abandoned his standard design for tollhouses on the road in favour of a little miniature castle. The tollhouse has recently been furnished in period style. In 1847 Robert Stephenson arrived to build his bridge to carry the railway from Chester to Holyhead. He opted for a revolutionary new design. The bridge consists of giant tubes, in effect hollow girders, and the trains run inside them. This was considered new technology, but even Stephenson couldn't resist following the earlier engineer's example by adding gothic towers. The site provides a rare opportunity to see the work of two of Britain's greatest civil engineers, side by side.

underground lake. The Miners' Tramway is not quite so colourful and stays on the level, but still includes immense man-made caverns. Here you are following the route used by miners in the mid-nineteenth century. If you want spectacle first and history second, take the Deep Mine ride; if you are mainly interested in the slate industry itself, then go for the other option. At the surface there are demonstrations of the craft of slate splitting and a reconstructed Victorian village.

Melin Pant-yr-Ynn, Bethania

£; May to October 2nd weekend in the month; Tel: 01766 830540

The mill may not be open very often but is still worth a visit to see the outside. This was originally a slate mill, built in 1846, before undergoing an unlikely transformation in 1881 to a woollen mill. The large overshot water wheel is still in working order. The mill now houses paintings of industrial towns by the artist Falcon D. Hildred.

Golan, Near Porthmadog
Brynkir Woollen Mill

Free; All year at time of writing, but winter closures likely; Garndolbenmaen, LL51 9YU; Tel: 01766 530236

This is an unusual and unusually interesting little mill. It started off as

a corn mill, until150 years ago it was converted into a woollen mill. The old overshot water wheel still turns but only for demonstration purposes. That does not, however, mean that water power has been forgotten. Now a turbine is used to supplement the electricity supply. Here, as in many small Welsh mills, all the processes are represented, from the willey to the loom, with many venerable machines, including mules, doublers and cheese and bobbin winders. The goods on sale in the mill shop all started off at the other end of the process as pure wool, so you really can say that you have seen the full range of processes.

LLANBERIS
Welsh Slate Museum

££; Easter to October daily; November to Easter Sunday to Friday; Tel: 01286 870630; Website: www.nmgw.ac.uk

The museum is based on the vast Dinorwig Quarry, begun in 1809, which reached a peak of activity a century later when it employed some 3000 men. The quarriers hacked away at the 915m (3000ft) mountain, Elidir Fawr, leaving shattered heaps of broken slate and an imposing series of levels linked by inclines. One of these inclines has now been restored to show the system as it was in its working days. Then the weight of trucks loaded with slate going down the mountain was used to haul the emp-

The Smith Rodley mobile crane began its working life in Glasgow in the 1930s and came to Llanberis via Wrexham and Blaenau Ffestiniog.

ties back up again. The quarries form the backdrop to the museum itself, based on the old workshops. The most imposing feature on the outside is the 15m (50ft) diameter water wheel that provided the power. The quarry was remarkably self-sufficient, right down to casting machine parts in their own foundry. Demonstrations of brass casting now form a regular feature in the museum year, and the sight of molten metal from the furnace being poured into prepared moulds is always exciting. There are demonstrations of slate splitting and dressing, a highly skilled craft, and a wide range of machinery on show in the workshop yard, including narrow gauge locomotives and a steam crane. A row of slate workers' cottages has been reassembled on site, and the modern world of museum presentation appears in the shape of a three-dimensional presentation of the dizzying life of the quarrymen on the high crags. The slate story can be continued in style from the site by steam railway.

Llanberis Lake Railway

££ return fare; Mid-March to November; Tel: 01286 870549; Website: www.lake-railway.freeserve.co.uk

The railway was built to serve the quarries, taking slate to newly established Port Dinorwig for shipment round the coast. The first line was a primitively constructed tramway that later gave way to the 1.2m (4ft) gauge Padarn Railway. One of the original locomotives, the *Fire Queen*, of 1848,

The former Dinorwig quarry workshops in their dramatic setting in the heart of Snowdonia are now home to the Welsh Slate Museum.

is preserved with other industrial locomotives at the Penryhn Castle Museum (p.147). When the quarries closed, the railway closed with them, then reopened as a passenger line, still using some steam locomotives that worked the quarry line, the oldest, *Elidir*, having arrived as a brand new engine in 1889.

Snowdon Mountain Railway

££££ return fare; Mid-March to November; Tel: 0870 458 0033; Website: www.snowdonrailway.co.uk

This really is quite unlike any other railway in Britain. It is the country's only rack and pinion railway, and long before metrication became commonplace it was built to a metric gauge of 800mm. The two facts are related, for when the engineers came to build the mountain railway in the 1890s, they naturally turned to Switzerland for expertise and locomotives. This led to a certain local confusion: faced with an air valve labelled 'luftventil', they simply called it the loft, and the name stuck. The differences to conventional lines do not end there. The locomotive works in a unique manner, pushing the train uphill but uncoupled and, instead of pulling it down, descends tender first but in forward gear, so that it acts as a brake. The engines even look odd, with boilers that slope when seen on the flat, but looking perfectly sensibly level when going uphill. None of this probably matters very much to the thousands who travel the line. The great thrill is the truly spectacular

climb to the summit of Wales' highest mountain. One word of warning, however: services do depend on the weather, and in the early and late parts of the year in particular the route to the summit may be blocked by snow, so a shortened service will be in operation, though even that is still splendid.

LLANFAIR

Old Llanfair Quarry Slate Caverns

££; Easter to mid-October; Tel: 01766 780247

This is one aspect of the slate industry, burrowing deep underground instead of quarrying at the surface. Work began here in 1877 and it was destined to last little more than a quarter of a century. In that time the miners and quarrymen created huge caverns supported by pillars of rock, giving them appropriate names such as 'the crypt' and, increasing in majesty, 'the cathedral'. It is difficult to believe that these chambers were all man-made.

LLANGOLLEN

Canal Wharf Boat Trips

££ Horse-drawn boat, £££ Motor boat; Easter to November; The Wharf, Wharf Hill; Tel: 01978 860702

What is now known as the Llangollen Canal was originally the Ellesmere Canal. Indeed, the branch to Llangollen was not even part of the

Boat trips along this beautiful section of the Llangollen Canal are available from the canal wharf at Llangollen.

main line. This was a navigable feeder: a narrow channel that brought water from a weir, in this case on the Dee, the Horseshoe Falls, to supply the rest of the canal. The line is carved into the hillside, twisting and turning to stay on the level. It soon became an attractive tourist route and horse-drawn boats carried passengers to enjoy the scenery, as they still do today. The longer trip by powered boat includes a crossing of Pontcysyllte (see p.143).

Llangollen Railway

£££ return fare; All year weekends, May to November daily; The Station, Abbey Road, LL20 8SN; Tel: 01978 860951

The preserved line runs from the old Llangollen station some 13km (8 miles) up the Dee valley.

MINERA

Minera Lead Mines

£ Visitor Centre and Meadow Shaft Site; Easter to October Tuesday to Sunday, August plus Mondays; Tel: 01978 751320

An area that was once one of the busiest lead mining areas in Britain is now a Country Park, but one where the old mining features have been

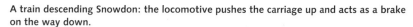

A train descending Snowdon: the locomotive pushes the carriage up and acts as a brake on the way down.

Telford's graceful suspension bridge. In construction, the chains were joined on a raft in the middle of the straits and raised into position by a gang of 150 men.

MENAI STRAITS
Road and Rail Bridges

Free; Open access

These are the companion pieces to the two Conwy bridges (p.140) carrying road and rail to Holyhead, but this time on a far grander scale. Telford's suspension bridge retains all its old majesty, though critics of modern engineering might care to note that before it eventually opened in 1826, it swayed alarmingly in the wind, and hurried remedial action was called for. An interesting little feature can be seen at the southern end, where a roadway is closed off by a rather Art Deco-looking iron gate – the date is actually 1820s not 1920s – one of Telford's original designs for toll gates on the Holyhead Road. Robert Stephenson's Britannia Bridge has fared less well, and its distinctive tubular structure has gone, destroyed in a fire.

excavated, restored and explained. The most striking feature is the engine house over the former Meadow Shaft, with its restored headstock. On the rest of the extensive site there are remains of ore dressing and separation plants. The visitor centre has displays, and the whole site is intended to give a notion of how the mine would have been at the height of its working life in the late nineteenth century.

PONTCYSYLLTE
Aqueduct

Free; Open access

This is one of the grandest features of any transport system in Britain. Over 300m (1000ft) long and rising 37m (120ft), it carries boats on the Llangollen Canal high above the River Dee. Designed by Thomas Telford and William Jessop, the water is held in an iron trough carried aloft on a parade of stone piers. Walking across on the towpath is dizzying, and travelling by boat – an experience rather like flying, as you cannot actually see the edge of the trough – is even more exciting. The latter experience can be enjoyed by taking the boat trip from Llangollen.

Parys Mountain, Anglesey

Free; Open access; Parking on the B5111 between Amlwch and Rhosybol

Once this was a green hill, much like other green hills on the island. Then, late in the eighteenth century, it was found to be exceptionally rich in copper ore. Soon there were over 1500 men at work, digging tunnels and shafts, opening quarries, digging away until all the ore had gone and half the mountain with it. Thousands of tons were removed every year, and now all that is left is this weird, lunar landscape, rocky and barren with yawning chasms, overhung by bare rock. A path leads to the summit, past the engine house where steam power was used to pump water from the workings and on to the tower of what was once a five-sailed windmill, also used for pumping. At the foot of the hill are precipitation tanks, still stained in brilliant colours by the ore. No one could call this ravished landscape pretty but it is hugely impressive. The ore was shipped from the nearby port of Amlwch, which is also worth a visit.

One of the extraordinary double-ended Ffestiniog locomotives, *Lloyd George*, leaving Porthmadog. This is a modern version, built in 1992.

PORTHMADOG

The port itself is of considerable interest. At the beginning of the nineteenth century the area at the mouth of the River Glaslyn was a swamp. It was William Madocks, an English Member of Parliament, who suggested building an embankment across the river. This could act both as a causeway and as a sea wall, behind which the land could be drained. The bank was duly built, becoming known as The Cob, and a harbour developed at the western end. It was originally called Port Madoc after the founder. The new town prospered as both a shipbuilding centre and as a port serving the developing slate mines and quarries at Blaenau Ffestiniog. But bringing slate down from the hills was no easy matter and thus a railway system was born, proving to be of immense historical significance.

Ffestiniog Railway

££££ return fare; February to December, but limited winter running; Harbour Station, LL49 9NF; Tel: 01766 512340; Website: www.festrail.co.uk

The Ffestiniog Railway was begun in 1832, as a line from Porthmadog to Blaenau Ffestiniog, but no one contemplated running steam locomotives on a line which, once it had been taken across The Cob, would have to climb up into the hills by means of steep inclines and sharp curves. So it was built to the same gauge as the quarry lines, a modest 59.7cm (23½in.). It mostly relied on gravity to take the laden trucks downhill, and horses to haul them back. The horses enjoyed a luxury ride downhill, travelling aboard 'dandy carts'. There were experiments with steam in the 1860s, but they were not very successful until Robert Fairlie came along and designed his double-ended locomotives. These extraordinary machines look like two locomotives that have reversed into each other and stuck together. What you have is two boilers and engine units, each mounted on its own bogie with a cab in the middle. They provide the power for the steep slopes and the manoeuvrability for the tight curves. Now that the old working line has become a preserved steam line, the double Fairlies are the stars of the show – along with the superb mountain scenery. Restoration of the through line to Blaenau Ffestiniog had its problems. Before restoration was complete, part of the line had been submerged by the construction of a reservoir. Originally, the line had meandered on its way, gaining height slowly: now the engineers were faced with a steep slope, too steep even for this line. So they came up with a solution that had first been tried in an even more mountainous terrain, on the Darjeeling Railway in the Himalayas. They created a loop, spiralling upwards, much like the ramp of a multi-storey carpark. This is the route that pioneered all narrow gauge development, and double Fairlies served mineral lines as far away as New Zealand.

History and scenery combine to make this one of the great railway experiences. There is a second railway in Porthmadog, which is just at the start of what promises to be a very exciting development, with trains running through the heart of Snowdonia. At the moment passengers get a hint of grandeur to come.

Welsh Highland Railway

££ return fare; Easter to November; Tremadog Road; see above for contact details

TREFRIW

Trefriw Woollen Mills

Free; All year Monday to Friday; Tel: 01492 640462; Website: www.trefriw-woollen-mills.co.uk

The mill buildings are comparatively modern, but the first water-powered mill was established here in 1859 and, as at Brynkir, water still plays a vital role with electricity being generated by a pair of turbines installed in the 1940s. Everything here is very traditional, again similar to Brynkir, but on a larger scale and including washing and dyeing. This is a genuine fleece in, cloth out process.

The cloth emerging from the power loom at Trefriw woollen mill has been woven using traditional Welsh designs.

TYWYN
Talyllyn Railway

£££ return fare; Mid-February to November; Wharf Station, LL36 9EY; Tel: 01654 710472; Website: www.talyllyn.co.uk

This has been a favourite line since I first travelled on it many years ago. Repeated visits have done nothing to diminish my enthusiasm. Like the Ffestiniog, it was built to link slate quarries in the hills to a port, but this was intended to work with steam locomotives from the first, if not throughout its length. When quarrying stopped in 1946, the line with its two solitary locomotives seemed doomed. However, it was saved, largely due to the efforts of that great writer on industrial history L.T.C. Rolt. It was the first successful railway preservation scheme in Britain – and the two

original engines of 1865 and 1866 were rescued along with the line itself. The narrow gauge line begins gently, but as it climbs, so it clings ever more precariously to the rocky slopes of the mountain until it reaches Nant Gwernol. Even that was not the end of the railway, though steam trains always terminated here. Walk on up the hill and you can still see an incline with its winding drum, the tramway and the stables for the horses that worked it, until at last you emerge by the quarries of Bryn Eglwys. Where, you might wonder, does Talyllyn come in? Where indeed? It lies several miles further on, and the railway does not, and never did, go there. As well as the attractions of the journey, there is an excellent museum at Tywyn Station.

The 1878 locomotive *Sir Haydn* **at Nant Gwernol, preparing for the return trip to Tywyn on the Talyllyn Railway.**

See Also
Beaumaris, Anglesey
Beaumaris Gaol and Courthouse
££; Easter to September; Steeple Lane, LL58 8EW; Tel: 01248 810921
The old gaol still has its treadmill in position. Six prisoners at a time 'walked' the outside of the wheel, partly as a punishment and partly for the practical purpose of pumping water for the gaol.

Betws-y-coed
Waterloo Bridge
Open access
The bridge carries the Holyhead Road, now the A5, across the Conwy. Designed by Thomas Telford, it is an elaborate cast iron structure with an inscription covering the full width of the arch, announcing that it was built in the year that the Battle of Waterloo was fought.

Dinas Mawddwy
Meirion Mill
Free; March to December; Tel: 01650 531311
Weaving can sometimes be seen in this woollen mill, though the main emphasis is on the shop. However, it is worth a visit, as it occupies the old railway station, and there are railway relics, including the wrought iron Victorian entrance gates: very grand for a modest station.

Llanddeusant, Anglesey
Llynon Mill
Free; June to October Tuesday to Saturday plus Sunday afternoons, October to March Tuesday, Thursday and Saturday,
April to June Tuesday, Thursday and weekend afternoons; Tel: 01407 730797
The only working windmill in Wales, this tower mill was built for a local surgeon in 1775.

Melin Howell
Free; Easter to September Monday to Friday all day, weekend mornings; Tel: 01407 730240
A restored watermill with an impressive overshot wheel.

Glan Conwy
Felin Isaf mill
£; Mid-March to Mid-November; Tel: 01492 580646
A fine pair of old watermills partly dating from the seventeenth century, together with an oat-drying kiln.

Llanuwchllyn
Bala Lake Railway
£££; April to September, daily in July and August, at other times check; Tel: 01678 540666
A narrow gauge railway in a wild, mountainous setting on the shores of the lake. It runs on the trackbed of the former Great Western line. There is a charming curiosity at Signal Halt: a director of the GWR lived on the far side of the lake, and when he wanted to catch a train he hoisted a flag, the train was stopped and he crossed in style in his steam launch. Sadly, modern passengers cannot enjoy that treat, but they can enjoy the scenery.

Stanley Embankment, Anglesey
Free; Open access
This immense earthwork was built under the direction of Thomas Telford to link Anglesey to Holyhead. The original tollhouse has been preserved, but moved to the Penrhos Coastal Park as a tea room.

SLATE

No industry has had a more dramatic impact on the landscape of Wales than slate. Others such as iron and coal may have created their own special surroundings, but often the buildings have crumbled, the spoil heaps grassed over. Yet slate remains, mountains of shattered waste that loom glumly over towns and villages on dark, sunless days but glisten and sparkle when sunshine follows rain. Slate has certainly been used as a building material since Roman times, but it was only in the latter part of the eighteenth century that it began to be worked on an industrial scale. The Penrhyn Quarry was developed from 1765 by Richard Pennant, and in fifty years it rose from a modest output of less than 2000 tons a year to over 70,000 tons a year. The quarry represents one form of slate winning, and here it is seen at its most spectacular. It rises up above Bethesda on the very edge of the Snowdonia National Park. The quarry itself consists of a series of ledges or galleries, one above the other, reaching up to a height of over 1500 feet, linked together by inclines. That is what one can see from the outside, but from these galleries tunnels were struck deep into the rock, accessed by shafts and drained by adits. A series of water balance hoists were in use, and a set has been preserved with the shaft headframe at the quarry. Originally the slate was removed by hand, but soon explosives came into regular use. A painting of 1832 shows a fantastic scene of rock faces and pinnacles, with crowds of men on all the galleries and working fly-like on the sheer rock faces.

Penrhyn was perhaps the biggest of all the Welsh quarries and it made a fortune for Pennant, who became Lord Penrhyn and built himself a sumptuous mock medieval castle near Bangor which, appropriately, features an immense slate bed, said to weigh a ton. The Castle is also home to an important collection of industrial locomotives.

Another quarry that could match Penrhyn for size was the Dorothea on the hillside above Nantlle. It began as a number of small pits which, over the years, merged to create ever-larger holes that were then subject to flooding. In 1899 a beam engine was ordered from the famous Cornish manufacturers Holman Brothers of Camborne. It nodded away, keeping the works open right through to 1956, and is now scheduled for preservation, a worthy survivor. At this quarry it is still possible to see the remains of the complex system of aerial ropeways that sent massive blocks of stone whistling over the heads of the workforce.

Mines played an equally important part in the industry, especially around Blaenau Ffestiniog. Mining enabled workers to get down to the best layers without having to remove immense quantities of unwanted rock. Once the good material had been

A traditional slate wagon in the yard at the Welsh Slate Museum at Llanberis. The 'cliff' behind the buildings on the right is actually the face of one of the quarries.

reached, it could then be taken out in bulk, creating huge caverns. The actual slate beds in the Ffestiniog area are up to 37m (120ft) thick, so the first stage in the operations was for miners to move in to begin driving levels, perhaps as little as 1.2m (4ft) high, which would then be widened out. After that, the 'rockmen' took over to start removing blocks of slate and sending them to the surface. The one disadvantage of mining was that a large amount of good slate had to be left behind as pillars supporting the roof of the caverns. The result, however, is that we

Nowhere can the effects of slate mining and quarrying be seen more clearly than here, in Blaenau Ffestiniog. The mountains have been sliced away in sheer faces and buried into through deep mines. But by far the greatest impact on the landscape is made by the vast quantities of waste slate rising above the houses.

are left today with an underground spectacular, which visitors can still see at the preserved old mines.

Once the slate was above ground it had to be dressed, i.e. cut into appropriate sizes. Slate can be split along natural fault lines and then be trimmed to the appropriate standard size, mainly for roofing. This was a highly skilled job, and the best men could produce slates no more than 0.16cm (1/16in.) thick. The processing of the slate usually took place in special slate mills, the grandest of which was the Cwmystradllyn factory, one of the grandest monuments to the slate industry of Wales. There are, however, untold numbers of other monuments, in the shape of slate roofs, slate buildings, slate gravestones and a tremendous range of artefacts from billiard tables to kitchen worktops that can still be seen all over Britain.

Where to see the remains of the slate industry

The principal museums are listed under Llanberis and Blaenau Ffestiniog.

Cwmystradllyn Slate Factory

The empty shell of this once great factory that served the nearby Gorseddau quarries can be found in a remote setting high in the hills above Porthmadog. It is reached by taking the minor road that leads into the hills from a turning near to the Brynkir Woollen Mill. The principal building has been rather fancifully called the cathedral of the Welsh slate industry. The main site, with its complex of watercourses, can be found at map ref. 124/550434.

Dorothea Quarry

The immense quarries can be seen near Nantlle on the B4418. The engine house for the Cornish engine is at map ref. 115/497532

Penrhyn Quarry

The quarries dominate the hillside to the south of Bethesda, offering a splendid view of terracing, inclines and hoists.

Penryhn Castle, Bangor

NT; £££ House and grounds, ££ Grounds and stable block; April to November; Tel: 01248 371337

The vast and ornate Norman-style castle, home to the Pennant family, houses the 1-ton slate bed made for Queen Victoria as a prize exhibit. A collection of early industrial locomotives, together with rolling stock from local slate quarries, is on display in the stable block.

SCOTTISH BORDERS AND LOWLANDS

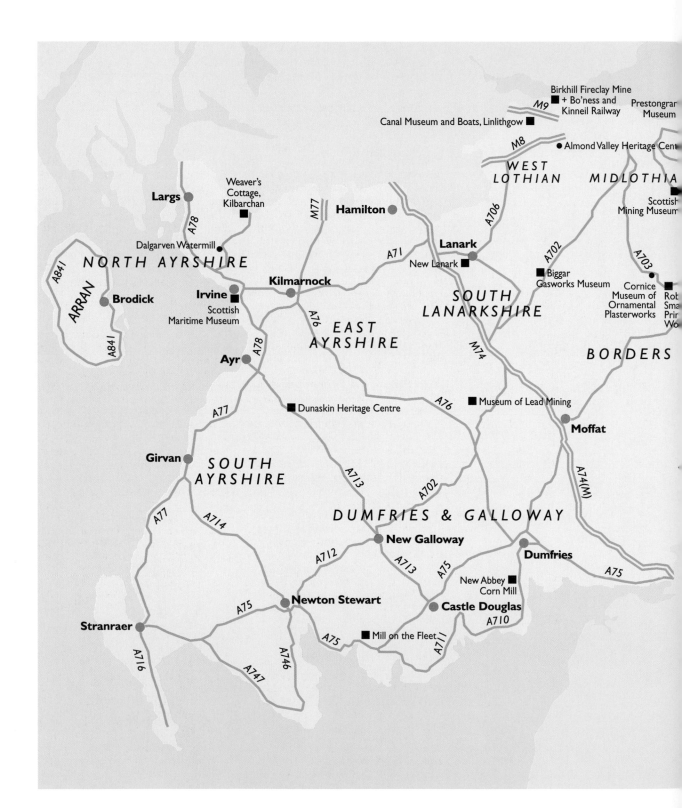

Birkhill Fireclay Mine
+ Bo'ness and
Kinneil Railway

Prestongrar
Museum

Canal Museum and Boats, Linlithgow

M9

M8

Almond Valley Heritage Cent

WEST
LOTHIAN

MIDLOTHIA

Scottish
Mining Museum

Largs

A78

A706

Weaver's
Cottage,
Kilbarchan

M77

Hamilton

Lanark

New Lanark

A702

A703

Dalgarven Watermill

NORTH AYRSHIRE

A71

SOUTH
LANARKSHIRE

Biggar
Gasworks Museum

Cornice
Museum of
Ornamental
Plasterworks

A841

ARRAN

A841

Brodick

Kilmarnock

Irvine

Scottish
Maritime Museum

A76

EAST
AYRSHIRE

Rob
Sma
Prir
Wo

BORDERS

A78

M74

Ayr

A77

Dunaskin Heritage Centre

A76

Museum of Lead Mining

Moffat

Girvan

SOUTH
AYRSHIRE

A713

A702

A74(M)

A77

A714

DUMFRIES & GALLOWAY

A712

New Galloway

A713

A75

Dumfries

A75

New Abbey
Corn Mill

Stranraer

A75

Newton Stewart

A75

Castle Douglas

A710

Mill on the Fleet

A711

A716

A747

A746

EAST LOTHIAN

Preston Mill

Haddington

A1

A1

Union Bridge

A6112

A68

A699

Galashiels

Lochcarron of
Scotland Woollen Mill

Kelso

Jedburgh

A68

Hawick

As in South Wales, this area has been subdivided into a multitude of small units, so all the following have been lumped together into one region, with apologies to those who might feel themselves slighted by a lack of respect for local identity: Dumfries and Galloway, East Ayrshire, East Lothian, East Renfrewshire, Midlothian, North Ayrshire, Renfrewshire, Scottish Borders, South Ayrshire, South Lanarkshire, West Lothian

Looking at a map of the area, it seems to consist of a great deal of empty space, and walking or driving through much of it does little to change that impression. Yet this has been a very busy region. The fleece from the hill sheep have given rise to a thriving woollen industry, and the growth of towns which, if they were not as brutally industrialised as some of those of Northern England, were still busy enough. Places such as Hawick and Galashiels grew rich as the mills multiplied. Even more importantly, a quite foreign material made an early appearance in the area: cotton from India and later from America. It began with the establishment of water-powered spinning mills in the eighteenth century, among them one that was to become so famous that both the mill and its village have now been declared a World Heritage site – New Lanark. To see where that story ended you should visit one of the great cotton towns, such as Paisley, where in giant mills such as Anchor Mills they made the cotton thread that filled countless work baskets. This is an area people always seem to rush through on their way to somewhere else, but it is one which well repays time spent on exploration.

BO'NESS

Birkhill Fireclay Mine

£ (Joint ticket with railway available); July and August Tuesday to Sunday, April to June plus September and October weekends; Bo'ness Station, Union Street, EH51 9AQ. Tel: 01506 822290, Website: www.srps.org.uk

Fireclay is, as its name suggests, a very heat-resistant form of clay, widely used for lining furnaces. It is often found, as

here, in close proximity to a coalfield. This is not a very deep mine, and visitors have to go down 130 steps to reach the workings – and, of course, climb the same 130 steps to get out again! Once down, expert guides provide the tour of the old workings. Access to the site is via the railway.

Bo'ness and Kinneil Railway

££ return fare; Opening hours as above; Contact details as above

This is more than just another steam railway, it is also home to a very impressive collection of steam locomotives, with a particularly good representation of industrial engines. The whole collection covers a range of almost a hundred years of development, from a North British saddle tank of 1887 to British Rail diesels. The rolling stock is equally important, with many items from the early years

A 1908 Caledonian Railway locomotive waits with its train at Bo'ness Station. The station itself and other buildings have come from many parts of Scotland.

BIGGAR
Biggar Gasworks Museum
HS; £; June to September afternoons; Tel: 01899 221050

This is one of those sites that should come complete with a huge asterisk to mark the entry, because there is a very real chance that readers will see the word 'gasworks' and move onto something less boring. After all, what can be interesting about a gasworks? Well, the answer is – a lot: in fact, this is a really good place to visit. For a start, you have to put yourself back mentally to the middle of the nineteenth century and imagine what it was like to live without gas – no street lights worth their name, no house lights except smoky lamps and candles, no cooking except the open fire or the kitchen range. Gas brought new benefits, and manufacturing it was of immense public benefit, not to mention a fascinating process. Small towns had to find the cash to build their own gasworks, or rely on enterprising businessmen. Biggar went down the latter route, and in 1839 the Biggar Gas Light Company was formed. It continued in business right up to nationalisation in 1949. They had one major modernisation in 1914, and what can be seen today is virtually the works as they were at that time.

Gas was made by heating coal in closed cast iron, later silica, containers known as retorts. These gave off the inflammable gases, but mixed in with tar, ammonia and sulphur compounds which all had to be removed through a series of washers, scrubbers and purifiers. Only then could the gas be sent on to fill the gas holders, in this case venerable structures of 1858 and 1879. Within their lacy iron framework, the holders expanded and contracted as gas was put in and taken out. What was left behind in the retorts was itself a valuable fuel: coke. Everything at Biggar is much as it was when manufacture stopped with the introduction of natural gas in 1973. Visitors cannot experience the heat, the flames, nor, indeed, the smell. But they can see what it was like in a video of the last working gas plant in Britain, on the island of Great Cumbrae. Having been lucky enough to see that plant just before it closed down, I can testify that Biggar is the next best thing to the real experience.

The retorts at Biggar gas works. They were installed in 1914 to replace the originals of 1839. There are nine retorts in all, which were heated for about six hours. All the firing was manual, so there was very little time for sitting around.

Preston meal mill. The grinding mill, with its breastshot wheel, is in the foreground, with the conical roof of the drying kiln behind it.

of Scottish railways. Add to this a well thought out exhibition on transport and it makes for a very satisfying visit. You can add to the day by taking a visit to tip your hat to one of the pioneers of steam. James Watt carried out many of his early experiments on the steam engine while staying in a cottage near to the home of his mentor, Dr John Roebuck. Roebuck lived in Bo'ness at Kinneil House, and a Watt steam cylinder has been preserved at the house.

EAST LINTON
Preston Mill

NTS; £; Mid-April to October Monday to Saturday and Sunday afternoon, October weekend afternoons; Tel: 01620 860426

This must be just about the most picturesque watermill in the whole of Britain. The appeal derives from contrasts: between the rich stone of the walls and the red pantiles of the roof, and between the conventional mill building itself and the drying kiln with its conical roof. The breast shot wheel is fed from a mill pond, now home to a large number of ducks and geese. Most of the present buildings date from the eighteenth century. Another important part of the rural economy in the past was the dovecote, or in Scotland, doocot. Doves were kept for food not display, and the nearby Phantassie Doocot is a short walk from the mill, where keys are available for viewing.

GALASHIELS
Lochcarron of Scotland Woollen Mill

Visitor Centre free, Guided tour £; June to September Monday to Saturday plus Sunday afternoon; Waverley Mill, Huddersfield Street, TD1 3BA; Tel: 01896 751100

Galashiels had become a major centre for manufacturing all kinds of woollens by the mid-nineteenth century when steam power took over from water. By then only one of sixteen mills still depended entirely on its water wheel. The history of the town and its mills is told in a largely pictorial exhibition at the visitor centre. The mill itself takes in yarn for weaving and finishing. There are tours of the working factory, which has an intriguing mixture of the old style power looms with their clattering shuttles and modern shuttleless looms.

GATEHOUSE OF FLEET
Mill on the Fleet

£; Late March to October; High Street; Tel: 01557 814099

With the rapid development of the cotton industry in the late eighteenth century, manufacturers began searching for likely sites for new mills. Scotland had one great advantage: labour was even cheaper here than it was in England. Birtwistle & Son built mills down by the river, and the scant remains of a three-storey mill can still be seen, together with the foundations of two others, all dating back to the 1780s. They employed 300 operatives with a weekly wage bill of just £50 – which averages out in modern terms at under 20p per person. Workers' houses were built in what was to become, inevitably, Birtwistle Street. Shortly afterwards, Thomas Scott & Co. arrived and built their mill, later converted into a sawmill making bobbins for the cotton industry. As a result, the building itself survived. It has two working water wheels, drawing water from a complex system of artificial watercourses known as lades. It now houses a permanent exhibition on the history of the town and temporary exhibitions.

INNERLEITHEN
Robert Smail's Printing Works

NTS; £; May to September Monday to Saturday plus Sunday afternoon, October all day Saturday plus Sunday afternoons; 7–9 High Street, EH44 6HA; Tel: 01896 830206

This wonderful curiosity is a Victorian printing works that originally had its machinery powered by water, but in a most unusual manner. The mill stream flows under the workshop and the wheel lowered into it when required. The restored machinery includes a number of remarkably ornate presses. Demonstrations of typesetting are regularly given, and visitors can try hand setting for themselves.

Robert Smail's printing works have been recreated much as they were a century ago, and old techniques, such as typesetting by hand, are still in use.

A handloom weaver at Kilbarchan seen at work using Kay's flying shuttle, worked by her right hand.

IRVINE

Scottish Maritime Museum

£; April to October; Harbourside, KA12 8QE; Tel: 01294 278283; Website: www.scottishmaritimemuseum.org

For many visitors the main attractions will be the vessels out on the water, including an old Clyde Puffer, bringing memories of Para Handy and the *Vital Spark*. Strictly speaking, maritime museums are not being described in this book, but this one is included because it has an important section on the shipbuilding industry. One of the great names in Scottish shipbuilding was Alexander Stephens of Linthouse, and the magnificent Engine Shop of 1872 has been dismantled and re-erected at Irvine. It is an outstanding example of Victorian industrial engineering, which when I visited was still being used as a store for the museum's collection. At the time of writing it is being arranged into displays. There was already enough there, however, to convince me that this was going to be a very exciting place indeed. A ship-worker's flat of 1914 has also been opened as part of the museum complex. There are two other branches of the Maritime Museum, at Braehead and Dumbarton, listed under Central Scotland.

KILBARCHAN

Weaver's Cottage, The Cross

NTS; £; April to September daily, October weekend afternoons; Tel: 01505 705588

The cottage was built in 1723 for a linen weaver in what was once a busy centre for handloom weaving – 800 looms were recorded at work here in the nineteenth century, some in cottages such as this, others in small workshops. The cottage has been restored and there are regular demonstrations of weaving on the hand loom.

NEW ABBEY

New Abbey Corn Mill

HS; £; Open all year, winter closed Thursday afternoons and Fridays and Sunday mornings; Tel: 01387 850260

The watermill was built around 1800 on the site of the former monastic grain mill. It has been restored to full working order and there are regular demonstrations for visitors. The remains of the Abbey, founded in 1273, and one of the most complete monastic churches to survive in Scotland, can be visited from the mill by paying a small extra charge for a joint ticket.

NEW LANARK

Visitor Centre

££; New Lanark; Open daily; Tel: 01555 661345; Website: www.newlanark.org

It is difficult to know where to start in describing what is to be seen here. For those who do not know the history of the site, it is best to look over the short essay on New Lanark and Robert Owen (p.156–7) to make it clear just why this place is so important historically. When I first came here it was simply a village where people lived. The main mill buildings were preserved in the sense that they were still standing and in use, but by a scrap dealer, and there were ominous signs of deterioration. All that has changed, thanks to the work of the New Lanark Conservation Trust. The houses were given improved interiors to make them more attractive for modern living and the most important buildings have either been incorporated into the museum area or have found new uses as hotel, shops and so on. As a result, the village is an odd mixture of theme park and living community. It has always been fascinating just to wander round New Lanark, and indeed it still is, but there are now exhibitions to see as well.

There have always been two interconnected aspects to the New Lanark story – the technological and the social history. The former is now represented by the installations in what was No.3 Mill. A water wheel turns

Water arrives along the launder at the right to fall onto the overshot wheel that provides the power for the New Abbey corn mill.

LINLITHGOW
Canal Museum and Boats

Museum free, Boat trips: £ 20-minute trip, £££ two and a half hour trip; Easter to September weekend afternoons; Canal Basin, Manse Road, EH49 6AJ; Tel: 01506 671215; Website: www.lucs.org.uk

The Edinburgh and Glasgow Union Canal was built at the very end of the canal age, with work starting in 1817. The museum is housed in the former stables and is the starting point for the exploration of this waterway by boat. It was built on the level all the way from Edinburgh to Falkirk, which involved a great deal of heavy engineering works. The longer boat trip takes visitors to see the mightiest of three imposing aqueducts. The Avon aqueduct is 244m (800ft) long, rises 24m (80ft) above the river and is carried on twelve arches. The shorter trip is taken on board a replica of a Victorian steamboat, but alas not powered by gently puffing steam but by modern diesel. It does, however, provide a most enjoyable introduction to the canal.

On most canals in Britain there has been little meaningful development since they were built, more repair and restoration than innovation. This canal is the exception. The eleven locks that linked it to the Forth and Clyde Canal to make the connection to Glasgow have long gone, but they have been replaced by an extraordinary contraption: the Millennium Wheel at Falkirk. Boats will go into one of two tanks, then the giant wheel will turn and deliver them to the next level. At the time of writing the wheel is almost ready for operation and a visitor centre will open at the site. It should be well worth a look. There is a certain continuity to this story: the Millennium Wheel is being constructed at the Butterley works in Derbyshire, founded in the eighteenth century by two great canal engineers, William Jessop and Benjamin Outram. They would have approved.

The canal centre is housed in the old stables, home to the horses that did the work on the canal before the arrival of motors. The replica steam launch can be seen behind the more traditional canal boat.

The aerial view of New Lanark clearly shows the river and the leat for the mill buildings, with the village housing on the right.

again and textile machinery is demonstrated, showing carding and mule spinning. On the social front there is a reconstruction of a worker's home of 1820 and of Robert Owen's own house. Education, the most important aspect of Owen's philosophy, has been remembered with a reconstruction of the old school room. The shop, forerunner of the co-operative movement, has also been given a period look. Modern display techniques have come into the centre. An audio visual show has an on-stage 'ghost' of Annie McLeod to tell her story of life in New Lanark, and The New Millennium Experience offers a ride into the future. A near perfect life is envisaged – much as Owen was convinced his ideas would lead to perfect societies. His experiment to put theory into practice in America ended in failure. As none of us will be here to check out the new prophecies, we can only hope they are right. Cynics might think that Utopia will be found where it is always to be found, somewhere round the next corner.

NEWTONGRANGE

Scottish Mining Museum

££; February to November daily; Lady Victoria Colliery, EH22 4QN; Tel: 0131 663 7519; Website: www.scottishminingmuseum.com

The museum is based on the Lady Victoria Colliery, first sunk in 1890–94. It used the latest technology of the age, surface buildings based on steel frames with brick cladding. The winding engine was also brand new – a horizontal duplex built in Kilmarnock, which needed a bank of seven boilers to keep it going. The pit was always very productive and constantly modernised until it finally closed in 1981. The present museum shows a day in the life of a nineteenth-century miner, and there is a recreation of a coal face showing mining methods. Newtongrange itself was very much a company town, with company-built houses and amenities.

PRESTONPANS

Prestongrange Museum, Morison's Haven

Free; April to October; Off the B1348 Prestonpans to Musselburgh road; Tel: 0131 653 2904; Website: www.eastlothian.gov.uk/museums/

The museum is based on a former colliery, developed on the site where Cistercian monks opened the first

recorded British coal mine in the twelfth century. The presence of coal led to the development of a wide range of other industries needing fuel for their furnaces. The list is extensive: potteries, brickworks, soap making, glass, chemicals, breweries, salt and drainage pipes. Each gets its place in the museum, which covers every aspect of the industrial life of the area. Some of the remains are extensive, such as the Hoffman kilns for brick making, but it is the colliery that dominates the scene. This is certainly the place for steam enthusiasts. Here is a massive beam engine, built by the famous Cornish firm Harvey of Hayle. It was supplied in 1874 and later enlarged. This is a real monster, with its steam cylinder of 178cm (70in.) diameter. It needed to be big since it was required to raise a pump rod weighing 100 tons at a rate of about three times a minute. Steam and diesel locomotives are given occasional outings on the old colliery rail system. The museum is not just about the past, it has an exhibition on space as well.

WANLOCKHEAD

Museum of Lead Mining

££; April to October daily; Tel: 01659 74387

This is not just a museum to visit and go away again; to really appreciate this site you have to spend a bit of time and expend a bit of energy in

The water bucket pump in its wild setting among the lead mines that spread across the moors around Wanlockhead.

walking around. In many ways, the best method to approach the area is to come, as I did on my last visit, on foot across the Lowther Hills. Then you get a real sense of what a lonely spot this is and what it must have been like when miners first arrived and established what was to become Scotland's highest village. The remains of mines, the transport system that served them and the surface buildings that surrounded the mines themselves are spread out along the valley. In among them is one unique survivor, the water bucket pump, restored and now preserved by Historic Scotland. This was a beam pump, with the bucket at one end and pump rods at the other. When the bucket filled with water, it pulled the beam down and raised the rods. Then at the bottom of the stroke a valve was opened, the bucket emptied and rose again ready for the cycle to restart. The museum has a wide range of artefacts and offers a guided tour of a drift mine that was opened up in the eighteenth century. Two of the old cottages have been restored, one in the style of 1740, the other of 1890. There are traces of precious metals among the lead, and visitors have the opportunity to pan for gold – and take home their finds.

Along the road is Leadhills, which for a time was linked to Wanlockhead by Britain's highest conventional railway and one of the shortest lived: opened in 1902, it was closed in 1938. Now part of the track bed is occupied by the Lowther Railway, open at weekends from May to September. The one other site not to be missed is the Miners Library at Leadhills. This subscription library was founded as long ago as 1741. Given the low wages of the miners, it shows just how strong the thirst for knowledge was. This is almost certainly the first library in the world to be organised by a working-class community.

WATERSIDE

Dunaskin Heritage Centre

££; April to October daily; Dalmellington Road, Patna, KA6 7JF; Tel: 01292 531144; Website: www.dunaskin.org.uk

The Doon valley is a peaceful and beautiful area now but was once busy with collieries and iron works. The Dalmellington Iron Company arrived in 1848 and soon developed into a major concern, employing 1400 people and eight furnaces. Although the furnaces have gone, the blowing engine house that held the steam engine used to provide blast for the furnaces survives. It was built in a rather elaborate Italianate style and now houses the visitor centre with displays on the industrial history of the area and an audio-visual show. Despite the iron works having closed in 1921, most of the surface remains that can be seen today, including the two soaring chimneys, date from the next phase when the site became a brickworks, continuing up to 1976. The open-air site encompasses Chapel Row cottage and a reconstruction of a coal mine. The museum also works with the Ayrshire Railway Preservation Group who have their collection of industrial locomotives at Minnivey on the outskirts of Dalmellington. They run trains

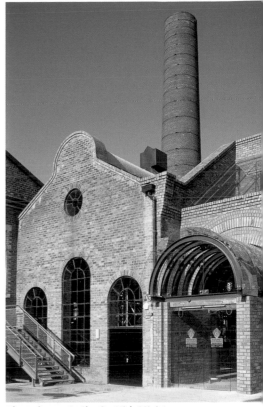

The entrance to the Scottish Mining Museum looks surprisingly modern, yet the buildings are part of the original development of the 1890s.

on part of the old iron company rail network. The railway and the heritage centre offer a joint ticket arrangement. The rail centre, however, has more limited opening hours – the first and last Sunday in May, the last Sunday in June, all Sundays in July and August, and the first Sunday in September.

See Also

Dalgarven Watermill, Kilwinning
£; Open daily; Tel: 01294 552448
A three-storey grain mill with a breast shot wheel, originally built in 1640 but rebuilt after a fire in 1880. The granary houses a museum of Ayrshire country life.

Almond Valley Heritage Centre, Livingston
£; Open daily; Tel: 01506 414957
The main centre of interest is the working farm, but the site also includes the Livingston watermill of 1790 and a shale mine.

Cornice Museum of Ornamental Plasterwork, Innerleithen Road, Peebles
Donation; All year weekdays; Tel: 01721 720212
Probably more craft than industry, but irresistible: a plasterer's casting workshop of *c.*1900 with ornate examples on display.

Union Bridge
Free; Open access
Crossing the Tweed between Paxton in Scotland and Loanend in England, it is Britain's oldest suspension bridge. It was the work of Captain Samuel Brown, who began his working life making anchor chains for the Royal Navy and then invented a patent wrought iron link for suspension bridges. It was completed in 1820.

NEW LANARK AND ROBERT OWEN

The story begins in Derbyshire where Richard Arkwright had established his new machinery in the mill at Cromford (see p.78). Armed with the protection of a patent, he was now anxious to enter agreements with other industrialists to open up more mills. One of these new partners was a Glasgow merchant, David Dale. The site he chose was by a famous beauty spot on the Clyde: the Corra Linn falls. Water power was in plenty here, and he set about building his mills. Now he had to recruit a work force and they needed somewhere to live. He built the village of New Lanark, much of it in the form of tenement blocks. Some such as those of Rosedale Street were built up against the hillside, so that they were four storeys at the front and two at the back. The name 'tenement' has come to suggest poor quality housing, but the tenements of New Lanark were fine structures with solid walls of granite. Even if nothing more had been done, it would still be an outstanding example of an early textile village. But things began to change in 1798 when a young Welshman, Robert Owen, was brought in as mill manager.

Dale had a reputation of being a good employer, which he undoubtedly was compared with other mill owners at the time. Yet he still relied heavily on children. He did not like the idea of the very young being set to work, but the good saintly men of the Charities insisted on sending children as young as six for the mill. They had good accommodation, decent food, medical care and a rudimentary education – but they still had to face a thirteen-hour working day. Robert Owen was to change all that. First he had to tackle the social conditions. He arrived to find a community blighted by crime and drunkenness. He turned away from the path taken by others. He did not punish the wrongdoers but set out to change the conditions in which the evils flourished. He began by insisting on cleanliness, not just in the streets but in the homes as well – and regularly made personal inspections of the workers' houses. He shut down the

A view of New Lanark c.1818 by John Winning. It is interesting to see how very little has changed since that time. The surrounding countryside, however, is given a rather romantic treatment, but it is easy to see why the Falls of Clyde were a popular tourist attraction.

Dancing demonstrations by the children were regularly laid on for New Lanark visitors at the Institution. The building was also used as a school, and the pictures of exotic animals on the wall give it quite a lively air. The painting is by G. Hunt, c.1828.

pubs and opened up the New Institution, where children and adults could all come to learn. He stopped the exploitation of the population by unscrupulous traders by opening up a shop where prices were fair and all profits were to be used for the good of the community as a whole. It was to be the inspiration for the nineteenth-century Co-operative movement.

The first striking change he introduced was a decision that no child should go to the mill until the age of ten. The youngest were to be sent to what we would now call a playgroup, and the five-year-olds would receive a good, general education. The children and the adults were also encouraged to take up pursuits such as dancing, though contemporary descriptions make it sound a rather joyless affair. The lives of the children were transformed. The poet Robert Southey came on a visit in 1819, and if he was not impressed by the formal concert put on for him, he was delighted by the infants who 'made a glorious noise'. He described how they 'crowded about Owen to make their bows and their little curtsies, looking up and smiling in his face; and the genuine benignity and pleasure with which he noticed them'. There were equally dramatic changes in the working of the mill. The accepted philosophy of the day was that a mill

would only be profitable if wages were kept low and hours long. Owen argued that if the work force were decently treated, they would respond by taking pride in their work. There was no point in working people to the point of exhaustion, for the quality would inevitably suffer. A well-motivated operative working civilised hours would, he claimed, actually produce more than the miserable wretch close to exhaustion. He proved his case in practice, but when the Peel Committee met in Parliament in 1816 to investigate mill working, they simply found his arguments literally incredible, and claimed he must have speeded up the machines not the workers. Owen was eventually to marry Dale's daughter and take over complete control of New Lanark. When he arrived at the mill, he set in motion one of the greatest social experiments of the age. However, when he left to try and establish a whole new community based on the principles of co-operation in America, establishing a town he called New Harmony, he was less successful. The experiment failed. But at New Lanark he showed the world that there were other ways of producing prosperity that did not include vicious exploitation; he even showed that profit and benevolence were not mutually exclusive. The tragedy of the nineteenth century was that so few learned the lessons.

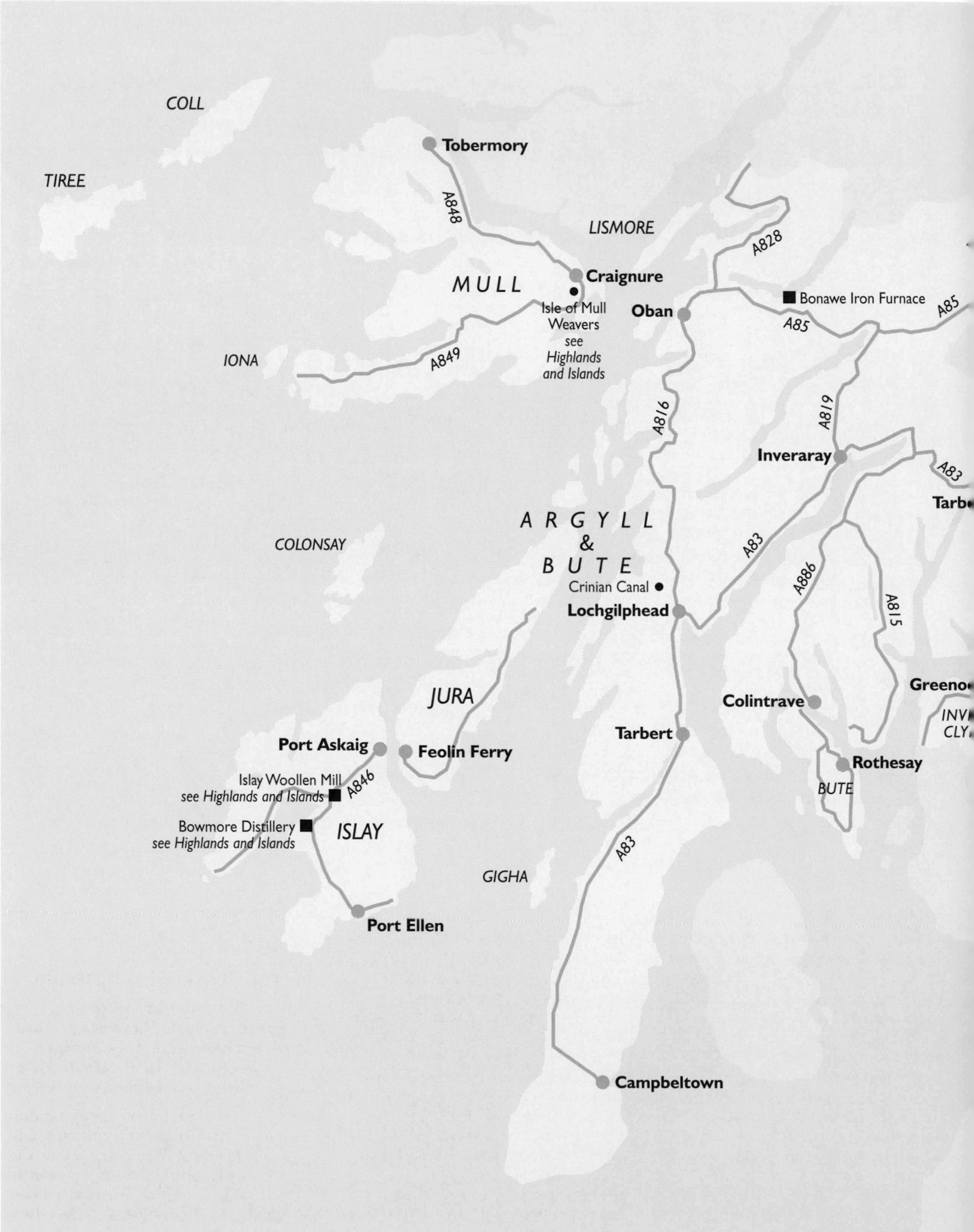

COLL

TIREE

Tobermory

A848

LISMORE

A828

MULL

Craignure

Isle of Mull
Weavers
see
*Highlands
and Islands*

Bonawe Iron Furnace

Oban

A85

A85

IONA

A849

A816

Inveraray

A819

COLONSAY

ARGYLL
&
BUTE

A83

Tarb

A83

Crinian Canal

Lochgilphead

A886

A815

JURA

Greenoc

Port Askaig

Feolin Ferry

Colintrave

INV
CLY

Islay Woollen Mill
see Highlands and Islands

A846

Tarbert

Rothesay

Bowmore Distillery
see Highlands and Islands

ISLAY

BUTE

Port Ellen

GIGHA

A83

Campbeltown

CENTRAL SCOTLAND

The following counties have been grouped together: Argyll and Bute, Clackmannanshire, East and West Dunbartonshire, Edinburgh, Falkirk, Fife, Glasgow, Inverclyde, North Lanarkshire

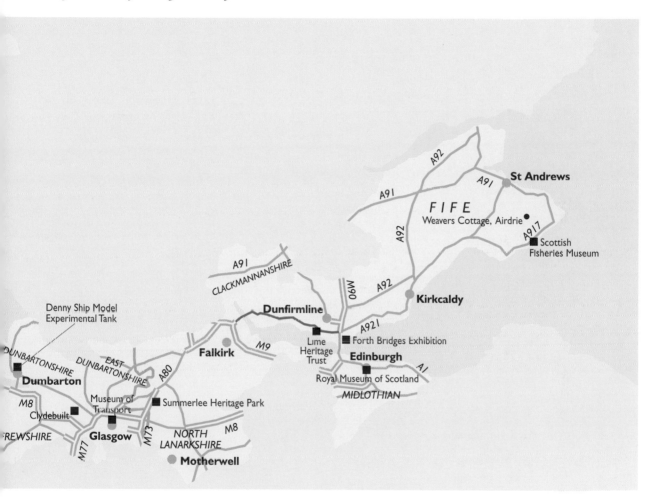

This is the region where industry flourished, encouraged by a wealth of natural resources, but it is also the most densely populated area of the country. The two great cities of Glasgow and Edinburgh have grown over the centuries and the space between them has gradually filled in as town merges with town. In the process much of the old has been lost. But recent years have seen a new enthusiasm for regaining the past, as the importance of this area to the whole development of the Industrial Revolution has been recognised. It was in Glasgow that James Watt made his crucial experiments that led to the development of an efficient steam engine. It was here that Britain's first paddle steamers made their tentative forays onto lochs and rivers, with Robert Burns himself as one of the first passengers when he took a trip on William Symington's experimental boat on Dalswinton Lake in 1788. Coal and steam are the keys to much of what we can see, whether it is the shipyards of the Clyde or the great engineering and iron works.

ANSTRUTHER

Scottish Fisheries Museum

££; April to September weekdays and Sundays, October to March weekdays and Sunday afternoons; St Ayles, Harbour Head, KY10 3AB; Tel: 01333 310628; Website: www.scottish-fisheries-museum.org

Fishing has always been a major industry in Scotland, and this museum tells the whole story. The main emphasis is, quite rightly, on the vessels that put to sea, and one of the museum's finest exhibits is undoubtedly the two-masted sailing drifter *Reaper*. She can

Reaper, **a traditional fishing boat of the type known as a fifie, moored up in Anstruther harbour.**

generally be seen down in the harbour or, better still, setting sail and going to sea. She is just one of a number of craft in the care of the museum. The buildings of the museum are grouped round a courtyard and are a varied selection, ranging from an eighteenth-century merchant's house to a nineteenth-century boat-building yard. The site, however, has a much longer association with fishing. In 1318 the Laird of Anstruther gave a parcel of land to the Abbey of Balmerino, and along with it went the rights for fishermen to lease booths and dry their nets. The exhibits tell a logical story, starting with the fish themselves and ending with their processing. It is a human story as much as one of developing technology. There are displays, for example, about the extraordinary lives of the herring lasses who followed the fleets and the fishermen as they in turn followed the migrating shoals around the coast of Scotland and down into England. The museum is a delight and anyone visiting it should take the opportunity to explore the fishing villages along this most beautiful coast, with their simple but effective harbours.

BONAWE

Bonawe Iron Furnace

HS; £; April to September Monday to Saturday plus Sunday afternoon; Off the A85 road to Lochawe;
Tel: 01866 822432

This is a remarkable survivor from the early years of the British iron industry. It is remarkable in that it has remained in such very good condition and, at first glance, equally extraordinary that it was ever built here at all. The iron ore was not found locally but shipped round the coast from Lancashire and Cumberland. It was begun by Richard Ford, who already had iron works at Furness, setting up here in the 1750s because there was land available for coppiced woodland from which charcoal could be made. It was charcoal rather than coke that fired this furnace. It was also cheaper to bring the ore to the furnace – you can see why this was the case at the site, where the charcoal sheds are very much larger than the ore sheds. The great stone furnace has a cast iron lintel over the tuyere arch with the initial 'F' for Ford and the date 1753, though the name of the place is given as 'Bunaw'. The structure itself is built against a bank, and material could be wheeled on the level from the stores to the charging house, then across a bridge to be tipped into the top of the furnace. Blast was provided by a water wheel driving giant bellows connected to the furnace through the tuyere arch. Ford had to build houses for the workforce, also constructing a school, a store, a church and a jetty. The furnace remained in use right up to 1874, simply because it produced iron of exceptionally high quality.

CHARLESTOWN

Lime Heritage Trust, Rocks Road

£; March to November Tuesday to Thursday plus Friday morning;
Tel: 01383 872722;
Website: www.CharlestownWorkshops.org

The Trust occupies restored workshops, part of the Earl of Elgin's Broomhall estate. This is particularly appropriate, since the development of the town was the work of the family: it was the 5th Earl who paid for the building of a harbour for the shipment of lime and limestone in the 1750s. This is now the inner basin, for the trade extended greatly over the years. Far and away the most imposing features in the landscape are the lime kilns themselves, fourteen of them in all, built shortly after work on the harbour was completed. Charles, Earl of Elgin then went on to build a model

The massive stone structure of the charcoal blast furnace, built in 1753, at the former Bonawe Iron Works.

The imposing row of lime kilns at Charlestown: since the photograph was taken, two of the kilns have been restored.

village for the work force, named Charlestown. Then, just in case anyone failed to make the connection, he arranged for the houses to be laid out so that they formed the initial CE. The Trust has a double function: it organises workshops on all aspects of the use of lime and limestone, and houses an exhibition that explains the historic importance of the local industry. There are guided tours on Sunday afternoons and Wednesday evenings in the summer.

COATBRIDGE

Summerlee Heritage Park, Heritage Way

Free; Open daily; Tel: 01236 431261

The park is based on the site of the former Summerlee iron works, served by a branch of the Monkland Canal, which runs through the middle of the complex. Although the exhibition hall was originally a crane shed, it now houses machinery and an immense model of the ironworks as it was a century ago – which is a great help in making sense of the excavated remains outside. Coal mining is represented by a recreated adit and a row of miners' cottages showing living conditions in 1860 and a century later. An electric tramway also runs through the site, with trams from Belgium and Germany, as well as Scottish trams. There is a small charge for tram rides.

DUMBARTON

Denny Ship Model Experimental Tank, Castle Street

£; All year Monday to Saturday; Tel: 01389 763444; Website: www.scottishmaritimemuseum.org

It probably seems obvious to us now that it is sensible to test the design of a ship's hull by using a small model before building the real thing, but this was something of an innovation even in the middle of the nineteenth century. Despite attempts to do tests in the previous century, the real breakthrough came with a series of scientific experiments carried out by the engineer William Froude in a purpose-built tank, paid for by the Admiralty. He showed that using a model and scaling down waves could produce an accurate reflection of how a real ship would perform on a real sea. William Denny, a shipbuilder on the Clyde, realised the importance of Froude's work and at once set about building a testing tank of his own in 1881. This is it, very much as it was when it was new. The tank itself is the length of a football pitch, and all kinds of wave conditions can be simulated. The models are made out of wax: these have the great advantage that they can be easily adjusted – a little added here, a touch shaved off there. One of the great delights of the place is the original machine for making the models. The model maker starts with the naval architect's drawings, and then traces round the contours. A mechanical linkage then translates this movement to cutters that shape the wax. It is beautiful, ingenious and it still works. So, too, does the tank, which although it is now run as part of the Scottish Maritime Museum, continues to be used for testing.

The Denny ship model experimental tank. Waves of different sizes can be created in the trough, and a number of model hulls can be seen.

GLASGOW

Museum of Transport, Kelvin Hall

Free; Open daily; 1 Bunhouse Road, G3 8DP; Tel: 0141 287 2720

Britain is fortunate in having a number of excellent transport museums of one sort or another, but none which covers as wide a range as this. There are exhibits that you will find elsewhere – horse-drawn vehicles, trams, buses, locomotives – and some that you certainly will not. Glasgow had its own underground railway system as early as 1896, when trains were pulled along by cables powered by mighty steam engines. It now runs more conventionally by electricity, but a section of the old subway system has been recreated in the museum, along with a reconstructed street scene from Kelvin Street. Even such familiar vehicles as motor cars have a different look, for there is a whole section devoted to cars made in Scotland. Powered vehicles, however, date back beyond the internal combustion engine. Here is one of Goldsworthy Gurney's steam drags, which was supposed to inaugurate a passenger service between Glasgow and Edinburgh in 1831, pulling a sixteen-seat trailer. It was not a success: supposed to dash along at a brisk 16km (10 miles) an hour, it ended up taking

three days for the journey. Although there is a huge amount to see, paradoxically perhaps the most exciting exhibits of all are models – not just any models but the ship models specially made at the yards for customers. Here you can see the vessels from the age of sail to the might of Cunard liners that carried the proud name of the Clyde around the world.

After visiting the museum, it is worth heading down to the city centre to see one of the original subway stations. St Enoch's was built like a miniature Scottish castle and now houses a travel centre. It is rather splendidly quirky, but it is not the quirkiest industrial building in Glasgow. Out on Glasgow Green is the former Templeton Carpet Factory, built as the Victorians imagined a Venetian palace should look. It is a riot of turrets and pinnacles, all decked out in polychrome brick and tile. It is no longer working but has happily been put to new uses without destroying its unique façade. Just across the Green is the People's Palace, a museum telling the everyday stories of Glasgow life, including the city's industrial life.

A section of the railway exhibits. In among the steam locomotives dating back to 1886, in a station setting, is a very special coach. This was built by the LMS in 1941 as a luxurious saloon car for King George VI. The flush doors are an unusual feature.

GLASGOW

Clydebuilt, Braehead

££; Open daily; Kings Inch Road,
G51 4BN; Tel: 0141 886 1013;
Website: www.scottishmaritimemuseum.org

This is a very new museum, designed to tell the story of the whole range of Clydeside industries – shipbuilding, textiles, iron and steel – and show how they relate to Glasgow and the river. It uses modern display techniques, all very interactive, showing everything from how to operate a triple expansion engine to how to rivet a ship's hull. The biggest display item is out on the water, the coastal steamer *Kyles*, built on the Clyde at Paisley in 1872.

NORTH QUEENSFERRY

Forth Bridges Exhibition

Free; Open daily; Queensferry Lodge Hotel,
Inverkeithing; Tel: 01383 410000

This offers an exhibition telling the history of the Forth bridges – and also provides an ideal viewpoint from which to see them. The first and most spectacular of the crossings is the famous rail bridge, built to a revolutionary design as the result of an accident. The accident did not happen here but further north, when the Tay railway viaduct collapsed in 1879 just

One of the most famous railway bridges in the world, crossing the Firth of Forth at Queensferry.

a year after its opening. The old plans were thrown out and the whole design was rethought to ensure nothing would go wrong here. The designers were Sir John Fowler and Benjamin Baker, and it is usually referred to as a cantilever bridge, though Baker always called it a 'continuous girder' bridge. In effect, it consists of three diamond-shaped trussies, linked by girders. Whatever name is used, it is one of the great pieces of Victorian engineering, and is as much admired today as it was when it first opened in 1890. It has to be said that the road builders of the twentieth century did a very good job as well.

See Also

Weavers Cottage, Wellwynd, Airdrie
Free; Monday to Tuesday, Thursday to
Saturday; Tel: 01236 747712
As the name suggests, this is a cottage refurbished much as it was around 1830, with occasional demonstrations of handloom weaving.

Crinan Canal
Free; Open access
This beautiful little canal was begun in 1793 to cut through the narrow neck of land between Lochgilphead and Crinan. It is only 14.5km (9 miles) long but it saves a 210km (130-mile) sea passage round the Mull of Kintyre. There are attractive harbours at either end, and the rocky hump of land in between was overcome by building thirteen locks to take vessels 27m (88ft) long by 6m (20ft) beam. It is a pleasure to explore and is still in regular use, though now mostly by pleasure boats instead of fishing boats.

SHIPS AND THE CLYDE

Probably no one will ever know when the very first ship was built on the Clyde, but we do know when the industry began to grow and, just as importantly, we know why. The first important factor is the river itself. The Clyde at Glasgow would never have been thought of as a shipbuilding centre in earlier times. When the old wooden bridge was replaced around 1350 by one of stone, the builders tried to charge users for the privilege of crossing it. However, many preferred to wade across and save their cash. Various attempts were made to widen and deepen the channel, and there was a new sense of urgency in the eighteenth century, when Glasgow began to develop as a port, with a particularly strong trade in tobacco. Unable to get their ships up river, the merchants developed new

facilities at Greenock and Port Glasgow. The demand still existed for improving navigation, and this was achieved by engineers narrowing the channel artificially. This increased the rate of flow in the river, scouring away the sandbanks and shoals to create a new deep channel. By the early nineteenth century much of the river was more like a canal than a natural waterway and became known as the Clyde Navigation. New quays were built in the heart of the city, which still survive today. Further connections were made inland with the building of the Forth and Clyde Canal, begun in 1768 under the direction of the engineer John Smeaton. You can still gauge its importance by visiting the basins at Bowling, with a custom house and moorings for seagoing ships. When the railway

One of the greatest ships ever built on the Clyde, the *Queen Mary*, seen in the early stages of construction at the John Brown shipyard.

arrived it had to build a swing bridge across the canal so as not to disrupt navigation. Even grander are the former company offices at Port Dundas, looking like some well-to-do gentleman's mansion. Further work on dredging was continued through the years, opening up the river to even larger craft. This also meant that big ships could now be built beside the Clyde.

The Forth and Clyde Canal was the scene of one of Britain's first attempts to use steam power to move a vessel over water when the tug *Charlotte Dundas* was put through its paces in 1812. The vessel was considered to have caused too much damage to the canal banks to be put into service. It was left to a young man, David Napier, whose father had an iron works at Dumbarton, to build an engine for *Comet*, a vessel that was rapidly to go into service on the Clyde. Napier was soon established as the leading manufacturer of marine steam engines. This was the vital change, for Scotland already had a tradition for engineering, and once the move was made from wooden hulls to iron, everything slotted into place. The area was rich in the necessary raw materials and had the expertise, and so began the tradition of building iron steam ships. The shipyards of the Clyde include some of the greatest names in British maritime history: Napier, Fairfield, Elder, Barclay and, most famous of all, John Brown. But it was not all iron and steam along the Clyde. Two of the best known ships ever to be built along the river could scarcely be more

In the early years of the 20th century, ships were assembled out of riveted plates. In this scene, photographed in 1919, rivet-heating fires are burning on the keelson.

different. In 1869 the Scott and Linton yard at Dumbarton built a handsome sailing ship, a clipper intended to break speed records on the oceans of the world, which she duly proceeded to do. She was the *Cutty Sark*. In 1934 John Brown launched ship No.534, given the name *Queen Mary*.

Any journey down the Clyde will reveal the traces of the old yards, but most are silent. In the working days it was an extraordinary sight. At modern yards such as Govan, ships are built in sections inside immense sheds. Up to quite recently even the grandest ships were constructed out in the open, not prefabricated but built up plate by iron plate to the accompaniment of the incessant racket of the riveters. Just as the yards have closed one by one, so, too, have the docks; Queen's Dock and the even bigger Prince's Dock have been abandoned, often filled in, leaving only a fraction of what was once there. Visiting them today is a rather forlorn experience. There are also traces of the famous yards and their slipways, but to understand the significance of the engineering work that went in to building everything from battleships to ocean liners you have to visit museums like the Scottish Maritime Museum. There is, however, still one way to get at least an idea of the immense extent of the Clyde yards, and that is to take one of the trip boats from the heart of Glasgow along the river, or as generations of Scots would have it, 'doon th' water'.

HIGHLANDS AND ISLANDS

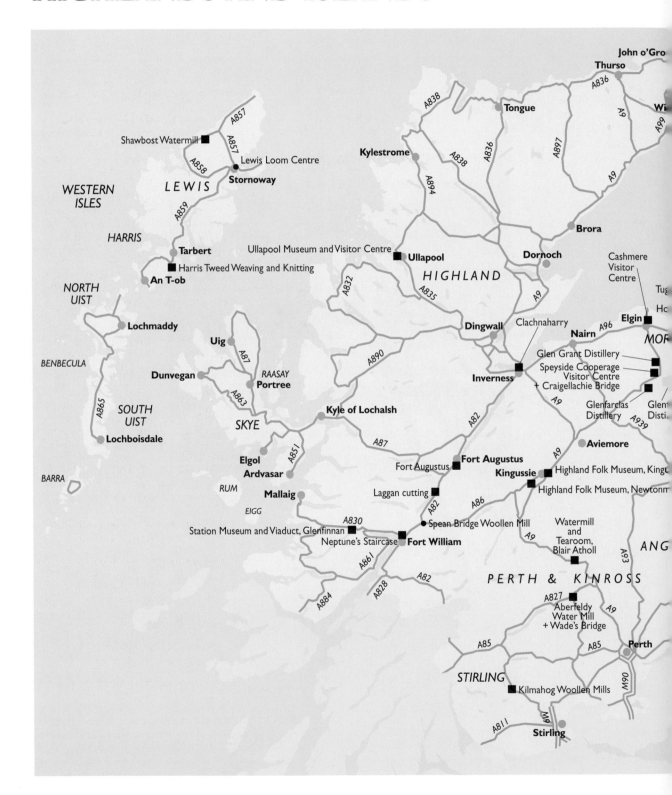

John o'Gro[...]
Thurso
A836
A9
Wi[...]
A99
A838
Tongue
A838
A836
A897
Kylestrome
A894
A9
Shawbost Watermill
A857
A857
A858
Brora
Lewis Loom Centre
WESTERN ISLES
LEWIS
Stornoway
Dornoch
Cashmere Visitor Centre
Ullapool Museum and Visitor Centre
Ullapool
HIGHLAND
A9
Tu[...]
Ho[...]
A859
HARRIS
Tarbert
A832
A835
Elgin
Harris Tweed Weaving and Knitting
An T-ob
Clachnaharry
Nairn
A96
MOR[...]
NORTH UIST
Dingwall
Glen Grant Distillery
Speyside Cooperage Visitor Centre
+ Craigellachie Bridge
Lochmaddy
Uig
A890
A87
BENBECULA
RAASAY
Dunvegan
Portree
Inverness
Glenfarclas Distillery
Glen[...]
Disti[...]
A865
A863
A939
SOUTH UIST
SKYE
Kyle of Lochalsh
A82
A9
Aviemore
Lochboisdale
A87
Highland Folk Museum, Kingu[...]
BARRA
Elgol
A851
Fort Augustus
Fort Augustus
Kingussie
Ardvasar
Laggan cutting
Highland Folk Museum, Newtonm[...]
RUM
Mallaig
A82
A86
A9
EIGG
Watermill and Tearoom, Blair Atholl
Spean Bridge Woollen Mill
Station Museum and Viaduct, Glenfinnan
A830
Neptune's Staircase
Fort William
A93
A861
ANG[...]
A828
A82
PERTH & KINROSS
A884
A827
Aberfeldy Water Mill + Wade's Bridge
A9
A85
A85
Perth
STIRLING
M90
Kilmahog Woollen Mills
A811
M9
Stirling

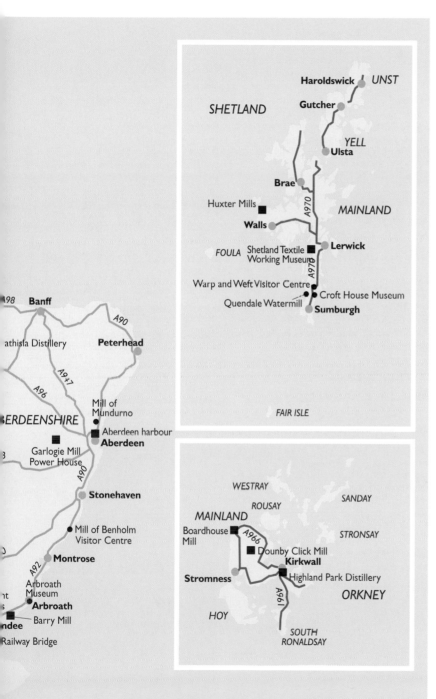

This section includes the following: Aberdeenshire, Angus, Dundee, Highland, Moray, Orkney, Perth and Kinross, Shetland, Stirling, Western Isles

Not many of the thousands who come each year to the Highlands of Scotland do so with the hope of finding some interesting industrial remains. The lure is the wild scenery and the freedom to roam the hills. But there is an interesting past to explore here as well, not least in the transport systems that developed in the eighteenth and nineteenth centuries. How many of the walkers who struggle up the Devil's Staircase on the steep walk out of Glencoe are aware that they are following the line of an old military road, part of a network created under General Wade? Inevitably in a largely rural area, such industries as existed were largely tied to the land: mills to process grain for flour and meal. Some of that grain went towards the area's most famous product, whisky. The old handcrafts of spinning, knitting and weaving still survive, especially on the islands, alongside the mechanised mills that were to supplant them. Even those who do not set out to explore these memories of an old working life may find that Highland weather can make them seem very attractive for a day's outing.

ABERFELDY
Aberfeldy Water Mill

£; April to October Monday to Saturday plus Sunday afternoons;
Tel: 01334 652514

Even before you step inside, you are aware that this is not an ordinary watermill. For a start, it is situated in the town and not near any obvious source of water. In fact, water comes from the Birks of Aberfeldy, over 0.4km (¼ mile) away, passing under the town to emerge at the mill before falling onto the overshot wheel. Where most mills are plain, this one is built in the gothic style with

The launder delivering the water to turn the overshot waterwheel for the mill in the centre of Aberfeldy.

pointed windows, a style that was very fashionable when the mill was built in 1825. The other striking feature is the pyramidal roof topped with a cowl that indicates that this is a meal mill, not a conventional grain mill on the English pattern.

This is a building in two parts. The first part is the kiln house. Here the oatmeal is loaded into the intake bin, then taken along horizontally by a screw feed, then vertically by a bucket elevator to the top of the 6m (20ft) high kiln. The dried oats are moved on again by a series of screws and elevators through dressing processes of sieving and shelling until they finally arrive at the grindstones. Altogether in its journey through the mill, the oats will have been passed along by four screw conveyors and five elevators, not to mention sack hoists. Not all of this can be seen in detail by visitors, but one can see enough of the complicated processing to show new respect to the morning porridge.

Wade's Bridge

Free; Open access

The bridge was built as part of the new system of military roads begun under General Wade in 1724, following the uprising of 1715. Most of the structures were plain and functional but this is a splendid exception. It was completed in 1733 with embellishments provided by the architect William Adam. Why so grand? Because it was also intended as a memorial to the general, who, according to two plaques, one in English and the other, not in Gaelic but in Latin, had built the finest roads in Britain since the time of the Romans,

BARRY

Barry Mill

NTS; ££; April to October daily, October weekends; Tel: 01241 856761

There has been a mill here since the sixteenth century but it was rebuilt in 1814 following a fire. It is an attractive building with an unusual circular kiln, topped by a conical roof. It continued in use up to 1982 and had now been restored, producing meal for animal food.

BLAIR ATHOLL

Watermill and Tearoom

£; April to October Monday to Saturday plus Sunday afternoons; Tel: 01796 481321

An opportunity here not only to see the production of stoneground oatmeal flour, but to discover how it is used in traditional Scottish recipes and to taste the result. Like many mills, this stands on a site that has been used for centuries, though the present buildings date from the 1830s. Two pairs of millstones are driven by a breastshot wheel. The gabled kiln is topped by a small ventilator.

DUNDEE

Tay Railway Bridge

Many people know the name who have never seen the bridge, since its collapse was recorded in excruciating verse by Scotland's worst poet, William McGonagall:

Beautiful Railway Bridge of the Silv'ry Tay!
Alas, I am very sorry to say
That ninety lives have been taken away
On the last Sabbath day of 1879,
Which will be remember'd for a very long time.

The replacement bridge by W.H. and Crawford Barlow was the longest railway bridge in the world when it was opened in 1887. Happily, it still stands, snaking away across the water for over 3km (2 miles).

ELGIN

Cashmere Visitor Centre, Newmill

Free; Open daily; Tel: 01343 554099

Alexander Johnston founded a woollen mill here in 1797. The oldest part of the mill complex has the elegant façade one would expect from that period, all well proportioned with tall windows on both floors and a central gable topped by a bell cote. Later additions include a boiler shop with its own roof tank, built in 1868, and weaving sheds of 1916. What makes this a particularly interesting site to visit is the fact that it is the one place that manufactures cashmere from fibre to garment. Originally cashmere was made exclusively from hair from Tibetan goats, but later the name came to be used for any material made from fine, very soft wool. All the processes are carried out here, from

Part of General Wade's military road system is now a footpath, on the West Highland Way climbing out of Glencoe.

The full range of machines, from carding the jute, through spinning to weaving and finishing is on display in the mill. It is difficult to believe that just a decade ago much of this mill was derelict, and it is good to see that so many of the original features have been preserved.

DUNDEE
Verdant Works

££; Open daily; West Henderson's Wynd, DD1 5BT; Tel: 01382 225282

Dundee's prosperity traditionally rested on the three Js – jam and journalism were two of them, the third was jute. The big mills still dominate large areas of the city, many now converted to homes or offices, but this one has been restored to present the history of an industry that once employed around 50,000 people in Dundee and sent its products all round the world.

The mill was built in 1833 to process and spin flax for linen manufacture. Jute was first brought over to Britain from India in 1791, but it proved difficult to spin by machinery and there was little interest. Then it was discovered that the brittle fibres could be softened by soaking them in oil and water. Dundee had a great deal of oil, as the port was used by whalers: whale oil proved ideal for the purpose. Gradually the linen industry declined and the jute industry grew. Verdant mill joined the trend and changed over to

manufacturing a range of jute products, from canvas to hessian. The new museum shows the different processes through which the raw material passes. The jute is first batched, sorted by colour and twisted into bundles. These are softened by machine and by soaking in the oil-water emulsion. Once that is complete, the remaining processes are not very different from those of any other textile manufacture, with carding, drawing, roving, spinning, weaving and finishing. The final processing is different, in that the cloth from the loom is calendered by being passed through heavy rollers to produce a smooth finish. The machinery is only a part of the story. The Verdant Works also has display areas looking at all parts of the social life of Dundee, from the mill girls to the 'jute barons' who created their own exclusive enclave a little way round the coast at Broughty Ferry.

TELFORD IN THE HIGHLANDS

Thomas Telford was born in Eskdale in the Scottish southern uplands. The son of a shepherd, he was apprenticed to a local stonemason. After gaining some experience, he headed down to London to further his career. He worked on such prestigious buildings as Somerset House, and his obvious intelligence and skill soon attracted the attention of men of influence. It was not long before he was giving up the practical work of a mason for the more important post of supervising the work of others. In 1786 he moved to Shropshire, where he was to become County Surveyor, a post which gave him the opportunity to design bridges, improve the local gaol and even try his hand at architecture with churches at Bridgnorth and Madeley. The great change in his fortunes came when he was appointed engineer to the Ellesmere Canal under the direction of William Jessop. Here his reputation as one of the outstanding engineers of the day was secured.

At the end of the eighteenth century the Highlands of Scotland had become a wretched region. The people had supported the Jacobite cause and paid the penalty for losing the war. It was clear to many that if the Highlands were to prosper, there needed to be radical changes. New types of work had to be found and the isolation of the region had to be ended. One of the first important tasks was to improve communications with the rest of Britain and throughout the region itself.

Among those who set out to do something practical was Sir John Sinclair, descendant of the Earls of Caithness and Orkney. His first idea was to develop the tiny settlement of Wick by building a harbour for fishing boats and establishing small industries round it. He called in Telford, and from that small beginning the engineer was introduced to the British Fisheries Society. This was to lead directly to a far more ambitious scheme.

Among the proposed projects for improving the Scottish fishing industry was a canal that would cut across the country from Fort William in the west to Inverness in the east. It would have the added advantage that it could be used by the navy to avoid the long and dangerous journey round the north coast. The government agreed to fund the scheme and Telford was appointed Chief Engineer for what was to become the Caledonian Canal. There was an additional benefit to be gained from the scheme, for it would also provide work for the locals who would be recruited to build it. Construction was authorised by Parliament in 1803 and work began. The canal follows an obvious route down the Great Glen. Much of the route makes use of natural lakes, Lochs Lochy, Oich, Ness and Dochfour, though some dredging was necessary to make them navigable by the ships that were to use the canal. It begins in the east at Corpach on the deep inlet of Loch Linnhe. Following that, it has to climb, first by a double lock,

Craigellachie bridge is of a satisfyingly crisp design, but Telford obviously decided it needed something extra to match the surroundings, so added castellated towers.

then by eight interconnected locks known as Neptune's Staircase, one of the most impressive engineering features on Britain's canals. There is another staircase of locks, five of them this time, at Fort Augustus, joining the canal to Loch Ness. The other major engineering features are not so immediately obvious. Between Lochs Lochy and Oich the ground rises very steeply, so Telford decided to go through it in a deep cutting. A small army of men was called in, replete with shovels and pickaxes to hack out the deep Laggan cutting. The work was begun in 1814 but not completed until 1821. The other great problem solved by Telford occurred at the western end. The Beauly Firth shelves very gently at the shoreline, far too gently to allow ships to approach. Consequently, if the ships could not reach the canal, the canal would have to go out to meet the ships. A great embankment was built out into the Firth and once it was consolidated, a channel was cut for the canal ending in a sea lock.

Long before the canal was finished, Telford was given a far more wide ranging brief. The government put in hand a scheme for building roads, bridges and harbours throughout the Highlands, once again with the dual aim of providing employment and improving

Neptune's Staircase on the Caledonian Canal. The capstans were originally used to open and close the heavy lock gates.

communications. Over the next few years Telford oversaw works which included over a thousand miles of new roads, the improvement of nearly 480km (300 miles) of military roads, 1000 bridges and more than 40 harbours and piers. Obviously he did not supervise all this work himself, but his guiding hand could be seen everywhere. He devised a new system of road building that ensured a good, solid, well-drained surface built on sound foundations. He produced standard designs for tollhouses and even for simple manses and churches. Although he was happy to entrust most bridges to local builders, there were a few important crossings that received his personal attention. One of the most imposing of all his Highland bridges crosses the Spey at Craigellachie. The harbours spread around the coast and out to the islands. Wick remains one of the most extensive schemes in which he was involved, though the most impressive works are the breakwater and north pier at Aberdeen. Those who travel the Highlands of Scotland today are more than likely at some time in their journeying to be using a road first laid out by Thomas Telford. He can literally be called a man who left his mark on the country of his birth.

Telford's Major Works

THE CALEDONIAN CANAL

The best way to appreciate the canal is to travel the full length. Boats are available for hire, the towpath can be walked or cycled, but listed below are the most important sites, all of which are freely accessible.

Neptune's Staircase, Banavie

The A830 crosses the bottom of the staircase. The locks enjoy a magnificent situation, under the shadow of Ben Nevis.

Laggan Cutting

This is best approached from the A82 at Laggan Locks at the end of Loch Lochy. A path leads out across the massive spoil banks for a view of the deep cutting.

Fort Augustus

The A82 crosses the canal on a swing bridge, and the staircase of locks rises steeply above it.

Clachnaharry

The eastern end of the canal and the start of the embankment pushing out to sea. The railway crosses the canal on a swing bridge, and down by the lock is a plaque with a poem in praise of Telford and the canal, written by Robert Southey.

ABERDEEN

The harbour has been greatly extended over the years. The north pier is the oldest part, the result of work by two great engineers. It was begun in 1775 by John Smeaton and extended by Telford between 1810 and 1816, during which time he also worked on the breakwater.

Craigellachie

This is one of Telford's most elegant bridges. The river is crossed in a single, shallow iron arch, with the ends of the bridge marked by little castellated towers. On one of these a plaque announces that the ironwork came from Plas Kynaston. This is the ironworks in Wales that provided the sections for the iron trough of the great Pontcysyllte (p.143). The castings for this bridge may well have begun their journey with a trip over the famous aqueduct. Visitors to Craigellachie might also like to visit the cooperage centre (see p.177).

ULLAPOOL

Museum and Visitor Centre
£; April to October Monday to Saturday, November to March Wednesday and Saturday; 7–8 West Argyle Street; Tel: 01854 612987
The museum is housed in one of Telford's churches. Exhibits include displays on the establishment of the port through the work of the British Fisheries Society.

The lonely railway station on Rannoch Moor, on the line from Glasgow to Fort William and on to Mallaig.

spinning and dyeing to finishing, and visitors get introduced to the processes by audio-visual and interactive displays before going on a tour of the works. What they find is a fascinating mixture of old techniques and the latest technology.

GARLOGIE
Garlogie Mill Power House

Free; May to September Thursday to Monday afternoons; Tel: 01771 622906

When steam power was first introduced into textile mills at the end of the eighteenth century, it came in the form of rotative beam engines. A substantial number of the later horizontal mill engines have survived in their original setting, but here is the one surviving beam engine in its engine house. Not a lot is known about it, though it almost certainly dates from the 1830s and was probably built in Glasgow. Ideally, of course, it would have a mill to go with it; unfortunately that was demolished in 1934. There is, however, a good audio-visual show to give the engine a context.

GLENFINNAN
Station Museum and Viaduct

£ Museum; June to September;
Tel: 01397 722295

The station is still part of the working railway system, on the line from Fort William to Mallaig. This was an extension of the West Highland Railway, which had made its way up from Glasgow by 1894 to reach Fort William and was then continued to Mallaig for the Skye ferry service. It was opened in 1901 and used the new technology of the twentieth century for important structures. The museum shows the history of the line but there is no substitute for the real experience of travelling it by train. In summer visitors can do so in style on a special steam hauled service. Although the scenery is magnificent throughout, the best of all for many travellers is the crossing of the Glenfinnan viaduct. It is 380m (416 yards) long, built out of concrete; what makes it especially exciting is the way in which it was built on a great sweeping curve. This always

results in crowds of photographers heading for the windows for the rare opportunity of photographing the engine on the viaduct from inside the train.

The earlier part of the line from the outskirts of Glasgow also goes through some stunningly beautiful Highland scenery. It crosses the wastes of Rannoch Moor, passing through one of Britain's loneliest stations.

HARRIS
Harris Tweed Weaving and Knitting

Free; All year Monday to Saturday; 8km (5 miles) south of Tarbert on Golden Road; 4 Plockropool; Tel: 01496 810563

Harris tweed is world famous as a hard-wearing woollen cloth, but it got its name by mistake. In 1826 a batch of cloth was sent from a mill at Hawick down to London, where a clerk saw the name 'tweel', a technical name for a type of coloured cloth. He misread it as 'tweed' and the name stuck. While tweed mills flourished in Scotland, some of the finest cloth of all was made on Harris using traditional methods, as it still is here. This is not production on the grand scale: weaving is limited to just two hand looms, but it is the real thing.

A passenger's eye view of a steam special crossing the Glenfinnan viaduct on the return run to Fort William.

Engineers at work on restoring the beam engine, which once powered the machinery of the Garlogie woollen mill.

ISLAY

Islay Woollen Mill, Bridgend

Free, Easter to October daily;
Tel: 01496 810563 (see Central Scotland map, pp.158–9)

I visited this mill out of general interest, and partly to get away from the local, peculiarly vicious insect population. What I found was an astonishing array of machinery that you might, with luck, see in a particularly well stocked textile museum. This is no museum, but a working mill that has scarcely been modernised since work started in 1883. The mill is like many small country mills, in that it carries out all the processes on site; therefore you can expect to find some machines working some days while others will be idle, but whenever you come you are assured that there will be something interesting to see. For anyone interested in the history of textile machinery, there are three groups of machine here of quite outstanding interest. The carder is one of the oldest – if not *the* oldest – still in use. It delivers the wool in long strips that then have to be joined together before they can go for spinning. In the early nineteenth century this was done

by hand, mainly by children. In later years it became part of a continuous process. However, here we find the intermediate stage: it is passed through a piecing machine, an extraordinary collection of rollers and conveyors that bring the strands together. Machines of this type were first patented by a Scottish inventor Robert Archibald in 1858, and this is one of his machines. There are, I believe only two others in Britain, but this is the only one in full working order.

The next stage in the process is to draw out the rovings from the piecing machine ready for spinning. At first sight the slubbing billy looks like a rather crude mule, and it is not dissimilar in operation. There is a row of bobbins on a standing frame which are turned by rollers. Spindles on a moving frame are also turned by rollers, but at a faster speed. The moving frame is pulled back by hand, drawing out the fibres. As far as is known, this particular machine is a unique survivor.

Most of us have heard of the spinning jenny, but who would expect to find not one but two in a working mill? In operation these are very like the slubbing billy and though they are

not unique, they are two of maybe half a dozen survivors. This is interesting for the non-expert, who cannot fail to be impressed by the ingenuity of these very old machines; for the enthusiast Islay Mill is an absolute must.

KILMAHOG

Woollen Mills

Free; Open daily; Tel: 01877 330268

There are two separate buildings very close together, both offering points of interest, even though they are now more concerned with selling than manufacturing. The Kilmahog Woollen Mill dates back to the early nineteenth century and still has its original 4.3m (14ft) diameter water wheel. Apart from the shop, inside there are displays on the history of clans and tartans. The neighbouring Trossachs Mill is now used for weaving, specialising in travel rugs, and visitors can see the resident weaver at work. There are memories of earlier times in a row of three single-storey weavers' cottages nearby.

KINGUSSIE

Highland Folk Museum

£; April to October Monday to Saturday; Duke Street, PH21 1JG; Tel: 01540 661307; Website: www.highlandfolk.com

The museum is centred on an eighteenth-century shooting lodge, and is mainly concerned with the social life of the Highlands and agriculture. The open-air site includes a reconstructed 'clack' mill. This was a grain mill powered by a horizontal mill set directly in the mill stream. The site is just one part of the museum and the rest can be found nearby at Newtonmore (see p.174).

LEWIS

Shawbost Watermill

Free; Open access; Tel: 01851 710208; Website: www.virtualhebrides.com

This is a former Norse-type mill. Water is brought to the site in a lade, lined with flagstones, and drives a horizontal wheel or tirl with eight paddles. The mill itself is an attractive building, oval in shape and built with drystone walls roofed with thatch. There is a small kiln nearby.

NEWTONMORE
Highland Folk Museum

££; April to September daily, September and October Monday to Friday; Contact details as at Kingussie (p.173)

This is the larger of the two folk museums, and like Kingussie, it is largely an open-air site with reconstructed buildings. Here, however, there is a far wider range of buildings, which include a reconstructed Highland township with rare breeds at the farm, clockmaker's and joiners' workshops, church and school. An estate sawmill from Laggan, with a 3.7m (12ft) overshot wheel, has also been rebuilt. In among the town buildings and the crofts are costumed museum staff, giving explanations and providing demonstrations of crafts such as handloom weaving. The site covers 32 hectares (80 acres) but there is no need to get sore feet, as free transport is provided in two replica vintage buses. More than 200 years of Scottish social and industrial history are explored on this one site.

The overshot water wheel and the former saw mill from Laggan being recreated by museum staff in the attractive parkland at Newtonmore.

Dounby click mill represents mill building at its simplest. Entrance is by the door on the left, and the horizontal wheel is under the arch on the right. When this picture was taken in summer, the stream had dried up.

ORKNEY

Boardhouse Mill, Birsay

£; April to September daily; On the A967 at the end of Loch of Boardhouse; Tel: 01856 721439

Although this is run by a Trust, it has all the atmosphere of a working mill. The three-storey mill was built in 1873 and powered by an overshot water wheel. Like all meal mills, there is a kiln incorporated into the main building and an array of elevators and cleaning machines. Grinding takes place using three pairs of millstones. As well as oatmeal, the mill also produces beremeal. Bere is an ancient form of barley grown in the area: there is evidence that it was known to the settlers who built the extraordinary neolithic village of Skara Brae, just a few miles away down the coast. My wife and I bought some and tried the traditional recipe for bere bannock cakes: we decided it was an acquired taste.

Dounby Click Mill

HS; Free; Open access; Just to the south of the B9057 Dounby to Georth road (map ref. 6/325228)

Orkney was only annexed to Scotland in 1471. Before that, it was part of Norway; visitors to these enchanted islands can still hear the rhythms of Scandinavia in the local speech. This tiny nineteenth-century watermill is also part of the earlier Norse heritage. Where most British mills have vertical wheels, this has a horizontal wheel or tirl dipping into the stream, with the vertical shaft driving the stones directly with no gears at all. Inside, a hopper drops grain on to the stones and the flour collects in a box let into the floor. And that's it. The building is as simple as the machinery, rough stone walls and a roof of thatch, lashed down to protect it from the gales that can whistle over this lonely, treeless moor.

SHETLAND

Huxter Mills, Sandness

Free; Open access; Map ref. 3/173572

Not perhaps the easiest site to find, but well worth the trouble. You have to take the A971 out to Sandness, which although it has an A designation, is mainly single track with passing places. You then look for a sign and head out across the fields following a series of way markers leading out towards the cliffs. Then you come to what looks like three little huts, built out of drystone walls, with thatch on the roofs. These are all Norse mills, each provided with a nine-paddle tirl, though only the lowest of the three still has its stones in place. All three are powered by the same stream from the nearby loch. Although it is impossible to do more than guess at a date, the mills are certainly well over a hundred years old. They stood on common grazing land and were used by the surrounding crofts.

MALT WHISKY

When in 1887 Alfred Barnard published his definitive work *The Whisky Distilleries of the United Kingdom*, he described his visits to 129 distilleries in Scotland. There may not be as many as that today but this is still an important industry and one that has not changed in its essentials since that time. Indeed, if you visit a distillery that featured in Barnard's book today and compare it with his illustrations, it is surprising how very similar they are. It is an industry that relies on just three very simple ingredients: grain, yeast and pure water. The finest whiskies are made using malt, though they can be blended with other grain spirits – or with other malts. But it is for their pure, single malt whiskies that the distilleries of the Highlands and Islands are rightly famous.

The first stage in the process is the production of malted barley. The barley is cleaned, then soaked in water and allowed to germinate, resulting in the starch being converted to sugar. At the appropriate moment, germination is stopped by drying in a kiln. Traditionally, peat has been used as the fuel, and this imparts a distinctive, smoky taste to the finished drink, a taste which is found at its most potent in some of the island malts. In the old style kilns the malt was spread on the floor above the furnace and regularly turned with wooden shovels. Ventilators are set in the roof, and a distinctive pagoda shape has become the familiar outline of the malting kiln. These days many distilleries buy in ready-malted barley from specialist maltings.

The next stage involves grinding the malted barley. Originally, this was done by grindstones, as in any grain mill, and in the older distilleries they would have been water-powered. The Strathisla distillery is one of the few where a water wheel can still be seen beside the kilns. Rollers later took over the task. The crushed

The typical pagoda roofs of the kilns at the Strathisla distillery. The water wheel adds to the very picturesque scene, though it has no practical use.

meal is then taken to a circular vat, the 'mash tun', where it is mixed with hot water to extract the sugar. Here, the quality of the water is all-important, thus the siting of a distillery was highly dependent on the right water being available. The spent grain or draff is removed and used as cattle food. It was not uncommon for distilleries to have their own farms, where they grew the grain and kept their cattle well fed from the waste product of the same grain. The liquid is now known as wort, and is taken on to washbacks, where yeast is added and fermentation begins. After a couple of days, the wort has an alcoholic strength of about 8% and is ready for distillation. This takes place in traditional copper stills. There are usually two stills involved, the 'low wines still' and the 'spirit still'. In each of these the strength of alcohol is increased, due to the fact that water and alcohol have different boiling points. The first distillation increases the strength to make 'low wines', roughly 20% alcohol, after which it is distilled again in the spirit still to emerge at a potent 68% – not to be confused with the proof strength listed on the finished product. The strength of the distillation is checked by a hydrometer in the spirit safe – and it really is a safe, for not even the still man can open it for a quick nip. He has to peer in through the padlocked glass door. Only a part of the distillate, the 'middle cut' is actually used for whisky making. The strength is now reduced by the addition of water.

That is the speedy part of the process. The next stage takes years. The whisky is stored in casks and allowed to mature for anything from eight years upwards. The nature of the cask has a real bearing on the final flavour. It is generally agreed that the finest results are obtained using casks that have previously been used for sherry. This may all sound as if it is getting a touch pretentious, but it is undoubtedly true that the nature of the casks makes an immediately recognisable difference. On a visit to the Macallan distillery some years ago, I was shown a range of whiskies that had been stored in different casks: the whisky from plain oak casks was rather pallid with not much aroma, but those which had come from sherry casks had an altogether richer colour and smell. Even the type of sherry used made a difference. The distillers were well aware of this, and had their own casks made, then shipped out to Spain with instructions on what was to be kept in them. They only got them back some years later when they were suitably ripened. As a result there could be a twenty-year gap between the cask being made and the first whisky taken out for bottling. Whisky is a valuable commodity and one that carries an extremely high excise duty, so the casks are kept securely in bonded warehouses.

There are now over thirty distilleries that have visitor centres and arrange tours. It is possible to see a large number by visiting areas such as the Spey valley, where you can follow a whisky trail – it is as well to decide in advance on who is going to do the driving, since most visits end with a dram. The following is a list of distilleries of particular historical interest, together with one associated site.

The gleaming copper stills at Bowmore Distillery, Islay. They look beautiful, but the design and choice of materials is dictated by years of experience, not aesthetics.

Bowmore Distillery, Islay

£; April to October Monday to Saturday, October to April Monday to Friday; School Street; Tel: 01496 810441
They have been making whisky here since 1779. This is one of the few places where visitors actually get a chance to see traditional floor maltings. An unusual feature is the swimming pool given to the local community and heated from the waste products.

Glenfarclas Distillery, Ballindalloch

££; June to September daily, October to May weekdays; Tel: 01807 500257
This typical Highland distillery has a long history, begun in 1836 when a local farmer decided to try a little distilling on the side. In 1865 it was taken over by John Grant, and it has been in the same family ever since. It enjoys a spectacular situation on the flank of Ben Rinnes, and the spring water from the moorland adds its quota to the taste of their fine malt whisky.

Glenfiddich Distillery, Dufftown

Free; All year Monday to Friday, Easter to October plus weekends; Tel: 01340 820373
This whisky has captured a big, international market, a fact reflected in the audio-video presentation and the tours, where you can select from a number of European languages and Japanese.

Glen Grant Distillery, Rothes

£; March to October daily; Tel: 01542 783318
Established in 1872, it was inherited by Major James Grant, who had travelled widely in India and South Africa, and formed a 'wilderness garden' that is also open to visitors.

Highland Park Distillery, Kirkwall, Orkney

£; March to October Monday to Friday, July and August plus weekend afternoons, November to February afternoon tours Monday to Friday; Tel: 01856 874619
The northernmost outpost of the whisky empire, established two centuries ago. This is another of the few places where visitors can actually see a floor malting in regular use.

Strathisla Distillery, Keith

££; February to March Monday to Friday, April to November Monday to Saturday plus Sunday afternoon; Seafield Avenue, AB55 5BS; Tel: 01542 783042; Website: www.chivas.com
This is the oldest working distillery in Scotland, established in 1786, and it looks it. In 1801 the Chivas brothers set up in business, using Strathisla malt as the basis for a blended whisky that they called Chivas Regal. Surprisingly little has changed here since the late nineteenth century, though it has to be admitted that the water wheel is purely decorative. There are few places that give a better picture of a Highland distillery of Barnard's time. It was then known as the Milton Distillery, and many of the buildings that can be seen in the illustration to his book can still be recognised today.

Speyside Cooperage Visitor Centre, Dufftown Road, Craigellachie

£; All year Monday to Friday, June to September plus Saturday; Tel: 01340 871108
This is a working site, repairing oak casks for the whisky industry. Visitors have a chance to see this highly skilled work in progress.

SHETLAND
Shetland Textile Working Museum, Weisdale Mill

£; May to September Tuesday to Saturday plus Sunday afternoons; On the B9075 at the head of Weisdale Voe, ZE2 9LW; Tel: 01595 830419

Although this certainly is a museum, and a very good one, it also has another function. It is run by the Shetland Guild of Spinners, Weavers and Dyers, who were formed to keep the traditional skills of the island alive. This is where that tradition is on display. Spinning and knitting have been central to the life of the island long before written records were kept, and children were taught knitting as early as three years old. This, however, is not just knitting as most of us know it. Although Shetland is famous for intricate patterns, such as Fair Isle, there is also a long tradition of knitting very fine lace. Handloom weaving was also common throughout the region but largely died away, as it did elsewhere, with the advent of mechanisation. The museum has artefacts, including the typical vertical spinning wheels that were once common throughout the regions, and there are displays of the finished products. Regular demonstrations take place at the museum.

The stunning colours of the wool are all the result of a return to traditional dyeing methods. These were produced using indigo, madder and such unlikely materials as onion skins.

See Also

Arbroath Museum, Signal Tower, Ladyloan, Arbroath
Free; All year Monday to Saturday, July and August plus Sunday afternoons;
Tel: 01241 875598
When work was completed on Robert Stevenson's Bell Rock Lighthouse in 1811, homes were built on shore for the lighthouse keepers. The complex now houses the museum, which deals with the lighthouse, the linen weaving industry, engineering and, of course, fishing and the famous and very appetising Arbroath smokies.

Mill of Mundurno, Bridge of Don
Free; Open during pub opening hours;
Tel: 01224 821217
A meal mill with three pairs of stones turned by a 4.3m (14ft) water wheel, together with a kiln, have been preserved in the pub grounds.

Mill of Benholm Visitor Centre, Johnshaven
£; Easter to October daily;
Tel: 01561 361969
A very handsome estate oatmeal mill, working up to 1982. The overshot water wheel and machinery have been restored, and it is also a centre for the park and woodland walks.

Isle of Mull Weavers, Craignure, Mull
Free; Easter to October daily; February to Easter plus November and December Monday to Saturday;
Tel: 01680 812381
(see Central Scotland map, pp.158–9)
This is just what the name suggests, a place where you can come and see weavers at work.

Lewis Loom Centre, Stornoway, Lewis
£; Open daily; Tel: 01851 703117
A working centre where the traditional ways of making woollen cloth, especially tweed, are demonstrated on spinning wheel and loom.

Croft House Museum, South Voe, Shetland
£; May to September daily;
Tel: 01595 695057
The complex consists of a thatched croft, outbuildings and a typical small Norse mill. The whole group recreates the self-contained lifestyle of the older crofting community.

Quendale Watermill, Shetland
£; May to September daily;
Tel: 01950 460550 / 460405
This is a large two-storey mill with an overshot wheel, built in 1868. It has been restored to working order with two pairs of stones, and also has a display of old croft tools.

Warp and Weft Visitor Centre, Hoswick, Shetland
Free; May to September Monday to Saturday and Sunday afternoons;
Tel: 01950 431215
No great surprise to find a collection of old looms in this former weaving shed, but it turns out to be rather more than that. There is also a collection of old radios and some fascinating historic photographs of life on Shetland.

Spean Bridge Woollen Mill
£; All year Monday to Friday, June to September plus Saturday;
Tel: 01397 712260
It is a slight exaggeration to call this a mill, since it consists of one weaver working in a former steading. It stands by the bridge itself, a handsome stone structure built in 1819 to a design by Thomas Telford.

Tugnet Ice House, Spey Bay
Free; May to September daily;
Tel: 01309 673701
The ice house is part of a fishery complex, which includes a boiler, dated 1783. Ice was an essential for preserving the fish. In the days before refrigeration, it had to be collected when available and stored in an insulated excavated cavern. This is the biggest in Scotland, with three vaulted bays and a covering of thatch. The lintel over the door has the date 1630 and a carving of a fish. There are displays on the salmon fishing industry.

GLOSSARY

WATER POWER

Horizontal or Norse mill: The rotating blades, or tirl, are set on a vertical axle and can drive the millstones without intermediate gearing.

Horizontal or Norse mill

Undershot wheel: The water hits the paddles near the bottom of the wheel, which turns it in the same direction as the flow.

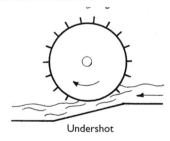

Undershot

Breastshot wheel: The water hits the wheel approximately half way up, and the wheel is moved by a combination of the force of the flow and the weight of water. It turns in the direction of the flow.

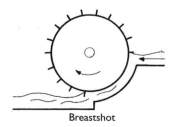

Breastshot

Overshot wheel: The water is brought to a point above the wheel, which has 'buckets' set round the rim. The weight of water falling into the buckets causes rotation in the opposite direction from the flow.

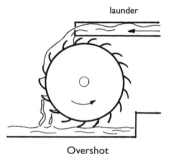

Overshot

A typical water-powered grain mill

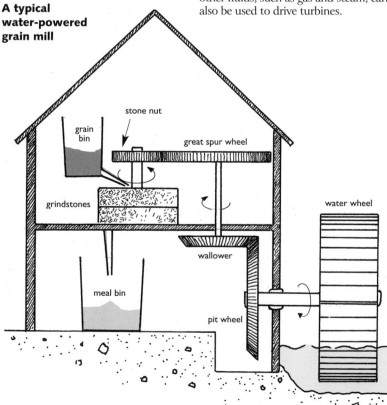

Pitchback wheel: Essentially similar to an overshot wheel, except that the buckets are shaped so that the wheel rotates in the direction of the flow.

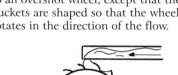

Pitchback

Turbine: Similar to a horizontal mill, in that the water turns blades on a shaft; other fluids, such as gas and steam, can also be used to drive turbines.

WIND POWER

Post mill: All the machinery is housed in the buck to which the sails are attached. The buck rotates on a central post, so that the sails can be brought into the wind.

Tower mill: The machinery is housed in a tower made of brick or stone. The sails are set on a separate rotating cap at the top of the tower.

Smock mill: Essentially the same as a tower mill, except that the tower is constructed of wood.

Fantail: A vane that turns in the wind. In tower and smock mills it is attached to the cap at the opposite side to the sails. When the sails are facing into the wind, the fantail is shielded. When the wind shifts, the vane turns, acting like a propeller to move the cap round to reposition the sails automatically. Fantails can also be attached to the ends of tail poles in post mills.

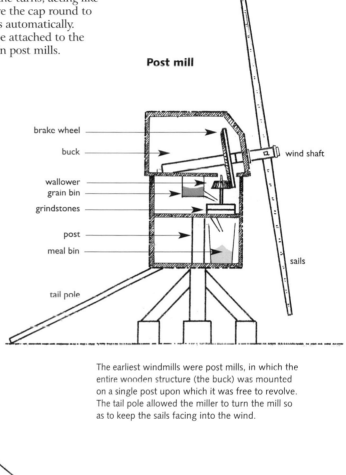

Post mill

brake wheel

buck

wind shaft

wallower

grain bin

grindstones

post

meal bin

sails

tail pole

The earliest windmills were post mills, in which the entire wooden structure (the buck) was mounted on a single post upon which it was free to revolve. The tail pole allowed the miller to turn the mill so as to keep the sails facing into the wind.

Tower mill

sails

fantail

brake wheel

wind shaft

wallower

grain bin

stone nut

great spur wheel

stones

meal bin

sails

In the case of a tower mill the body of the mill, containing the grain and meal bins and the grindstones, was a fixed structure, usually of brick or stone, and only the cap carrying the sails, wind shaft and brake wheel rotated. In early tower mills the cap was turned with the help of a chain fixed to the rim of the cap; later, the addition of a fantail on the back of the cap meant that the cap automatically turned to keep the sails facing into the wind.

STEAM POWER

Beam engine: An engine in which a piston is attached by a connecting rod to one end of an overhead beam. As the piston moves up and down, so the beam rocks, activating a mechanical linkage at the opposite end of the beam.

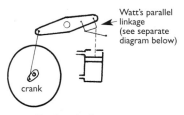

Single-cylinder
rotative beam engine

The rotative beam engine used the expansive power of steam, injected alternately above and below the piston, to provide power on both the downstroke and the upstroke. In order to achieve this, it was, of course, necessary for the top of the cylinder to be sealed, and the piston had to be linked to the beam by a rigid rod, rather than a flexible chain as in the single-action engines.

Atmospheric or Newcomen engine: An engine in which steam is condensed below the piston, creating a partial vacuum, so that air pressure forces the piston down in the cylinder. The engine is limited to pumping, as it requires the weight of pump rods to move the beam back to its original position to repeat the cycle.

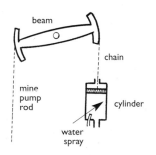

Newcomen
atmospheric beam engine

The Newcomen engine, properly speaking, was an atmospheric rather than a steam engine. For it was atmospheric pressure on the top of the piston, forcing the piston down when the steam in the bottom part of the cylinder was condensed by the cooling effect of the water spray, which provided the power stroke. The weight of the pump rod on the other end of the beam then raised the piston again, drawing a new charge of steam into the bottom of the cylinder.

Boulton and Watt beam engine: An improvement on the Newcomen engine, in that the steam is condensed in a separate condenser. The cylinder is closed and the piston moved up and down by the expansive power of steam.

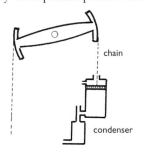

Watt single-action beam engine

Watt's single-action beam engine operated on a similar principle, though the addition of a separate condenser meant that heat was no longer wasted heating up the cold cylinder at the completion of each stroke.

Horizontal engine: Engine that has no overhead beam but instead drives machinery directly though a connecting rod from the piston.

Compound engine: An engine using high pressure steam in two or more cylinders. The steam first enters the high pressure cylinder and is then passed to the low pressure cylinder or cylinders. Where the cylinders are in line, it is a tandem compound; where they are side by side, it is a cross-compound engine. Beam engines can also be compounded.

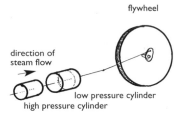

Horizontal
tandem-compound engine

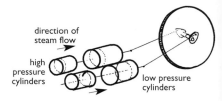

Horizontal twin
tandem-compound engine

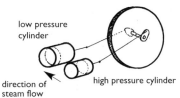

Horizontal
cross-compound engine

The various types of compound engines all used high-pressure steam and operated on a similar principle, which minimised wastage of energy by adding a second, larger, low pressure cylinder or cylinders that utilised the residual pressure of the steam after it emerged from the high pressure cylinder or cylinders.

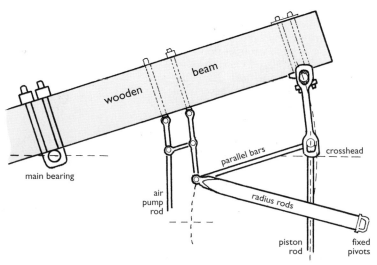

The parallel linkage invented by Watt allowed the rod to move vertically through the seal in the top of the cylinder even though the end of the beam to which it was pivoted moved in an arc.

MINING

Adit: A tunnel cut into the mine workings below water level to act as a drain.

Bell pit: A mine where a shaft is sunk down to the mineral stratum, then excavated all round the bottom of the shaft, creating a bell-shaped chamber.

Deep mine: A mine developed from a shaft, with galleries reaching out horizontally, often linked together by other shafts underground.

Drift mine: A mine dug in horizontally from a hillside to reach the mineral.

Gin or whim: A mechanical device for raising and lowering material in a shaft, which can be powered by hand, animals or steam power.

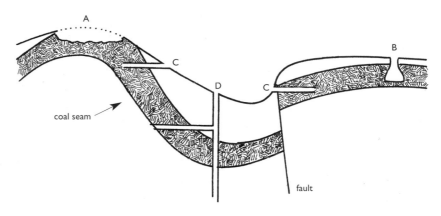

Types of coal mine
A – Open cast mine, slicing off the top of the surface
B – Bell pit, cut down from the surface to the coal seam and worked outward from the bottom of the shaft
C – Drift mine cut from the hillside into the seam
D – Deep mine with vertical shaft and horizontal galleries

IRON AND STEEL

Blast furnace: The furnace used for smelting iron ore. The ore is mixed with a suitable fuel, originally charcoal, later coke, and raised to a high temperature by blowing air through the fire.

Cast iron: Iron with a high carbon content, generally around 4 per cent, which appears from the blast furnace in a molten state and can be run into moulds for casting. It is brittle.

Puddling: A method for converting cast iron, or pig iron, to wrought iron. Invented in 1784 by Henry Cort, the metal is heated in a reverbatory furnace, one where the metal is never in direct contact with the fuel. The molten metal is constantly stirred to burn off the carbon, then removed and rolled into shape.

Steel: A form of iron with a low carbon content, typically between 0.25 and 1.4 per cent. It can be strengthened by the addition of other elements, such as manganese and tungsten.

Wrought iron: Very pure iron, which is malleable and can be shaped by forging.

A typical blast furnace

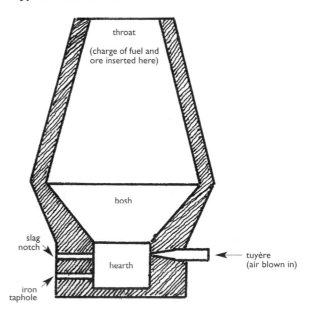

TEXTILES

Carding: This process precedes spinning, and is used to roughly align the fibres. Originally this was achieved by drawing the fibres between cards studded with wire; later carding engines were introduced using a rotating drum.

Spinning wheel: The simplest spinning wheel consists of a wheel, turned either by hand or by foot treadle, which rotates a spindle. Unspun wool is placed on the spindle and pulled away by the spinner. As it leaves the rapidly rotating spindle, it is both twisted and stretched.

The jenny: A spinning machine invented by James Hargreaves in the 1760s. The hand-operated wheel turned a number of spindles, and the fibres were held in a clasp, moving away from the spindles. After the fibres had been drawn out, the clasp was reversed and the spun fibres wound on.

The water frame: Invented by Richard Arkwright, this was the first cotton spinning machine to be powered by water wheel. The fibres were drawn out by being passed through rollers moving at different speeds, before passing to the spindle for twisting. The machines were first installed at Cromford, Derbyshire in 1771.

The mule: This spinning machine invented by Samuel Crompton in 1779 combined the rollers of the water frame with the moving carriage of the jenny.

Hand loom: This is actually a surprisingly complex spinning machine, thus the following description is a simplification: warp threads are wrapped round a roller at the back of the loom and fixed to the cloth take-up roller at the front. They are carefully set in place, and they pass through eyes in moveable heald shafts. Alternate threads are raised and lowered by means of a foot treadle. This creates a space through which a shuttle can be passed, trailing the weft threads

Spinning Wheel

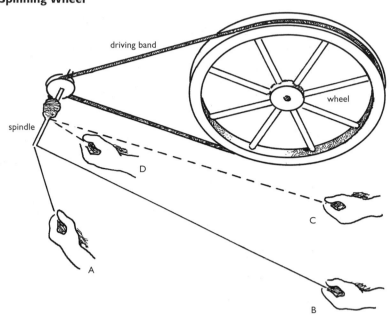

The large wheel is linked to the spindle by a cord-driving band. The spinner starts by drawing out the thread along the spindle, which causes it to spiral and twist, A. It is then drawn out to B. The hand moves across towards the wheel to C, and the thread is wound on, D.

Spinning Jenny

Spinnning with the jenny. The spinner turns the wheel by hand to rotate the spindles A and pull the draw bar B to draw out the threads.

behind it. After each pass of the shuttle, the weft threads are beaten into place.

The flying shuttle: Patented by John Kay in 1733, this spinning machine consisted of a long board running across the front of the loom along which the shuttle ran. At each end of the board were boxes, with moveable metal rods, known as pickers. These were joined by cord to a picking peg, hanging in front of the loom. By jerking the peg one way or the other, the weaver could send the shuttle flying across from picker to picker.

Jacquard loom: A spinning machine invented by Joseph Marie Jacquard in 1801, the loom could be used for the production of complex weaving patterns. It used punched cards to determine the order in which the different healds were raised and lowered.

Fulling stocks: First introduced in the thirteenth century, the stocks were used to shrink the cloth from the loom and compact it. Worked by a water wheel, the stocks were heavy wooden hammers. The cloth was placed in a trough with water and pounded by the stocks, which had curved heads to keep the cloth moving.

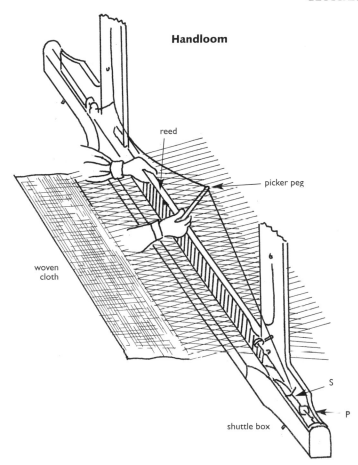

Handloom

This shows Kay's flying shuttle. The shuttle, S, is shown in the shuttle box, on the right. In the box is a spindle with a picker, P, which can slide along it and which is attached to the picker peg. When the weaver jerks the peg, shown held in the right hand, the picker sends the shuttle flying across the shuttle board to the shuttle box on the other side, carrying with it the yarn which forms the weft of the cloth. The weaver then uses his left hand to pull the reed back towards his body, beating the newly inserted weft back up to the edge of the cloth.

Site Index

SUBJECT INDEX

Sites are listed under their main features of interest, and not cross-referenced. For example, Cheddleton Flint Mill appears under 'Pottery' but not under 'Mills, Other'.

Animal Power
Beaumaris Gaol, 145
Greys Court, Rotherfield Greys, 53
Harwich Treadwheel Crane, 81

Breweries and Distilleries
Bass Museum, Burton-upon-Trent, 65
Bowmore Distillery, Islay, 177
Glenfarclas Distillery, Ballindalloch, 177
Glenfiddich Distillery, Dufftown, 177
Glent Grant Distillery, Rothes, 177
Highland Park Distillery, Orkney, 177
Speyside Cooperage Visitor Centre, Craigellachie, 179
Strathisla Distillery, Keith, 177

Bridges and Viaducts
Causey Arch, Stanley, 100, 106
Clifton Suspension Bridge, Bristol, 36
Conwy Bridges, 140
Craigellachie, 171
Forth Bridges Exhibition, North Queensferry, 163
Glenfinnan Viaduct, 172
Knaresborough Viaduct, 99
Maidenhead Railway Bridge, 53
Menai Straits, 143
Ribblehead Viaduct, 99
Royal Albert Bridge, Saltash, 25
Stratford-upon-Avon Tramway Bridge, 61
Tay Railway Bridge, 168
Tyne Bridges, Newcastle-upon-Tyne, 102
Union Bridge, 155
Wade's Bridge, Aberfeldy, 168
Waterloo Bridge, Betws-y-Coed, 145

Canals
Anderton Lift, Northwich, 110
Barton Aqueduct, Barton-upon-Irwell, 112
Birmingham Canal, 57, 59
Boat Museum, Ellesmere Port, 109
Bratch Locks, Staffs & Worcester Canal, 59
Brecon & Abergavenny Canal, 130–1
Bridgewater Canal, 17, 112, 119
Bude Canal, 28
Buxworth Basin, 79
Caen Hill Locks, Devizes, 34
Caledonian Canal, 10, 170, 171
Canal Museum, Foxton, 70
Canal Museum, Stoke Bruerne, 69
Canal Wharf, Llangollen, 142
Claverton Pumping Station, 32
Crinan Canal, 169
Crofton Pumping Station, 34
Cromford Canal, 78
Dapdune Wharf, Wey Navigation, 47
Dundas Aqueduct, Limpley Stoke, 34

Galton Valley Canal Heritage Centre, Birmingham, 59
Harecastle Tunnel, Trent & Mersey Canal, 65
Hatton Locks, Grand Union Canal, 59
Kennet & Avon Canal Trust Museum, Devizes, 34
Linlithgow Canal Centre, 153
London Canal Museum, 50
Longdon-on-Tern Aqueduct, 59
Lune Aqueduct, 119
Marple Locks, Peak Forest Canal, 110
National Waterways Museum, Gloucester, 37
Pontcysyllte, Llangollen Canal, 143
Powysland Museum & Canal Centre, Welshpool, 137
Sapperton Tunnel, Coates, 37
Shardlow, 79
Shropshire Union, 64
Standedge Visitor Centre, Marsden, 96
Stourport Canal Basin, 59
Thames & Severn Canal, Chalford, 37
Whaley Bridge, 110

Coal Mining
Astley Green Colliery Museum, 112
Big Pit, Blaenavon, 123
Cefn Coed Colliery Museum, Crynant, 124
Elliot Colliery, New Tredegar, 125
Elsecar Heritage Centre, 93
Haig Colliery, 120
Hopewell Colliery Museum, Coleford, 37
National Coal Mining Museum, Overton, 97
Prestongrange Museum, Prestonpans, 153
Rhondda Heritage Park, Trehafod, 129
Scottish Mining Museum, Newtongrange, 154
Snibston Discovery Park, Coalville, 71
South Wales Miners Museum, Cynonville, 124
Woodhorn Colliery Museum, Ashington, 105

Copper and Tin
Aberdulais Falls, 123
Blue Hills Tin Streams, Trevellas Coombe, 26, 28
Botallack Engine Houses, 27
Caradon Hill, 27
Geevor Tin Mine, Pendeen, 24
Kidwelly Industrial Museum, 134
King Edward Mine, Troon, 22
Levant Steam Engine, Pendeen, 24, 26
Parys Mountain, Anglesey, 143
Poldark Mine and Heritage Complex, Wendron, 28
Saltford Brass Mill, 32–3
Sygun Copper Mine, Beddgelert, 139
Tolgus Tin, Portreath, 25

Industrial Museums, General
Almond Valley Heritage Centre, Livingston, 155
Amberley Museum, 42
Arbroath Museum, 179
Armley Mills, Leeds, 96
Avoncroft Museum of Historic Buildings, Stoke Heath, 56, 90
Bewdley Museum, 55
Black Country Living Museum, Dudley, 26, 60
Bradford Industrial Museum, 94
Bristol Industrial Museum, 36
Dean Heritage Centre, Upper Soudley, 37
Derby Industrial Museum, 78
Discovery Museum, Newcastle-upon-Tyne, 103
Dunaskin Heritage Centre, Waterside, 155
Highland Folk Museum, Kingussie, 173
Highland Folk Museum, Newtonmore, 174
Ironbridge Gorge Museums, 17, 62–3, 107
Kelham Island Museum, Sheffield, 11, 98
London Transport Museum, 51
Magna, Rotherham, 97
Morwellham Quay, 29–30
Museum of East Anglian Life, Stowmarket, 85
Museum of Lincolnshire Life, Lincoln, 89
Museum of Science and Industry in Manchester, 114
Museum of Transport, Glasgow, 162
Museum of Welsh Life, St Fagans, 128
National Museum of Wales, Cardiff, 127
North of England Open Air Museum, Beamish, 101, 107
Nottingham Industrial Museum, 73
Pewsey Heritage Centre, 34
Royal Museum of Scotland, Edinburgh, 107
Science Museum, London, 18, 51, 107
Summerlee Heritage Park, 161
Swansea Maritime and Industrial Museum, 129
Thinktank, Birmingham, 60
Ullapool Museum and Visitor Centre, 171
Wayside Folk Museum, Zennor, 28
Weald and Downland Open Air Museum, Singleton, 43, 45
Wigan Pier, 115

Iron and Steel
Abbeydale Industrial Hamlet, Sheffield, 98
Bersham Heritage Centre and Ironworks, 139
Blaenavon Ironworks, 123
Bonawe Iron Furnace, 160
Cyfarthfa Castle, Merthyr Tydfil, 125
Derwentcote Steel Furnace, Hamsterley, 100
Dyfi Furnace, Furnace, 134
Finch Foundry, Sticklepath, 30
Florence Mine, Egremont, 120
Forge Mill, Redditch, 55, 57
Joseph Parry's Cottage, Merthyr Tydfil, 125
Millom Folk Museum, 121

PICTURE CREDITS